the **law** *of*
tax-exempt
organizations

Eleventh Edition

2017 Cumulative Supplement

the **law** *of* tax-exempt organizations

Eleventh Edition

2017 Cumulative Supplement

Bruce R. Hopkins

WILEY

Published by John Wiley & Sons, Inc., Hoboken, New Jersey.
Published simultaneously in Canada.

For general information about our other products and services, please contact our Customer Care Department within the United States at (800) 762-2974, outside the United States at (317) 572-3993 or fax (317) 572-4002.

Wiley publishes in a variety of print and electronic formats and by print-on-demand. Some material included with standard print versions of this book may not be included in e-books or in print-on-demand. If this book refers to media such as a CD or DVD that is not included in the version you purchased, you may download this material at http://booksupport.wiley.com. For more information about Wiley products, visit www.wiley.com.

Library of Congress Cataloging-in-Publication Data:

ISBN 978-1-118-87369-4 (main edition)
ISBN 978-1-119-34518-3 (supplement)
ISBN 978-1-119-34517-6 (ePDF)
ISBN 978-1-119-34513-8 (ePub)

Cover Design: Wiley
Cover Image: © iStock.com/photo168

Printed in the United States of America
10 9 8 7 6 5 4 3 2 1

Contents

CONTENTS

CONTENTS

CONTENTS

CONTENTS

Preface

This is the second Preface in a supplement accompanying the eleventh edition of this book. This 2017 cumulative supplement essentially covers developments in the federal law of tax-exempt organizations for the period ending at the close of 2016.

The IRS's Tax Exempt and Government Entities Division has resumed issuance of annual work plans. There had not been one of these work plans since the one issued in fiscal year 2013; it is good to see these plans emerge again. The work plan for fiscal year 2016 was issued on October 1, 2015. This plan was somewhat marred, like the prior year's "program letter," by an overabundance of management-speak. This work plan, however, addressed some forthcoming program activity, as does its more exuberant successor for fiscal year 2017, both of which are summarized in this cumulative supplement.

The IRS has issued other interesting publications (summarized herein), including a memorandum from Rulings and Agreements concerning a toughening of the processing time lines now being followed in connection with applications for recognition of exemption, a memorandum from the Division regarding the use of one or more political activities referral committees, and a notice pertaining to mission-related investing by private foundations. The streamlined application process, utilizing Form 1023-EZ, seems to be operating fairly well, although it continues to be battered by substantial criticism, such as that leveled by the National Taxpayer Advocate (noted herein).

The IRS continues to issue private letter rulings illustrating its positions on application of the commerciality doctrine (some of them questionable), the private inurement and private benefit doctrines, the lack of qualification for exempt status as a business league, absence of the requisite charitable class, housing organizations, the lessening-burdens-of-government principle, the conduit rules in connection with foreign grantmaking, application of the unrelated business rules, and regulation of nonprofit governance (these continuing to be, in the view from here, incorrect).

An issue has come to the fore again in relation to the time frame covered by this supplement: the matter of "conversion" from nonexempt (for-profit) status to nonprofit, tax-exempt status. The IRS seems to have evolved to the position that, once an enterprise is formed as a for-profit entity, it can never be reconstituted as an exempt organization; there are two recent private letter rulings on the point. This is certainly not the law. This issue was bizarrely highlighted when a group of U.S. senators wrote to the IRS and the Department of Education asserting that conversions of for-profit schools to exempt schools are resulting in "sham nonprofits," and constitute fraud and tax evasion.

Since the main volume was published, some notable cases have been decided (again, all summarized herein), resulting in opinions concerning the necessary attributes of an entity qualifying as an *organization*, preliminary to considerations as to whether it is tax-exempt; the concept of a *corporation*, which generally subsumes the concept of a *nonprofit corporation*; the strict scrutiny test to apply in evaluating race-based affirmative action programs in the public higher education context; the lawfulness of the contraceptive mandate and its religious exceptions as applied to nonreligious tax-exempt entities; application of the strict scrutiny test in the free speech context (perhaps the "sleeper" opinion of the Supreme Court's last term); application of free speech principles in the realm of the processing of applications for recognition of exemption; and the use of a corporation sole as an abusive tax shelter.

The Senate Committee on Finance, on August 5, 2015, released its report on the Committee's bipartisan investigation of the IRS's handling of applications for recognition of tax exemption submitted by political advocacy organizations. The essence of this report is that, during 2010–2013, IRS management was delinquent in its responsibility to provide effective control, guidance, and direction over the processing of these applications. Two federal courts of appeals, however, are of the view that this matter goes beyond management issues and is in the realm of violation of free speech principles by reason of viewpoint discrimination.

The Government Accountability Office (GAO), in a report issued in July 2015, concluded that there are "several areas" where the Division's controls intended to enable it to properly select tax-exempt organizations for examination "were not well designed or implemented." The GAO recommended that the Division undertake several actions to rectify these deficiencies.

The Finance Committee and GAO reports are summarized in this cumulative supplement.

The Finance Committee also undertook an investigation of some small tax-exempt museums. The inquiry letters and the findings of the Committee as submitted to the IRS on May 17, 2016, are summarized herein.

The Protecting Americans from Tax Hikes Act of 2015 was enacted near the close of that year, bringing several new and revised rules concerning the law of tax-exempt organizations, all of which are summarized in this cumulative supplement.

The GAO also issued a report concerning the nature of IRS guidance and the lack of procedures within the agency as to selection of types of guidance. This report, which has considerable implications for the law of tax-exempt organizations, is summarized as an addition to Appendix A of the book.

Two recent developments have not been added to the book just yet (although both are summarized in the January 2017 *Nonprofit Counsel*). One development is the new country-by-country reporting regime and its impact on tax-exempt organizations. The regulations that detail this reporting requirement were issued in final form in July 2016; the principal underlying statutory authority for this reporting is IRC § 6038. The other development is the import for exempt organizations of the new audit regime for partnerships; this body of law was created by the Bipartisan Budget Act of 2015 and revised by the PATH Act of 2015.

The potential for tax reform looms. As a consequence, a table has been added, this of proposed and House of Representatives–enacted law revisions in the tax-exempt organizations law setting.

My thanks go to my development editor, Brian Neill, and the production editor, Abirami Srikandan, for their assistance and support in connection with this cumulative supplement.

BRUCE R. HOPKINS

the **law** *of* tax-exempt organizations

Eleventh Edition

2017 Cumulative Supplement

CHAPTER ONE

Definition of and Rationales for Tax-Exempt Organizations

*§ 1.1 DEFINITION OF *NONPROFIT* ORGANIZATION

(a) *Nonprofit Organization* Defined

p. 5. *Insert as fourth paragraph, before heading:*

Use of the word *corporation* in the law context usually means both nonprofit and for-profit ones, unless clearly stated otherwise. This point was nicely illustrated in the case of a tax-exempt teaching hospital that is organized as a nonprofit corporation under state law and is tax-exempt under the federal tax law as a charitable corporation. It is required to pay Federal Insurance Contributions Act (FICA) taxes. An exclusion is available from the FICA taxes for students at educational institutions.[6.1] An IRS regulation, promulgated in 2005, basically states that medical residents are not students for this purpose. The hospital sued for a refund of FICA taxes it paid before the effective date of the regulation; the IRS eventually conceded this point. The parties disagreed, however, as to the interest rate that applies with respect to the tax refund.[6.2] A lower interest rate applies to corporations. The hospital asserted that it was entitled to a higher rate of interest on its tax refund, on the grounds that the statutory reference to *corporations* in this context is inapplicable to nonprofit organizations that happen to be organized as corporations. The court involved surveyed the contents of several dictionaries, concluding that the word *corporation*, "standing alone, ordinarily refers to both for-profit and nonprofit entities without distinction."[6.3] It essentially reached the same conclusion on the basis of the Internal Revenue Code definition (although it is not really a definition) of the term.[6.4] The court further engaged in an extensive textual analysis of the interest rate provision, again rejecting the hospital's

---

[6.1] IRC § 3121(b)(10).
[6.2] IRC § 6621(a)(1).
[6.3] Maimonides Medical Center v. United States, 809 F.3d 85, 87 (2nd Cir. 2015).
[6.4] IRC § 7701(a)(3).

arguments and concluding that the hospital's readings of the section "wreak havoc on the statutory language."[6.5]

§ 1.2 DEFINITION OF *TAX-EXEMPT* ORGANIZATION

*p. 7, note 20, last line. *Delete closing parenthesis and period, and substitute:*

, *vac'd and rem'd sub nom.* Diebold Found., Inc. v. Comm'r, 736 F.3d 172 (2nd Cir. 2013), *rev'd and rem'd*, 776 F.3d 1010 (9th Cir. 2014), T.C. Memo. 2016-154 (Aug. 15, 2016) (two private foundations held liable for income taxes as transferees of a transferee)).

*p. 8, note 22. *Insert following existing text:*

Also *Constitutional Law*, Chapter 1.

p. 9, note 33, second paragraph. *Delete and substitute:*

The staff of Congress's Joint Committee on Taxation, on December 7, 2015, issued its estimates of federal tax expenditures for fiscal years 2015–2019 (JCX-141-15). The income tax charitable contribution deduction is the ninth largest of these expenditures, at $260.1 billion. The charitable deduction tax expenditure is broken down into the categories of education ($35 billion), health ($26.7 billion), and other ($198.4 billion).

The largest of the tax expenditures, ahead of the charitable deduction, are the net exclusion of pension contributions and earnings ($881.5 billion); the exclusion of employer contributions for health care, health insurance premiums, and long-term care insurance premiums ($769.8 billion); the reduced rates of tax on dividends and long-term capital gain ($689.6 billion); deferral of active income of controlled foreign corporations ($563.6 billion); the deduction for mortgage interest on owner-occupied residences ($419.8 billion); the deduction of nonbusiness state and local government income taxes, sales taxes, and personal property taxes ($342.3 billion); the subsidies for insurance purchased through health benefit exchanges ($322.5 billion); and the tax credit for children ($267 billion).

*§ 1.4 POLITICAL PHILOSOPHY RATIONALE

p. 11, last paragraph, third line. *Delete* ; more accurately *and substitute* , namely.

p. 13, last line. *Delete first* of.

p. 14, third complete paragraph, eighth line. *Insert* the federal *following* of.

p. 16, last paragraph, eighth line. *Delete* inexplicably ignored *and insert* trimmed.

p. 17, note 80. *Insert as second paragraph:*

An unavoidable aspect of tax exemptions is narrowing of the tax base. This phenomenon is most notable at the state and local level, in connection with real estate tax exemptions for charitable organizations. The Lincoln Institute of Land Policy reported, based on its study made available in August 2016, that these governments "forgo roughly 4 to 8 percent of total property tax revenues each year" due to these exemptions. Some local governments ask exempt organizations to make payments in lieu of taxes, to contribute to the "cost of the public services they consume." The report states that, as of 2012, at least 218 localities in 28 states had received PILOTs, amounting to more than $92 million annually. These political philosophical principles can fade into mere platitudes, if remembered at all, in the face of practical needs, such as money.

[6.5] Maimonides Medical Center v. United States, 809 F.3d 85, 91 (2nd Cir. 2015). Likewise, United States v. Detroit Medical Center, 833 F.3d 671 (6th Cir. 2016).

CHAPTER TWO

Overview of Nonprofit Sector and Tax-Exempt Organizations

*§ 2.1 Profile of Nonprofit Sector   § 2.2 Organization of IRS

*p. 23, second paragraph, seventh line. *Delete* later *and insert* below.

*§ 2.1 PROFILE OF NONPROFIT SECTOR

*p. 27. *Delete first two complete paragraphs and substitute:*

Charitable giving in the United States in 2015 is estimated to have totaled $373.3 billion.[65.1] Giving by individuals in 2015 amounted to an estimated $264.6 billion; this level of giving constituted 71 percent of all charitable giving for the year. Grantmaking by private foundations is an estimated $58.5 billion (16 percent of total funding). Gifts in the form of charitable bequests in 2015 are estimated to be $31.8 billion (9 percent of total giving). Gifts from corporations in 2015 totaled $18.5 billion (5 percent of total giving for that year).

Contributions to religious organizations in 2015 totaled $119.3 billion (32 percent of all giving that year). Gifts to educational organizations amounted to $57.48 billion (15 percent); to human service entities, $45.21 billion (12 percent); to foundations, $42.26 billion (11 percent); to health care institutions, $29.8 billion (8 percent); to public-society benefit organizations, $26.9 billion (7 percent); to international affairs entities, $15.75 billion (4 percent); to arts, culture, and humanities entities, $17 billion (5 percent); and to environmental and animals groups, $10.7 billion (3 percent). Two percent of this total (about $7 billion) involved gifts to individuals, such as corporate contributions of medicine.

[65.1] These data are from *Giving USA 2016*, published by the Giving USA Foundation, and researched and written under the auspices of the Center on Philanthropy at Indiana University.

§ 2.2 ORGANIZATION OF IRS

p. 32. *Insert following first paragraph, before heading:*

(c) EO Division's FY 2016 Work Plan

The Tax Exempt and Government Entities Division, on October 1, 2015, issued its work plan for fiscal year 2016. This work plan identifies TE/GE's five key areas of focus in the coming months. The first area is *continuous improvement*. It is written that one of the Division's guiding principles involves "sustaining a continuous improvement feedback loop" so as to effectively allocate resources. TE/GE's "partnership" with the IRS's Lean Six Sigma Office has, according to this report, led to "many improvements" in the Division's procedures. One example is the trimming of the time taken to process applications for recognition of exemption.[92.1]

Forthcoming projects include evaluation of the Form 1023-EZ process to determine potential improvements, development of a program to make Forms 990 available in Modernized e-File format, finding efficiencies in closing unit processes, simplifying tax forms and enhancing their digital functionality, and refining information document requests to reduce the length of examination processes.

Another of these areas is *knowledge management*. The Division is developing a "knowledge management framework." This entails gathering information from employees and staffing the "knowledge networks" (what the IRS likes to refer to as K-Nets). The IRS has begun building knowledge libraries within each K-Net, containing technical resources searchable by key issue areas and resource types.

A third area is *risk management*. The Division is working with the IRS's Office of the Chief Risk Officer to ensure that managers and management officials receive risk awareness training. It completed "risk registers" where managers identified risks within their offices and ways to mitigate existing and potential risks. It also introduced the Risk Acceptance Form and Tool to senior management, which is to help the Division document business decisions in the context of its "risk appetite and acceptance." Overall, the Division is implementing mitigation strategies and/or plans to "lessen the likelihood of the risk manifesting or the impact should it manifest."

The fourth area is fostering a culture of *data-driven decision-making*. These steps have been taken: the focusing of examination plans on strategic areas or issues where the Division believes there may be greater risk of noncompliance, and development of "a pilot project to analyze data from Form 1023-EZ applications to identify trends and patterns."

The last of these areas is *employee engagement*. This involves "empowering employees and managers, maintaining an effective recognition program, and strengthening our leadership team's visibility, transparency and interaction with employees."

[92.1] See § 26.1(a)(iii).

*(d) EO Division's FY 2017 Work Plan

The IRS, on September 29, 2016, unveiled the TE/GE FY 2017 Work Plan. A message from the TE/GE commissioners stated that the work of the Exempt Organizations Division is being conducted in the context of the IRS's Future State strategy, the vision of which foresees a "transformed taxpayer—and employee—experience: easily accessible web-based information that provides pre-filing education, user-friendly technology that makes filing easier, expeditious case handling and resolution if the IRS makes post-filing contact with the taxpayer, a better-equipped and engaged work force, and more."

(i) EO Determinations. In FY 2016, EO Determinations focused on its objectives to improve the processing of applications for recognition of exemption and enhance customer satisfaction. These programs have been implemented:

- *Erroneous Revocation Prevention.* On May 3, 2016, EO Rulings and Agreements formalized procedures to identify and prevent erroneous automatic revocations before posting to EO Select Check. The IRS reports that, since March 2015, it has reviewed 13,933 potential auto-revocations and prevented 3,202 erroneous revocations through June 2016.
- *Rejection of Incomplete Applications.* The IRS, on November 18, 2015, began rejecting incomplete applications. This process is said to educate applicants as to the requirements of a complete application and assure review of completed applications by revenue agents in a more efficient and expeditious manner. The IRS has rejected 2,588 incomplete applications through June 2016.
- *Social Welfare Organizations Notice Implementation.* The new notice requirement for social welfare organizations became operational on July 8, 2016, with the release of regulations, a revenue procedure, and interim guidance.[92.2] Through August 2016, the IRS has successfully processed over 400 of these notifications.
- *Form 1023-EZ User Fee.* The IRS reduced the user fee for Form 1023-EZ users. This change was implemented on July 1, 2016. Through the third quarter of FY 2016, EO received 33,549 Form 1023-EZ cases (58 percent of overall Form 1023 cases) and closed 33,909 Form 990-EZ cases, including 31,840 cases approved (94 percent) and 1,705 cases rejected (5 percent). The IRS anticipates that reduction of this user fee will result in an increase in its use.
- *FY 2016 Determinations Results.* Through the third quarter of FY 2016, EO Determinations continued to close more applications than it received. The average age of the open inventory (73 days) continued to decrease, while the quality of the work is said to remain consistent. EO Determinations approved 93.6 percent of all closed cases and denied less than 1 percent. The most common reasons for denial were private benefit and private inurement, substantial nonexempt purposes, and violation of the commerciality doctrine.

[92.2] See § 26.3A.

In FY 2017, EO Determinations will continue to improve the processing of applications and the new social welfare organizations notice (Form 8976). The projected increase in applications is expected to "almost entirely" be in the Form 1023-EZ "workstream,"[92.3] while Forms 1023 are projected to slightly decline. Other form receipts, such as Forms 1024 and 8940, are expected to increase slightly in FY 2017. Applications overall are projected to total "just over" 88,000.

The IRS stated that it will "continue to mitigate Form 1023-EZ applicant compliance risks with pre-determination application reviews and evaluation of the pre-determination data." The agency is said to "continue to utilize data from Form 1023-EZ pre-determination reviews and will consider future adjustments to the application, instructions, and pre-determination program."

(ii) Knowledge Management. In its continued effort to increase the technical knowledge base of EO employees, the IRS has several knowledge management initiatives planned for FY 2017. The IRS continues to prepare and post technical Issue Snapshots for EO employees and the public. Five of these snapshots have been completed, including abatement of Chapter 42 first-tier taxes and the definition of disqualified person (IRC § 4946), and the IRS has over 20 snapshots in development.

The EO Determinations Quality Assurance function will continue to review and evaluate EO Determinations cases for correctness and consistency. Areas for improvement will be identified and developed.

(iii) Correspondence. The IRS is projecting a 1 percent increase in taxpayer correspondence in FY 2017 based on new tax law and the new Form 8976 workstream. The agency anticipates improvements in "cycle time and open and overage inventory in FY 2017, resulting from increased efficiencies." The IRS continues to "reduce open correspondence inventory with the goal of responding and resolving submissions timely to match demand."[92.4]

[92.3] See § 26.1(h).
*[92.4] The EO Examinations component of these work plans is the subject of § 27.7(a)(vi), (vii).

CHAPTER THREE

Source, Advantages, and Disadvantages of Tax Exemption

*§ 3.2 Recognition of Tax Exemption

*§ 3.2   RECOGNITION OF TAX EXEMPTION

*p. 46, note 27. *Delete* **2014-10, 2014-2 I.R.B. 293 § 4.01** *and substitute* **2016–5, 2016-1 I.R.B. 188.**

*p. 46, first complete paragraph, sixth sentence. *Delete and substitute:*

In addition, for an organization to be regarded as an exempt social welfare entity, it must give notice to the IRS[29]; the same is the case as regards exempt political organizations.[29.1]

---

[29] IRC § 506. See § 26.3A.
[29.1] IRC § 527(i). See § 26.11.

CHAPTER FOUR

Organizational, Operational, and Related Tests and Doctrines

§ 4.1 FORMS OF TAX-EXEMPT ORGANIZATIONS

(a) General Rules

p. 63. *Insert as fifth paragraph:*

Perhaps the best illustration of this body of law came in connection with a court opinion finding that an organization did not exist for tax-exempt organization law purposes.[23.1] The court observed that, during the years at issue, neither this individual nor those assisting him "maintained financial records, kept minutes, drafted organizing documents or bylaws, requested an employer identification number, or put in place any structures that would be expected from a continuing organization." No state organizational requirement was met. Federal annual information returns were either not filed or filed late. The court also stated that "there was no separation between [this individual] and his activities." He was the "sole researcher, analyst, producer, service provider, and scientist (and was later defined as the only director and officer)." He had control of all of the funds involved (none of which were devoted to charitable purposes), which were deemed to be gross income to him personally.

*§ 4.2 GOVERNING INSTRUMENTS

*p. 66, third complete paragraph, last line. *Delete period and insert following footnote number:*

or a supporting organization.[52.1]

*p. 67, carryover paragraph. *Insert as last sentence:*

If a limited liability company, the organizing document will be an operating agreement.

[*23.1] George v. Comm'r, 110 T.C.M. 190 (2015).
[*52.1] See § 12.3(c).

*(d) Dissolution Requirements

*p. 71, second complete paragraph, second line. *Insert footnote following period:*

87.1

> Reg. § 1.501(c)(3)-1(b)(4).

*p. 71, second complete paragraph, ninth line. *Insert footnote following period:*

87.2

> *Id.*

*p. 71, note 88, first line. *Delete* **Reg.** *reference and substitute* **Id.**

§ 4.5 OPERATIONAL TEST

(a) Basic Rules

p. 86, note 211. *Insert following existing text:*

> See § 26.1(i).

p. 86, first complete paragraph. *Insert as last sentence:*

By contrast, a charitable organization was allowed by the IRS to maintain its exempt status, even though it was a "dormant shell" (because it transferred all of its then assets for charitable purposes), inasmuch as additional funds were to be received by it (as to which it had an "identifiable legal right in the future") and it had a "specific plan" to continue its charitable operations. [211.1]

p. 86, note 212. *Insert following existing text:*

> Likewise Community Education Found. v. Comm'r, T.C. Memo. 2016–223 (Dec. 12, 2016).

*(c) Quantification of Activities

*p. 88. *Insert as second complete paragraph, before heading:*

In a certainly troublesome and seemingly incorrect ruling, the IRS concluded, as to an organization that has been operational for at least three years, that it does not qualify for exempt status as a social welfare organization because 100 percent of its expenditures were for political campaign activities in one year, even though it expended 100 percent of its volunteer time on exempt functions in the ensuing two years, because this organization did not make any exempt function expenditures in those two years.[221.1]

*(e) Aggregate Principle

*p. 90, note 238, first line. *Insert* **718** *following fourth period.*

[211.1] Priv. Ltr. Rul. 201448026.

*[221.1] Priv. Ltr. Rul. 201615014. Shortly thereafter, the IRS issued a private letter ruling analyzing an organization's total activities based solely on categories of time expended (Priv. Ltr. Rul. 201639016).

*§ 4.9 STATE ACTION DOCTRINE

*(a) Doctrine in General

p. 97, note 288. *Insert* See *before existing text.*

§ 4.11 COMMERCIALITY DOCTRINE

(d) Contemporary Application of Doctrine

p. 124, second complete paragraph, first line. *Delete* The IRS *and insert* A court.

p. 125, line 31. *Delete* and.

p. 125, line 32. *Delete* period *and substitute* semicolon.

p. 125, line 32. *Insert following footnote number:*

an organization that functioned as a licensing agency for products devised by children in contests, where it serves to further children's education and establish a social network to further children's education funding;[517.1] an organization that was said by the IRS to be competing with for-profit companies (although that point was not explained) and had an "insubstantial" amount of charitable gifts (this observation was not explained either);[517.2] and an organization that is "marketing and selling support services for a fee" and is (ostensibly) competing with a for-profit organization.[517.3]

p. 126, carryover paragraph. *Insert as first sentence:*

The IRS ruled that the fact that an organization collected testimonials on its website is evidence that the entity is being operated in a commercial manner.[518.1]

p. 126, second complete paragraph. *Insert as second sentence:*

For example, a court simply concluded (or assumed) that an activity labeled *recreational* is "inherently commercial" and decided on that basis that an organization providing recreational therapy could not qualify as a tax-exempt charitable entity.[524.1]

[517.1] Priv. Ltr. Rul. 201545029.

[517.2] Priv. Ltr. Rul. 201548021.

[517.3] Priv. Ltr. Rul. 201548025.

[518.1] Priv. Ltr. Rul. 201540019.

[524.1] GameHearts v. Comm'r, 110 T.C.M. 454 (2015).

CHAPTER FIVE

Nonprofit Governance

§ 5.7 IRS and Governance

§ 5.7 IRS AND GOVERNANCE

*p. 133, paragraph, third line. *Insert following* statutes:

, augmented by court opinions

*p. 133, paragraph, seventh line. *Insert* board composition and, *following* on.

(a) Matter of Agency Jurisdiction

p. 149. *Insert as second complete paragraph:*

In what appears to be the most direct case on point, an appellate court held that the Federal Energy Regulatory Commission did not have the statutory authority to make or enforce its order endeavoring to dictate the composition of the board of a public benefit corporation, a form of nonprofit corporation.[79.1] The agency took the position that the nonprofit organization violated its rules concerning independent system operators (ISOs); its order dictated replacement of the board. The court of appeals ruled that the FERC "has no authority to replace the selection method or membership of the governing board of an ISO."[79.2] The court, having found the FERC's position "breathtaking," wrote that the agency "commit[ed] . . . an absurdity."[79.3] The court added that the FERC was "overreaching," that its attempt to order the nonprofit entity to change its board was an "extreme measure," and that the agency was "stretching" in asserting its authority over this aspect of nonprofit governance.[79.4]

[79.1] California Independent System Operator Corporation v. Federal Energy Regulatory Commission, 372 F.3d 395 (D.C. Cir. 2004).

[79.2] *Id.* at 398.

[79.3] *Id.* at 402.

[79.4] *Id.*

(c) IRS Ruling Policy

p. 153. *Insert as second paragraph:*

When a small board is presented to the IRS as part of the application-for-recognition-of-exemption process, the agency often attempts to persuade the entity to expand its board as a condition of exemption. In some instances, the applicant organization refuses to change the board composition.[101.1] In other instances, the organization will comply with the request, only to have the IRS deny recognition of exemption on other grounds.[101.2]

p. 153. *Insert as last sentence of existing second paragraph:*

The IRS ruled that a five-person board consisting only of family members was a violation of the private benefit doctrine because the organization is governed "by a small group of individuals who have exclusive control over the management of [its] funds and operations."[110.1]

p. 154, carryover paragraph. *Insert as third complete sentence:*

The IRS in one private letter ruling, while not revoking exemption on this basis, went out of its way to highlight the fact that an organization does not have a conflict-of-interest policy or a document-retention-and-destruction policy, noting also that it lacks any internal control reports, an annual report, or audited financial statements.[112.1]

p. 154, carryover paragraph. *Begin new paragraph with fourth line.*

[101.1] E.g., Priv. Ltr. Rul. 201507026.

[101.2] E.g., Priv. Ltr. Rul. 201541013.

[110.1] Priv. Ltr. Rul. 201540019.

[112.1] Priv. Ltr. Rul. 201543019.

CHAPTER SIX

Concept of *Charitable*

§ 6.2 Public Policy Doctrine   § 6.3 Collateral Concepts

§ 6.2 PUBLIC POLICY DOCTRINE

(d) Other Forms of Discrimination

p. 173, second complete paragraph, second sentence. *Insert footnote at end of sentence:*

[109.1] In the aftermath of the Supreme Court's ruling that there is a constitutional right to same-sex marriage, with this right to marry a "fundamental right inherent in the liberty of the person, and under the Due Process and Equal Protection Clauses of the Fourteenth Amendment" (Obergefell v. Hodges, 135 S. Ct. 2584, 2604 (2015)), tax-exempt charitable, educational, and religious organizations are contemplating the notion that their exemption may be jeopardized if they engage in practices contrary to same-sex marriage protections. The Department of the Treasury, on October 21, 2014, issued proposed regulations to implement the *Obergefell* decision in a variety of tax law contexts (REG-148998-13).

(e) Affirmative Action Principles

p. 175, first complete paragraph. *Delete last sentence, including footnote.*

p. 175. *Insert as second complete paragraph:*

The Court subsequently articulated a tougher strict scrutiny test that courts are to use in evaluating race-based affirmative action programs in the public higher education context.[125] The prior version of the test, the Court stated, "does not permit a court to accept a school's assertion that its admissions process uses race in a permissible way without a court giving close analysis to the evidence of how the process works in practice."[125.1] It added that, in reviewing an affirmative action program, a court must "verify that it is necessary for a university to use race to achieve the educational benefits of diversity."[125.2] The reason that this test

---

[125] Fisher v. Univ. of Texas at Austin, 133 S. Ct. 2411 (2013).

[125.1] *Id.* at 2421.

[125.2] *Id.*

is now more difficult to meet is that there must be a "careful judicial inquiry into whether a university could achieve sufficient diversity without using racial classifications."[125.3] This case was remanded, with the court of appeals holding that the university's affirmative action race-influenced admissions program is constitutional.[125.4] The majority wrote: "We are persuaded that to deny [the university] its limited use of race in its search for holistic diversity would hobble the richness of the educational experience in contradiction of the plain teachings of *Bakke* and *Grutter*."[125.5] On June 29, 2015, the Court announced it would again review this case.[125.6] The Court, on June 23, 2016, voted (4-3) to uphold the affirmative action program at the university.[125.7]

§ 6.3 COLLATERAL CONCEPTS

(a) Requirement of *Charitable Class*

p. 179, note 153, last sentence. *Delete and substitute:*

A similar situation arose in the case of an organization formed to provide funding for the treatment, education, and therapies for an individual with autism (Priv. Ltr. Rul. 201519035). A nonprofit day care center failed to achieve recognition of exemption where the only children (four) enrolled in the entity's program were those of its board members (Priv. Ltr. Rul. 201218041).

p. 179, note 156. *Insert following existing text:*

An organization was denied recognition of tax exemption as a charitable entity because those it was (ostensibly) serving, "undocumented aliens" and "American workers," were not members of a charitable class (Priv. Ltr. Rul. 201527043), as was an organization established to assist "homeowners," without those to be assisted confined to low-income individuals (Priv. Ltr. Rul. 291519034).

[125.3] *Id*. at 2420.

[125.4] Fisher v. Univ. of Texas at Austin, 758 F.3d 633 (5th Cir. 2014).

[125.5] *Id*. at 659–660.

[125.6] Earlier, the Court held that a ban on racial preferences in admissions to a state's public colleges and universities, added to the states' constitution as the result of a statewide referendum, is constitutional (Schuette v. Coalition to Defend Affirmative Action, 134 S. Ct. 1623 (2014)).

[*125.7] Fisher v. Univ. of Texas at Austin, 136 S. Ct. 2198 (2016).

CHAPTER SEVEN

Charitable Organizations

§ 7.4 PROVISION OF HOUSING

p. 203. *Insert as second paragraph:*

Likewise, a nonprofit corporation was formed to purchase, rehabilitate, sell, and lease housing properties. It did not impose restrictions on who may rent these properties, although it advised the IRS that it will give preference to low- and moderate-income families, first-time home buyers, and veterans. All of its income will be derived from "appreciated values received from the sale or rent of rehabilitated properties." This organization is an "affinity partner" with what apparently is a for-profit company. It presented itself as a "profitable opportunity" for the company, stating it will increase the company's "scope of services" and will assist the company in "marketing of new sales opportunities." The IRS quite correctly ruled that the organization's programs are not charitable and that it is not serving a charitable class.[107.1]

§ 7.6 PROMOTION OF HEALTH

(a) Hospital Law in General

p. 208. *Insert as first complete paragraph, before heading:*

A subsequent report from the IRS to Congress, dated January 28, 2015, offered comparisons among tax-exempt, taxable, and government-owned hospitals.[148.1] This report provided information regarding charity care and bad-debt expenses, and contains information about exempt hospitals' community benefit activities: (1) charity care provided by exempt hospitals was in excess of $12 billion, $8.9 billion of such care was provided by government-owned hospitals, and $1.4 billion

---

[107.1] Priv. Ltr. Rul. 201534020.

[148.1] This report, based on data for calendar year 2011, was mandated by the Patient Protection and Affordable Care Act § 9007(e)(1).

in care was provided by taxable hospitals; (2) non-Medicare bad-debt expenses of exempt hospitals totaled $8.7 billion, government-owned hospitals' bad-debt expenses were $4.6 billion, and such expenses for taxable hospitals were $1.9 billion; and (3) the costs of community benefit activities of exempt hospitals were $62.5 billion, comprising 9.67 percent of total expenses.

(b) Additional Statutory Requirements for Hospitals

p. 209, note 159. *Insert following existing text:*

The IRS issued guidance providing hospital facilities with clarification as to how a facility may comply with this provider list requirement (Notice 2015-46, 2015-28 I.R.B. 64).

(f) Health Maintenance Organizations

p. 214, note 196, last line. *Insert following closing parenthesis and before period:*

, although the IRS reclassified an HMO (Medicaid-only type) from an IRC § 501(c)(3) entity to an IRC § 501(c)(4) HMO, after the plan merged with a commercial enrollment-based plan (Priv. Ltr. Rul. 201538027)

(l) Health Insurance Exchanges

p. 222, note 257. *Insert following existing text:*

The Supreme Court held that these tax credits are available to qualified individuals irrespective of whether the health insurance is acquired from a state exchange or an exchange established by the federal government (King v. Burwell, 135 S. Ct. 2480 (2015)).

§ 7.7 LESSENING BURDENS OF GOVERNMENT

*p. 230. Insert as second complete paragraph:

Congress established the Medicare Shared Savings Program to be conducted through accountable care organizations in order to promote quality improvements and cost savings in health care.[304.1] Consequently, participation in the MSSP by an ACO furthers the charitable purpose of lessening the burdens of government.[304.2] By contrast, federal law does not provide an objective manifestation that the federal government considers non-MSSP-related ACO activities to be its burden, so that these types of ACOs are not tax-exempt by reason of lessening the burdens of government.[304.3]

p. 231. *Insert as last paragraph:*

An organization claiming to be charitable because it is lessening the burdens of government had its tax exemption revoked.[317.1] The entity was established

---

[*304.1] See § 7.6(m).
[*304.2] E.g., Notice 2011-20, 2011-6 I.R.B. 652.
[*304.3] Priv. Ltr. Rul. 201615022.
[317.1] Priv. Ltr. Rul. 201531022.

to purchase claims for refunds by fuel tank owners or contractors to clean up spillage from underground storage tanks where approval for reimbursement was made by a state's department of environmental quality. The IRS said that the organization failed to show that it was lessening the burden of a government, the fuel tank owners are not members of a charitable class[317.2] and the financing program the organization developed is commercial in nature.[317.3] The IRS wrote that this organization "provides more relief to the burden of the fuel tank owners and consultants than to the burden of the government." Private inurement was also found in the form of a flow of fees to an entity owned by the organization's founder.[317.4]

p. 231, note 314. *Delete 293, 305 and insert 294, 306.*

§ 7.14 FUNDRAISING ORGANIZATIONS

(c) Other Exemption Issues

p. 252, carryover paragraph, last sentence. *Insert comma after* donees *and before note number, and delete* and.

p. 252, carryover paragraph, last sentence, last line. *Delete period and insert comma; insert the following after existing text:*

and that an organization providing fundraising and marketing services to unrelated charitable entities could not be tax-exempt because it was primarily engaged in commercial activity.[510.1]

§ 7.16 OTHER CATEGORIES OF CHARITY

An *agriculture research organization* is a type of public charity. This is an entity that is engaged in the continuous active conduct of agricultural research (as defined in the Agricultural Research, Extension, and Teaching Policy Act of 1977) in conjunction with a land-grant college or university or a non-land grant college of agriculture. For a contribution to an agricultural research organization to qualify for the 50-percent limitation,[588] during the calendar year in which a contribution is made to the organization, the organization must be committed to spend the contribution for the research before January 1 of the fifth calendar year which begins after the date of the contribution.[589]

[317.2] See § 6.3(a).

[317.3] See § 4.11.

[317.4] See § 20.4.

[510.1] Priv. Ltr. Rul. 201507026.

[588] See *Charitable Giving* § 7.5.

[589] IRC §§ 170(b)(1)(A)(ix) (added by the Protecting Americans from Tax Hikes Act of 2015 (Pub. L. No. 114-113, Division Q) § 331(a)) and 509(a)(1). It is intended that this provision be interpreted in like manner to and consistent with the rules applicable to medical research organizations (see § 7.6(d)).

(f) Other Types of Charitable Organizations

p. 262. *Insert following existing text:*

One of the many ways to qualify as a tax-exempt charitable entity is to engage in activities consisting of the "erection or maintenance of public buildings, monuments, or works."[590] An organization sought recognition of exemption as a charitable entity with a program of development and distribution of open source software. The IRS declined to recognize exemption in this case because anyone can use the software for any purpose (including commercial, personal, recreational, lobbying, and/or political campaign purposes), and the organization's undertakings do not serve a charitable class, educate individuals, or amount to the performance of qualifying scientific research.[591] The entity advanced the argument that it is operating in a charitable manner inasmuch as production of the software is "effectively" the "erection of a public work." The IRS disagreed, taking the position that the concept of public works does not encompass intangibles and that software is not a facility.

---

[590] Reg. § 1.501(c)(3)-1(d)(2).
[591] Priv. Ltr. Rul. 201505040.

CHAPTER EIGHT

Educational Organizations

*§ 8.1 FEDERAL TAX LAW DEFINITION OF *EDUCATIONAL*

*p. 263, second complete paragraph, second line. *Insert* law *following* tax.

*§ 8.2 *EDUCATION* CONTRASTED WITH *PROPAGANDA*

*p. 266, first complete paragraph, second line. *Delete* presentation *and insert* communication.

*p. 266, first complete paragraph, line 15. *Delete* opinion *and substitute* opinion(s).

*p. 267, carryover paragraph. *Insert* as *last sentence:*

This court subsequently concluded that, using these factors, messages were "indicative that the method used to communicate the position is not educational," such as distortion of facts and use of "inflammatory language and disparaging terms."[33.1]

§ 8.3 EDUCATIONAL INSTITUTIONS

(b) Museums *Tax Law*

p. 270, third paragraph, first line. *Insert before existing text:*

(i) *Law in General.*

p. 272. *Insert following first complete paragraph, before heading:*

---

*33.1 Parks v. Comm'r, 145 T.C. 278, 317–318 (2015).

(ii) Senate Finance Committee Investigation. Reacting to media reports raising the possibility that some tax-exempt museums are operating with minimal benefit to the public while facilitating substantial charitable deductions, the Senate Finance Committee has initiated investigations. These inquiries started with letters sent to several small museums around the end of November 2015.

These letters ask, with respect to the museum's most recent five years, for information about the museum's normal operating schedule (including the total number of hours in each of these years the museum was open to the public). The Committee wants to know the total number of visitors each year to the museum and any amount charged to visit the museum.

The letters request a description of how the museum obtained its artwork. Identification is asked of any donor who provided more than 5 percent of the artwork held by the museum, as well as a statement of that donor's role in overseeing the museum (such as director or trustee).

The Committee is asking about the legal entity that holds title to the museum building and other property; if the building is rented, the legal entity to which the museum pays rent; whether any property tax is being paid on museum property; and whether trustees, directors, or donors have physical access to the museum when it is closed to the public and, if so, whether the museum is reimbursed for this access.

Other questions pertain to whether the museum loans artwork to other museums or charities, whether the museum loans donated artwork to the donor, the provision of the museum's policy on acceptance of restricted gifts, whether the museum is involved in partnerships or displays artwork in cooperation with other museums, the methods the museum uses to value donated artwork, and whether the museum provides valuation information to donors.

The concluding question is whether the museum has awarded any grants during the past five years.

*The findings of this investigation, based on responses from 11 museums, were summarized in a letter from the chairman of the Committee to the IRS dated May 17, 2016.

One principal area of inquiry was the manner in which museums make their art available to the public. The Committee's findings are that museums operate in "many fashions" and provide a "varying degree of public access" to their collections. Some museums are said to have as many as 500,000 visitors annually. Others are working to increase attendance and expand their facilities. Still others have "robust" artwork loan programs, have active grant programs supporting artists and art education organizations, or make their collections viewable online.

Conversely, some of these museums are "not readily accessible" to the public. Of "particular concern" to the Committee are museums that are "lightly advertised" and require reservations "weeks or months in advance." This approach is characterized as "narrowing the visitor pool to a small group of patrons." Some museums keep "short hours."

The other main area of inquiry concerns the extent to which founders and donors enjoy privileges. One of the findings in this area is that "many founding donors continue to play an active role in management and operations of the museum, although many have professional staff and are working to further professionalize their organizations." Some museums "sit on land that is owned by the founding donor"; in other instances, museum buildings are adjacent to the donor's private residence. Some museums obtained all or most of their collection from a single founding donor or family.

"In many cases," the report states, the "founding donor continues to have an active role in management of the museum, either by serving on the board of directors or by serving as president of the museum." These factors have, as to the Committee, "raise[d] questions about the nature of the relationship between the donor and museum that perhaps merit further scrutiny." Chairman Hatch wrote that he "remain[s] concerned that this area of our tax code is ripe for exploitation" and asked for the IRS's views on "private museums and the agency's efforts to ensure that private museums have sufficient guidance to conduct their operations."

Some of the specific findings in this report are (1) overall, the total number of hours museums are open each week ranges from 20 to 48; the average number of hours open for each of the past five years ranged from 768 to 2,832; (2) some museums, in addition, accommodate school groups and other private visitors; some have outdoor areas with expanded access hours; (3) some museums have "highly irregular schedules"; some were closed for extended periods due to construction or exhibit installation; (4) one museum stated it expected over 500,000 visitors in 2015; another reported 35,000 visitors annually; four museums said their annual average number of visitors was 5,700 or less; (5) nine museums stated they do not charge an admission fee; (6) seven museums indicated that they actively participate in partnerships with other museums to display artwork; (7) the responses as to how the artwork was obtained ranged from gifts by founding donors (or their private foundations), purchases of art, or loans of private collections; (8) nine of these museums stated that they use outside professional appraisers to value donated artwork; (9) as to the facility, some museums own the property, some have rent-free access to the property, and some have ownership and rental combinations; (10) several museums stated that trustees, directors, and/or donors have access to the museum outside of normal operating hours but never for personal purposes; and (11) seven museums indicated that they make grants such as in connection with visiting scholar programs or the awarding of prizes; one museum reported that it has made grants in excess of $3 million to more than 75 exempt organizations during the past five years.

CHAPTER NINE

Scientific Organizations

*§ 9.1   Federal Tax Law Definition of *Science*

*§ 9.1   FEDERAL TAX LAW DEFINITION OF *SCIENCE*

*p. 287, second complete paragraph, first line. *Insert* revenue *following* IRS.

CHAPTER TEN

Religious Organizations

§ 10.1   CONSTITUTIONAL LAW FRAMEWORK

(a) General Constitutional Law Principles

p. 301, note 66. *Insert following existing text:*

Yet a federal district court ruled that the contraceptive mandate violates the RFRA (and equal protection principles), because the mandate, as applied to a nonreligious, nonprofit organization and its employees with contrary religious views, is equally offensive to them as it is to those who are protected by the exemption for religious employers, resting that conclusion on the jurisprudence equating certain moral beliefs with religion (see § 10.2(a), text accompanied by notes 131, 132) (March for Life v. Burwell, 2015 WL 5139099 (D.D.C. 2015)).

p. 301. *Insert as fourth complete paragraph, before heading:*

The Court considered the constitutionality, from the standpoint of free speech principles, of a town's sign code. Signs concerning "qualifying events," including church services, were treated less favorably than other categories of signs. The Court held that this sign code is content-based on its face; its provisions were said to be able to stand only if they survive the strict scrutiny test. This required the town to prove that its restrictions, including those on churches, further a compelling governmental interest and are narrowly tailored to achieve that interest. The town was unable to do that; the code was struck down.[71.1]

*(c) Internal Revenue Code Provisions

***p. 304, note 97.** *Insert as last sentence:*

This lawsuit was refiled on April 6, 2016, with the reason for lack of standing apparently resolved (Freedom From Religion Foundation, Inc. v. Lew, 3:16-cv-00215 (W. D. Wis.). This lawsuit , on October 24, 2016, survived the government's motion to dismiss.

[71.1] Reed v. Town of Gilbert, Arizona, 135 S. Ct. 2218 (2015).

*§ 10.2   FEDERAL TAX LAW DEFINITION OF *RELIGION*

*p. 305, fourth paragraph, third line. *Insert* **well** *following* authored.

*§ 10.3   CHURCHES AND SIMILAR INSTITUTIONS

*(b) Associational Test

*p. 317, note 194. *Delete* 131 S. Ct. 1676 *and insert* 562 U.S. 1286.

§ 10.5   CONVENTIONS OR ASSOCIATIONS OF CHURCHES

p. 320, note 214. *Insert following existing text:*

The IRS ruled that employees of a tax-exempt elder care facility being operated for the benefit of elderly and infirm members of a religious order are, by virtue of control of the facility by a church, deemed to be employees of a church or a convention or association of churches by virtue of being employees of an organization that is tax-exempt and controlled by or associated with a church or a convention or association of churches (Priv. Ltr. Rul. 201537025).

CHAPTER ELEVEN

Other Charitable Organizations

§ 11.9 Endowment Funds

§ 11.9 ENDOWMENT FUNDS

(b) College and University Endowments

p. 340, first line. *Insert before existing text:*

(i) IRS Compliance Check.

*p. 340. Insert as fourth complete paragraph, following third heading:

Two federal government studies of college and university endowment funds have been recently published.

p. 342. *Insert following first paragraph, before heading:*

(ii) CRS Report. The Congressional Research Service, in a report made public on December 4, 2015, provided background information on college and university endowments, and summarized various options for changing their treatment under the federal tax law.

This report discussed college and university endowment fund basics, with the term *endowment* defined simply as an "investment fund maintained for the benefit of the educational institution." Definitions are provided for *true endowments*, otherwise known as *permanent endowments*, including those with restrictions imposed by donors. Also referenced are *term endowments* and *quasi endowments*.

For 2014, $226.6 billion (44 percent) was held in true endowments and $119 billion (23 percent) was in quasi endowments. Of the true endowment balance, $210.3 billion was donor-restricted. The term endowment balance was $17.9 billion.

At the close of fiscal year 2014, endowment balances for the 832 institutions included in the National Association of College and University Business Officers–Commonfund Study of Endowments totaled $516 billion. Endowment assets are concentrated, with 11 percent of institutions holding 74 percent of all endowment assets. Institutions with the largest endowments (Yale, Princeton, Harvard, and Stanford) each hold more than 4 percent of total endowment assets. For this fiscal year, endowments earned an average return of 15.5 percent.

An increasing proportion of endowment funds has been invested in alternative investments, including private equity and hedge funds. Large endowments, the report observes, are more likely to invest their funds in alternative strategies.

Spending from endowments, this report states, "supports various higher education activities." For 2014, the payout rate for these institutions was 4.4 percent. The report states that, "[o]n average, in recent years, institutions with the largest endowments have tended to have payout rates that exceeded average payout rates for institutions with smaller endowments."

College and university endowments are tax-exempt, either because they are components of exempt institutions of higher education or they have their own recognition of exemption. Contributions to these endowment funds are generally tax-deductible. Investment earnings of these funds generally are not taxable.

The CRS report observed that there are a number of options relating to the tax treatment of endowments should policymakers decide to "change the status quo." As always, "[p]olicy options considered may depend on the overarching policy objective." The report notes one of the options: "Leaving current-law tax treatment of endowments unchanged." Here are four other policy options discussed in this report.

One option is to impose an annual payout requirement on endowment funds. Often, the proposal is to have a minimum 5 percent payout rate, similar to that required of private foundations. In this context, of course, there are proposals to force colleges and universities to use endowment resources to reduce the cost of higher education and make college education more accessible. As discussed in the report, there are many complexities attending this proposal, such as restricting a payout requirement to certain types of endowments, tying the payout to investment earnings, measuring a payout over a multiyear period, or associating a payout with metrics such as tuition levels or student need. Critics of this approach note that most endowment gifts (around 90 percent) are restricted as to use by donors.

Another option is to tax endowment earnings. One approach would be to follow the tax-rate regime used in the unrelated business income tax context (current maximum rate of 35 percent). Another approach would be to utilize the rules applicable in the private foundation setting (an excise tax on investment income at a 1 or 2 percent rate). As the report notes, a tax on endowment earnings "would generate additional federal revenues."

A third option is to reduce the value of the charitable deduction for gifts to endowments, on the basis of the lapse in time between an endowment gift and its ultimate use for charitable purposes. The report notes that "this type of adjustment could become complex." A refinement would be to limit the deduction reduction to gifts of a certain size.

The fourth of these policy options changes the law for certain offshore investments. The report focuses on the use of blocker corporations, referencing a proposal to disallow the use of blockers by introducing look-through rules to determine the source, and thus the taxation, of earnings.

CHAPTER TWELVE

Public Charities and Private Foundations

§ 12.3 Categories of Public Charities   § 12.4 Private Foundation Rules

§ 12.3 CATEGORIES OF PUBLIC CHARITIES

(a) Institutions

p. 356, third complete paragraph, sixth line. *Insert following first footnote reference:*

agricultural research organizations;[136.1]

*(b) Publicly Supported Charities

*p. 363, note 193. *Insert another §; insert , 509(a)(1) before period.*

*(c) Supporting Organizations

*p. 367, fifth complete paragraph, last line. *Insert footnote at end of line:*

[222.1] Additional requirements in connection with these integral part tests were proposed on February 18, 2016 (REG-118867-10). Final regulations concerning the payout requirements for Type III supporting organizations that are not functionally integrated with respect to their supported organizations were issued on December 21, 2015 (T.D. 9746).

*p. 369, note 238, first line. *Delete of and insert semicolon.*

[136.1] IRC §§ 170(b)(1)(A)(ix), 509(a)(1). See § 7.16(f), text accompanied by notes 588, 589.

§ 12.4 PRIVATE FOUNDATION RULES

(d) Jeopardizing Investments

p. 376. Insert as third complete paragraph:

Also, outside the context of program-related investments, private foundations may take their charitable purposes into account in formulating investment policy (*mission-related investing*). That is, when exercising ordinary business care and prudence in deciding whether to make an investment, foundation managers may consider all relevant facts and circumstances, including the relationship between a particular investment and the foundation's charitable purposes. Foundations are not required to select only investments that offer the highest rate of return, the lowest risks, or the greatest liquidity as long as the foundation managers exercise the requisite ordinary business care and prudence under the facts and circumstances prevailing at the time of the investment in making investment decisions that support, and do not jeopardize, the furtherance of the private foundation's charitable purposes.[316.1]

[316.1] Notice 2015-62, 2015-39 I.R.B. 411.

CHAPTER THIRTEEN

Social Welfare Organizations

§ 13.1 Concept of *Social Welfare*   *§ 13.2 Requirement of *Community*

§ 13.1 CONCEPT OF *SOCIAL WELFARE*

(b) Benefits to Members

p. 389, first complete paragraph, line 10. *Delete* and.

p. 389, first complete paragraph, line 12. *Delete period and substitute comma; insert the following after footnote number:*

and an organization providing assistance to those owning recreational residences in a national forest had its exemption as a social welfare entity revoked because its activities were almost exclusively for the benefit of its membership.[46.1]

*§ 13.2 REQUIREMENT OF *COMMUNITY*

*(b) Broader Requirement of *Community*

*p. 396, second paragraph. *Insert as last sentence:*

By contrast, the IRS ruled that an entity could not qualify as an exempt social welfare organization inasmuch as its sole function was maintenance of a private road that was essentially a common driveway for its four members' homes; the benefit to the "larger community" was said to be "minor and incidental."[110.1]

[46.1] Priv. Ltr. Rul. 201518018.
*[110.1] Priv. Ltr. Rul. 201623013.

CHAPTER FOURTEEN

Business Leagues and Like Organizations

§ 14.1 CONCEPT OF *BUSINESS LEAGUE*

(a) General Principles

p. 403. *Insert as second complete paragraph:*

The IRS is attempting to discourage the use of small boards, in the case of public charities, by portraying the practice as an inherent form of private benefit.[13.1] The agency has made one attempt to import that proposition into the law concerning tax exemption for business leagues. On that occasion, the IRS ruled that an organization did not qualify as an exempt business league, in part because the organization had a self-perpetuating governing board; in that instance, the IRS lamented the absence of "oversight of an independent board."[13.2] Nonetheless, among the federal tax law criteria for business leagues, there is no requirement of an "independent board" (whatever meaning that term may have in this context).

§ 14.2 DISQUALIFYING ACTIVITIES

(c) Performance of Particular Services

p. 421, carryover paragraph, line 16. *Delete and.*

p. 421, carryover paragraph, line 18. *Delete period and substitute semicolon; insert the following after footnote number:*

an organization the membership of which is confined to franchisees affiliated with a specific business corporation;[186.1] and an organization operating a farmers' market.[186.2]

[13.1] See § 5.7(c).

[13.2] Priv. Ltr. Rul. 201349021.

[186.1] Priv. Ltr. Rul. 201540017.

[*186.2] E.g., Priv. Ltr. Rul. 201639016.

CHAPTER FIFTEEN

Social Clubs

§ 15.1 Social Clubs in General

§ 15.1 SOCIAL CLUBS IN GENERAL

(b) Club Functions

p. 430, second paragraph. *Insert as fourth sentence:*

For these reasons, a club, organized only because that form is required by state law to enable a restaurant of which it is a part to serve alcoholic beverages, was denied recognition of exemption as a social club on the grounds that it is not operated exclusively for pleasure and recreation, there is no requisite mingling of members, there is private inurement regarding the owners of the restaurant, and the sole function of this ostensible club is to sell alcohol to the public.[13.1]

p. 430, second paragraph, last line on the page. *Delete* **For this reason** *and insert* **Similarly.**

*p. 431, carryover paragraph. *Insert as last sentence:*

Of course, the entity must be a true *club,* as opposed to, for example, a nonprofit entity formed to operate a restaurant and bar, accessible to the public, in circumvention of law in a dry county.[15.1]

[13.1] Priv. Ltr. Rul. 201515035.
[*15.1] E.g., Priv. Ltr. Rul. 201605021.

CHAPTER SEVENTEEN

Political Organizations

*§ 17.6   Taxation of Other Exempt Organizations

p. 456, note 8. *Insert as second paragraph:*

As to gifts made after December 18, 2015, the gift tax exclusion is available for transfers of money or other property to tax-exempt social welfare organizations (see Chapter 13), labor organizations (see § 16.1), and business leagues (see Chapter 14) (IRC § 2501(a)(6), added by Protecting Americans from Tax Hikes Act of 2015 (Pub. L. No. 114-113, Division Q) § 408(a), (b)). No inference is to be drawn from this law change as to whether transfers to these entities prior to this effective date are subject to the gift tax (id. § 408(c)).

*§ 17.6   TAXATION OF OTHER EXEMPT ORGANIZATIONS

*p. 465, first complete paragraph, lines 2 and 3. *Delete* public charities engaging in any amount of *and insert* charitable organizations engaging to any extent in.

CHAPTER EIGHTEEN

Employee Benefit Funds

§ 18.3 Voluntary Employees' Beneficiary Associations

§ 18.3 VOLUNTARY EMPLOYEES' BENEFICIARY ASSOCIATIONS

p. 484, first complete paragraph. *Insert as seventh sentence:*

Where the exempt sponsor is dissolving, the VEBA's assets may be distributed as taxable lump-sum payments among the participants without triggering excise tax.[76.1]

p. 484, first complete paragraph. *Insert as penultimate sentence:*

Indeed, a VEBA, without any remaining participants and that has paid all benefits that were due, may terminate by distributing its remaining assets to charitable organizations.[77.1]

p. 484, last paragraph. *Insert as second sentence:*

For example, the IRS, having determined that a welfare plan's membership is not voluntary, because the plan excludes certain employees from participation in it, held that the plan cannot qualify as an exempt VEBA because it is discriminatory.[79.1]

[76.1] Priv. Ltr. Rul. 201528038. This excise tax (IRC § 4976(a)) was avoided inasmuch as the amounts to be distributed did not give rise to a disqualified benefit (IRC § 4976(b)(1)(C)), in part because these amounts were not the subject of an employer plan deduction (IRC § 419) in any year, since the employer had been tax-exempt.

[77.1] Priv. Ltr. Rul. 201545026.

[79.1] Priv. Ltr. Rul. 201515036. The statute on which the IRS relied (IRC § 50(b)(1)) addresses discrimination only in favor of employees who are highly compensated.

CHAPTER NINETEEN

Other Categories of Tax-Exempt Organizations

*§ 19.6 Cemetery Companies
§ 19.19 Qualified Tuition Programs
§ 19.20 ABLE Programs

§ 19.22 Governmental and
Quasi-Governmental Entities

*§ 19.6 CEMETERY COMPANIES

*p. 510, carryover paragraph. *Insert as second complete sentence:*

A mutual cemetery company which also engages in charitable activities, such as the burial of paupers, is regarded as operating in conformity with this rule.[172.1]

§ 19.19 QUALIFIED TUITION PROGRAMS

p. 530, first complete paragraph, eighth line. *Insert following* equipment:

(including computer or peripheral equipment, computer software, and Internet access and related services)

p. 530, note 374. *Insert following existing text:*

The text in parentheses reflects law as added by the Protecting Americans from Tax Hikes Act of 2015 (Pub. L. No. 114-113, Division Q) § 302(a).

p. 532. *Insert as first complete paragraph:*

In the case of a designated beneficiary who receives a refund of any higher education expenses, any distribution that was used to pay the refunded expenses is not subject to tax if the beneficiary recontributes the refunded amount to the qualified tuition program within 60 days of receiving the refund, only to the extent that the recontribution is not in excess of the refund.[392.1]

---

*[172.1] *Id.* The IRS ruled that a grant of property, including an historic cemetery, to an exempt charitable organization was a charitable activity for purposes of cemetery company tax law (Priv. Ltr. Rul. 201605019).

[392.1] IRC § 529(c)(3)(D), added by the Protecting Americans from Tax Hikes Act of 2015 (Pub. L. No. 114-113, Division Q) § 302(c). The PATH Act also repealed the so-called aggregation requirement applicable to distributions from qualified tuition programs, effective for distributions made after December 31, 2014 (§ 302(b)). These programs were unable to adjust their systems to retroactively accommodate the new method of calculating the earnings portion of a distribution before the due date of the reporting form (Form 1099-Q for 2015); consequently, the IRS notified these programs that it will not impose penalties (IRC § 6693) solely because of a reported earnings computation in 2016 that does not reflect this repeal (Notice 2016-13, 2016-7 I.R.B. 314).

§ 19.20 ABLE PROGRAMS

p. 532, third complete paragraph, first line. *Delete* The newest category *and substitute* One of the newest categories.

pp. 532–533, last paragraph beginning on p. 532. *Delete fourth sentence (including footnote) and substitute:*

A beneficiary is not required to be a resident of the state that established the account.[403]

p. 533, note 415. *Insert following existing text:*

The Department of the Treasury promulgated proposed regulations to accompany IRC § 529A (REG-102837-15). An IRS hearing on this proposal was held on October 14, 2015.

    The IRS issued interim guidance as to three provisions of the proposed regulations, concerning reporting requirements, which will be eased when the final regulations are issued (Notice 2015-81, 2015-49 I.R.B. 784).

§ 19.22 GOVERNMENTAL AND QUASI-GOVERNMENTAL ENTITIES

(b) Income Exclusion Rule

p. 535, second paragraph. *Insert as last sentence:*

    Similarly, this status was accorded to an integrated faculty group practice corporation, formed to deliver high-quality, cost-effective patient care, established by a state university and the state's teaching hospital facility to provide a more strategically, financially, and clinically integrated enterprise.[427.1]

*p. 536, note 433. *Insert following existing text:*

    The Department of the Treasury, on February 23, 2016, issued proposed regulations that provide guidance regarding definition of the term *political subdivision* for purposes of the tax-exempt bond rules (IRC § 103) (REG-129067-15). This proposal continues, without substantive change, the longstanding requirement that a political subdivision be empowered to exercise at least one of the generally recognized sovereign powers, plus requires that a political subdivision serve a *governmental purpose* and be *governmentally controlled*. In general, American Bar Association Section of Taxation, "Comments on the Definition of Political Subdivision for Tax-Exempt Bonds and Other Tax-Advantaged Bonds," 69 *Tax Law.* (No. 2) 313 (Winter 2016).

(d) State Instrumentalities

p. 540, first complete paragraph. *Insert as last sentence:*

The IRS used these criteria in ruling, for example, that a charter school did not qualify as a state instrumentality.[461.1]

---

[403] The Protecting Americans from Tax Hikes Act of 2015 (Pub. L. No. 114-113, Division Q) § 303 repealed IRC § 529A(b)(1)(C), which imposed a residency requirement.

[427.1] Priv. Ltr. Rul. 201528010.

[461.1] Priv. Ltr. Rul. 201519027.

CHAPTER TWENTY

Private Inurement and Private Benefit

*p. 548, second complete paragraph, fourteenth line. *Delete* (or entity).

*p. 548, second complete paragraph, sixteenth line. *Delete* it *and insert* the organization.

§ 20.1 CONCEPT OF PRIVATE INUREMENT

*p. 550, first complete paragraph, ninth line. *Insert* general *following first* the.

p. 550, note 29. *Insert following existing text:*

Occasionally, the IRS applies the private inurement doctrine, in a case involving a transaction or arrangement with an insider, without making any judgment as to the reasonableness of the matter (e.g., Priv. Ltr. Rul. 201548021).

*§ 20.3   DEFINITION OF *INSIDER*

*p. 552, second paragraph under heading, sixth line. *Delete* founders,.

*p. 552, second paragraph under heading, seventh line. *Delete* certain.

*p. 555, note 71. *Move* Sound Health Ass'n *citation to be first item in footnote.*

*§ 20.4 COMPENSATION ISSUES

*(b) Determining Reasonableness of Compensation

*p. 560, note 107, first line. *Insert following* Also:

H.W. Johnson v. Comm'r, 111 T.C.M. 1418 (2016);

*p. 560, note 109, second line. *Delete* T.C. Memo. 2015-53 (Mar. 23, 2015) *and substitute* 109 T.C.M. 1245 (2015).

§ 20.5 OTHER FORMS OF PRIVATE INUREMENT

*p. 564, second paragraph, second line. *Delete* are *and insert* involve.

*(e) Equity Distributions

p. 567, carryover paragraph. *Insert following existing text:*

Earlier, a limited dividend housing corporation, under close supervision of a state, was denied exemption as a social welfare entity[152.1] because it was operated on a for-profit basis (the private inurement rule not being expressly applicable at the time).[152.2] Similarly, a "sweat equity housing cooperative association," formed pursuant to state statute to engage in restoration of historic properties, was denied recognition of exemption as a charitable entity because its board members had possessory interests in properties owned by the organization and were potentially eligible for cash distributions on dissolution.[153.3]

(h) Tax Avoidance Schemes

p. 569. *Insert as last sentence of carryover paragraph:*

In still another of these situations, a tax-exempt organization founded and managed by an accountant had its exemption revoked because the accountant concealed receipts from his practice to avoid payment of federal income tax, by treating some payments as having been made to the charitable entity.[175.1]

p. 573. *Insert following last complete paragraph:*

(n) Still Other Forms of Inurement

Promotion of the career advancement of an individual (an insider) within a nonprofit entity was ruled by the IRS to be a form of private inurement; an entity

---

[152.1] See Chapter 13.
[152.2] Amalgamated Housing Corp. v. Comm'r, 37 B.T.A. 817 (1938), *aff'd*, 108 F.2d 1010 (2nd Cir. 1940).
[153.3] Priv. Ltr. Rul. 201640022.
[175.1] Priv. Ltr. Rul. 201544028.

seeking classification as a charitable and religious organization was supporting the candidacy of its pastor for the position of a bishop of a church and was denied recognition of exemption on this basis.[204.1]

§ 20.12 PRIVATE BENEFIT DOCTRINE

*(a) General Rules

*p. 582, second complete paragraph, second line. *Insert* formally *following* law.

*p. 582, second complete paragraph, fourth line. *Delete* can be *and insert* is.

*p. 583, second complete paragraph. *Insert as last sentence:*

Similarly, a nonprofit organization, formed to provide training to softball and baseball umpires, and to coordinate and schedule games and tournaments, is also involved in assigning umpires to games and promoting ethical standards among baseball officials; this organization was denied recognition of exemption as a charitable or educational entity, in part because it is serving the private interests of the umpires, who are paid for their services.[299.1]

*p. 583, last paragraph, first line. *Insert* permissibly *following* may.

*p. 583, last paragraph, fourth line. *Italicize* quantitatively incidental.

*p. 584, first line. *Italicize* qualitatively incidental.

(b) Incidental Private Benefit

p. 586, first complete paragraph, nineteenth line. *Delete* And an *and insert* An.

p. 586, first complete paragraph. *Insert as last sentences:*

A nonprofit organization was ruled to be in violation of the private benefit doctrine where its purpose was provision of scholarships for students attending an art academy, as well as funding the acquisition of equipment for the school; the academy was structured as a for-profit entity, started by the principal officer of the nonprofit organization.[324.1] Unwarranted private benefit was also found where a scholarship-granting organization was making grants only to members of one family (and descendants of the founder of the organization); a court allowed revocation of this entity's tax exemption.[324.2]

[204.1] Priv. Ltr. Rul. 201523022.
[*299.1] Priv. Ltr. Rul. 201617012.
[324.1] Priv. Ltr. Rul. 201514011.
[324.2] Educational Assistance Found. for the Descendants of Hungarian Immigrants in the Performing Arts, Inc. v. United States, 111 F. Supp. 3d 34 (D.D.C. 2015) (on appeal).

*(c) Joint Venture Law

*p. 591, note 358. *Insert following existing text:*

The IRS issued guidance that provides safe harbor conditions under which a management contract does not result in private business use of property financed with governmental tax-exempt bonds or cause the modified private business use test for property financed with qualified 501(c)(3) bonds to be met (Rev. Proc. 2016-44, 2016-36 I.R.B. 316). This new approach to the concept of private business use may have a broader application, in that the rules concerning management contracts in the context of joint ventures involving tax-exempt organizations, when evaluating the presence of private benefit, may be somewhat loosened.

CHAPTER TWENTY-ONE

Intermediate Sanctions

*§ 21.9 Rebuttable Presumption
of Reasonableness

§ 21.10 Excise Tax Regime

*§ 21.9 REBUTTABLE PRESUMPTION OF REASONABLENESS

*p. 611, carryover paragraph, fifth line. *Insert* the board *following the comma.*

*p. 611, carryover paragraph, sixth line. *Insert* the board *following second* and.

§ 21.10 EXCISE TAX REGIME

p. 613. *Insert as last paragraph:*

In one instance, the IRS concluded that the first-tier excise tax due under these rules, in connection with an automatic excess benefit transaction, should not be abated, because the disqualified person (a limited liability company) did not exercise ordinary business care and prudence when it relied on the oral advice of a public charity's legal counsel.[163.1] The IRS stated that the disqualified person failed to offer any evidence showing that its reliance on the advice of legal counsel was reasonable. There was no information about the lawyer's expertise, there was no evidence that the LLC provided necessary and accurate information to a lawyer, the LLC itself did not seek legal advice, there was no information indicating that the LLC considered legal advice when pursuing the transaction (a loan), and the LLC did not provide any facts indicating the circumstances that would tend to support a finding of reasonable cause.

[163.1] Tech. Adv. Mem. 201503019.

CHAPTER TWENTY-TWO

Legislative Activities by Tax-Exempt Organizations

*§ 22.3 Lobbying by Charitable Organizations

§ 22.6 Legislative Activities of Business Leagues

*§ 22.3 LOBBYING BY CHARITABLE ORGANIZATIONS

*(b) Concept of *Lobbying*

*p. 629, first complete paragraph, second line. *Insert* communications that are *following* between.

*(d) Expenditure Test

*p. 633, third complete paragraph. *Insert as last sentence:*

On the basis of the principles illustrated in examples in the tax regulations, a court held that a communication *refers to* a ballot measure "if it either refers to the measure by name or, without naming it, employs terms widely used in connection with the measure or describes the content or effect of the measure."[71.1]

§ 22.6 LEGISLATIVE ACTIVITIES OF BUSINESS LEAGUES

(a) Business Expense Deduction Disallowance Rules

*p. 644, first paragraph, second line. *Insert footnote following* with:

[170.1] The IRS is of the view that this phrase is to be construed broadly (e.g., Priv. Ltr. Rul. 201616002), citing Snow v. Comm'r, 416 U.S. 500 (1974); Conopco v. United States, 572 F.3d 162 (3rd Cir. 2009); and General Mills v. United States, 554 F.3d 727 (8th Cir. 2009); one court of appeals has ruled it should be read narrowly (Boise Cascade v. United States, 329 F.3d 751 (9th Cir. 2003)).

p. 646, note 196. *Delete third sentence and substitute:*

This $50 amount is indexed for inflation; for tax years beginning in 2017, the amount is $113 (Rev. Proc. 2016-55, 2016-45 I.R.B. 707 § 3.41).

[*71.1] Parks v. Comm'r, 145 T.C. 278, 309 (2015).

CHAPTER TWENTY-THREE

Political Campaign Activities by Tax-Exempt Organizations

§ 23.2 Prohibition on Charitable Organizations

*§ 23.5 Political Activitiies of Social Welfare Organizations

*§ 23.7 Political Activities of Business Leagues

*p. 657, paragraph, second line. *Insert* affirmatively *following* not.

*p. 657, paragraph, fourth line. *Insert* tax *following* The.

*p. 657, paragraph, sixth line. *Insert* and state *following* federal.

§ 23.2 PROHIBITION ON CHARITABLE ORGANIZATIONS

*(a) Scope of the Proscription

*p. 659, second complete paragraph, second line. *Insert* recognition of *following* deny.

(b) Participation or Intervention

p. 659, last paragraph. *Insert footnote at end of last sentence:*

16.1 The use of one or more PARCs was announced in mid-2015, in a memorandum from the Director, Exempt Organizations Division (TEGE-04-0715-0018 (July 17, 2015)), where it was stated that a PARC consists of three General Schedule grade 14 managers, who will receive "appropriate training" and serve as committee members for two years. A PARC is to review and recommend referrals for audit in an "impartial and unbiased manner." The "inventory volume of political activities referrals" will determine the number of PARCs established and the time commitment required of the members of a PARC. It is not known whether the PACI is continuing by that name and thus whether use of PARCs is an element of an ongoing PACI.

(c) Voter Education Activities

p. 666, note 53. *Insert following existing text:*

The IRS ruled that a nonprofit organization planning on conducting a series of ostensibly educational symposia failed to qualify for tax exemption because, as to the first of these events, representatives of only one political party, some of whom were candidates for public office, were invited to participate as speakers (Priv. Ltr. Rul. 201523021).

*§ 23.5 POLITICAL ACTIVITIES OF SOCIAL WELFARE ORGANIZATIONS

*(a) Allowable Campaign Activity

*p. 679, note 148. *Insert following existing text:*

Congress thereafter prohibited the IRS from issuing guidance concerning candidate-related political activity (Fiscal Year 2016 Omnibus Appropriations Act (Pub. L. No. 114-113), Division E § 127; Fiscal Year 2017 Financial Services and General Government Appropriations Act (Pub. L. No. _____) § ___).

*§ 23.7 POLITICAL ACTIVITIES OF BUSINESS LEAGUES

*p. 681, note 164. *Insert prior to existing text:*

IRC § 162(e)(1)(B).

*p. 681, note 164. *Insert following existing text:*

Citing this IRC provision, the IRS ruled that a business corporation, maintaining a political action committee, may not deduct as a business expense charitable contributions made to match its employees' charitable gifts, inasmuch as its charitable gifts are intended to incentivize political contributions by its employees to the PAC; the agency stated that the corporation's gifts to its PAC and its matching charitable gifts are "inextricably linked," so that the latter types of gifts are being made in connection with political campaigns (Priv. Ltr. Rul. 201616002).

CHAPTER TWENTY-FOUR

Unrelated Business: Basic Rules

*§ 24.1 INTRODUCTION TO UNRELATED BUSINESS RULES

***p. 687, second complete paragraph, third line.** *Insert footnote following period:*

[11.1] See § 4.5(c).

***p. 689, note 29.** *Insert following existing text:*

Thus, the IRS ruled that income to be received by a private foundation on satisfaction of debts of legal fees earned by its founder, now deceased, will not be unrelated business income because the foundation will only be a passive recipient of the income; the unrelated business that was regularly carried on to generate the fees was conducted by the founder's law firm, not the foundation (Priv. Ltr. Rul. 201626004).

*§ 24.2 DEFINITION OF *TRADE OR BUSINESS*

*(b) Requirement of Profit Motive

***p. 691, second complete paragraph, first line.** *Insert footnote following first sentence:*

[52.1] The instructions accompanying Form 990-T (see § 28.10) state: "Generally, an activity lacking a profit motive is one that is not conducted for the purpose of producing a profit or one that has consistently produced losses when both direct and indirect expenses are taken into account."

*p. 692, note 56. *Insert as first sentence:*

A similar arrangement involved a religious organization and a charitable remainder trust of which it is the remainder beneficiary (Priv. Ltr. Rul. 201636042).

*p. 692, note 58. *Insert following existing text:*

This matter of the requirement of a profit motive in the exempt organizations context closely parallels the law distinguishing bona fide businesses from hobbies ("hobby loss" rules (IRC § 183). Not all courts agree with the IRS's interpretation of these rules, however; an appellate court characterized the approach as "goofy" (Roberts v. Comm'r, 820 F.3d 247, 250 (7th Cir. 2016)). In *Roberts*, the court of appeals stated that the rule should be that if an activity is in an "industry known to attract hobbyists" and "loses large sums of money year after year that the owner of the business deducts from a very large income that he derives from other (and genuine) businesses," a presumption arises that the activity is a hobby (*id.* at 254). *Roberts* also is an authority for the position that two consecutive years of losses is an insufficient basis for concluding absence of a profit motive. Likewise, Estate of Stuller v. United States, 811 F.3d 890 (7th Cir. 2016).

*(j) Concept of *Investment Plus*

*p. 701, last paragraph, fifth line. *Delete* **may.**

*p. 701, last paragraph, last line. *Insert footnote at end of line:*

[140.1] The concept of *investment plus* was subsequently applied by another court, which embellished the arrangement by referring to it as a "partnership-in-fact" (Sun Capital Partners III, LP v. New England Teamsters & Trucking Industry Pension Fund, 2016 WL 1253529 (D. Mass. 2016)).

*§ 24.3   DEFINITION OF *REGULARLY CARRIED ON*

*(b) Determining Regularity

*p. 703, first complete paragraph, second line. *Delete* **commercial.**

§ 24.5   CONTEMPORARY APPLICATIONS OF UNRELATED BUSINESS RULES

(a) Educational Institutions

p. 718. *Insert as first complete paragraph:*

The IRS held that an event, where vendors offer arts and crafts, a farmers' market, entertainment, and refreshment booths to the public, sponsored by a tax-exempt alumni association operating to provide financial support to a public college, is an unrelated business.[325.1] The association funds a scholarship program and provides financial support for maintenance of certain college facilities. The IRS rejected the alumni association's contentions that the event is a substantially

---

[325.1] Tech. Adv. Mem. 201544025.

related activity because it has the potential for student recruitment, generating donors, and endearing the college's alumni to that institution, and it lessens the burdens of government and relieves the distress of the elderly (the majority of the attendees of the event are over age 55).[325.2]

*(h) Advertising

*p. 733, third paragraph, third line. *Delete* by means of.

*(i) Fundraising

*p. 739. *Insert as first complete paragraph:*

The IRS ruled that a fundraising event conducted by a tax-exempt alumni association, held every weekend for the benefit of a public college, is an unrelated business.[526.1] The association funds scholarships and other financial aid for the college's students and provides financial support for college facilities, including a computer room in the library and maintenance of the football field. The association's principal argument was that the event contributes importantly to its exempt purposes by attracting potential students and donors to the college's campus, endearing the college to its alumni and others, and developing civic support for the college. The IRS dismissed these assertions as being "merely speculative," noting that the event's website contains only statements about use of the funds raised.

*(l) Sales of Merchandise

*p. 747, first paragraph. *Insert as second sentence:*

Similarly, the IRS determined that an exempt conservation and preservation organization, selling a product through its online store, by print catalog, and at various retail outlets, with almost no provision of educational information, was engaging in an unrelated business.[589.1]

*§ 24.9   UNRELATED DEBT-FINANCED INCOME

*p. 757, last paragraph, fifth line. *Insert* substantially *following* is.

*p. 761, note 719. *Insert following existing material:*

Regulations were proposed, on November 22, 2016, with respect to allocations of items by partnerships that have debt-financed property and have one or more (but not all) qualified tax-exempt organization partners (REG-136978-12); this proposal would amend existing regulations to facilitate compliance, regarding certain allocations resulting from specified common business practices, with the statutory law.

[325.2] It is said that this alumni association derives "substantially all" of its revenue from operation of this event, yet there is no discussion about the association's ongoing exempt status.

*[526.1] Tech. Adv. Mem. 201544025.

*[589.1] Tech. Adv. Mem. 201633032.

*§ 24.10   TAX STRUCTURE

*p. 763, first complete paragraph, first line. *Insert* tax *following* income.

*p. 763, third complete paragraph, first line. *Delete* 731.

*p. 763, fourth complete paragraph, second line. *Insert* taxable *following* business.

*§ 24.11   DEDUCTION RULES

*p. 764. *Insert as third complete paragraph:*

   The American Institute of Certified Public Accountants, on June 27, 2016, by letter to the IRS's Chief Counsel's Office, submitted guidelines for allocating expenses, by tax-exempt organizations in the computation of the unrelated business income tax, in connection with dual-use facilities. The focus is on determination of the expenses that are deductible in ascertaining net taxable income. The AICPA guidelines are: (1) deductible expenses must bear a proximate and primary relationship to the conduct of the unrelated activity; (2) deductible expenses include direct and indirect costs; (3) indirect costs are fixed expenses (those that do not change when the unrelated activity is or is not conducted) and variable expenses (those that can increase or decrease when the unrelated activity is or is not conducted); (4) the methodology for allocating expenses relating to dual-use facilities and personnel should be reasonable and consistently followed from year to year, and should not cause double-counting of an expense; (5) the methodology for allocating expenses relating to dual-use facilities and personnel should be based on the character of the expense involved; (6) facility costs (rent, mortgage interest, insurance, taxes, security, and utilities) should be apportioned on the basis of the portion of the facility used (square footage and time) for each activity; (7) personnel costs (salary, benefits, and taxes) should be apportioned based on the time expended on each activity; (8) information technology costs (software, computer services, and Internet) should be apportioned on the basis of allocation of personnel to the activity; and (9) office expenses (supplies, printing, postage, and subscriptions) should be apportioned based on allocation of personnel to the activity.

CHAPTER TWENTY-FIVE

Unrelated Business: Modifications, Exceptions, and Special Rules

§ 25.1 Modifications
§ 25.2 Exceptions

§ 25.3 Special Rules

§ 25.1 MODIFICATIONS

(h) Rent

p. 772, first complete paragraph. *Insert as last sentence:*

For example, the IRS ruled that revenues paid by vendors at an event, sponsored by a tax-exempt alumni association, were not rent, largely because of the extensive services provided the vendors that go "far beyond" services "usually rendered for occupancy only."[38.1]

§ 25.2 EXCEPTIONS

(j) Low-Cost Articles

p. 787, note 190. *Delete sentence and substitute:*

The IRS calculated that the low-cost article threshold for tax years beginning in 2017 is $10.70 (Rev. Proc. 2016-55, 2016-45 I.R.B. 707 § 3.30(1)).

(l) Associate Member Dues

p. 788, note 200. *Delete sentence and substitute:*

For tax years beginning in 2017, this threshold is $162 (Rev. Proc. 2016-55, 2016-45 I.R.B. 707 § 3.29).

[38.1] Tech. Adv. Mem. 201544029.

§ 25.3 SPECIAL RULES

p. 789, third paragraph. *Insert as third sentence:*

For example, with respect to tax-exempt voluntary employees' beneficiary associations, investment income, employer contributions, and other income received by a VEBA set aside to pay plan benefits is exempt function income.[217.1]

p. 789, third paragraph, fourth sentence. *Delete* **For example, a tax-exempt voluntary employees' beneficiary association** *and substitute* **By contrast, an exempt VEBA.**

[217.1] E.g., Priv. Ltr. Rul. 201512006.

CHAPTER TWENTY-SIX

Exemption Recognition and Notice Processes

§ 26.1   RECOGNITION APPLICATION PROCEDURE

*p. 796, second paragraph, third line. *Delete* of exemption.

*p. 796, note 8, first line. *Delete* 2015-9, 2015-2 I.R.B. 249 *and substitute* 2016-5, 2016-1 I.R.B. 188.

*p. 796, note 8, fourth line. *Delete* 2015-6, 2015-1 C.B. 194 *and substitute* Rev. Proc. 2016-6, 2016-1 I.R.B. 200.

*p. 796, note 8, lines 9 and 10. *Delete* 2015-8, 2015-1 I.R.B. 235 *and substitute* 2016-8, 2016-1 I.R.B. 243.

*p. 796, note 10, third line. *Delete* 2015-9, 2015-2 I.R.B. 249 *and substitute* 2016-5, 2016-1 I.R.B. 188.

*p. 797, note 11. *Delete* 2015-9, 2015-2 I.R.B. 249 *and substitute* 2016-5, 2016-1 I.R.B. 188.

*p. 797, note 12. *Delete* 2015-2, 2015-1 I.R.B. 105 *and substitute* 2016-2, 2016-1 I.R.B. 102.

*p. 797, note 13. *Delete* 2015-9, 2015-2 I.R.B. 249 *and substitute* 2016-5, 2016-1 I.R.B. 188.

*p. 797, note 14, second line. *Insert parenthesis following* Three.

*p. 797, note 14, third line. *Delete or and insert , or (r) (see § 7.6(b))* before the *period.*

*p. 797, first complete paragraph, third line. *Insert* often *following* is.

*p. 797, first complete paragraph. *Insert as third sentence:*

Certain organizations seeking recognition as a charitable entity are eligible to file a streamlined application.[14.1]

*p. 797, note 15, third line. *Delete , (9) (see § 18.3).*

*p. 797, note 15, fourth line. *Delete , (17) (see § 18.4); at end of line insert:*

Rev. Proc. 2016-5, 2016-1 I.R.B. 188 § 3.07.

*p. 797, note 16. *Delete* 2015-9, 2015-2 I.R.B. 249 § 3.04 *and substitute* 2016-5, 2016-1 I.R.B. 188 § 3.07.

*p. 797, note 19. *Delete* 2015-9, 2015-2 I.R.B. 249 § 3.06 *and substitute* 2016-5, 2016-1 I.R.B. 188 § 3.09.

*p. 797, note 20. *Delete* 2015-9, 2015-2 I.R.B. 249 § 3.05 *and substitute* 2016-5, 2016-1 I.R.B. 188 § 3.08.

*p. 797, note 20, fourth line. *Delete first* or; *insert* (29) (see § 19.18) *following comma.*

*p. 797, note 21. *Delete* 2014-9, 2014-2 I.R.B. 281 § 3.07 *and substitute* 2016-5, 2016-1 I.R.B. 188 § 3.10.

*p. 797, first complete paragraph. *Insert as last sentences:*

ABLE accounts are required to submit notices to the IRS on establishment of accounts.[21.1] Organizations seeking reinstatement of tax exemption after automatic revocation for nonfiling of returns or notices are subject to special rules.[21.2] An organization that is identified or designated as a terrorist organization is ineligible to apply for recognition of exemption.[21.3]

*p. 797, note 22, lines 4 and 5. *Delete* 2015-4, 2015-1 I.R.B. 144 *and substitute* 2016-4, 2016-1 I.R.B. 142.

*p. 797. *Delete last paragraph.*

*p. 798, note 24. *Delete* 2015-9, 2015-2 I.R.B. 249 *and substitute* 2016-5, 2016-1 I.R.B. 188.

[14.1] Rev. Proc. 2016-5, 2016-1 I.R.B. 188 § 3.04. See § 26.1(h).
[21.1] See § 26.8.
[21.2] Rev. Proc. 2016-5, 2016-1 I.R.B. 188 § 3.11. See § 28.6.
[21.3] Rev. Proc. 2016-5, 2016-1 I.R.B. 188 § 3.14. See § 26.11.

*p. 798, note 29. *Delete* 2015-9, 2015-2 I.R.B. 249 *and substitute* 2016-5, 2016-1 I.R.B. 188.

*p. 799, first paragraph, second line. *Delete* or ruling.

*p. 800, note 45. *Delete* 2015-9, 2015-2 I.R.B. 249 *and substitute* 2016-5, 2016-1 I.R.B. 188.

*p. 801, first complete paragraph, fifth line. *Delete* may *and substitute* will.

*p. 801, first complete paragraph, sixth line. *Delete* or may retain it and request the necessary information.

*p. 801, note 56. *Delete* 2015-9, 2015-2 I.R.B. 249 §§ 4.05, 4.05(1) *and substitute* 2016-5, 2016-1 I.R.B. 188 § 4.05.

*p. 801, note 58. *Delete* 2015-9, 2015-2 I.R.B. 249 *and substitute* 2016-5, 2016-1 I.R.B. 188.

*p. 801, note 59. *Delete* 2015-9, 2015-2 I.R.B. 249 *and substitute* 2016-5, 2016-1 I.R.B. 188.

*p. 801. *Insert as fourth paragraph:*

The IRS will accept for processing a completed streamlined application[60.1] from an eligible organization that has a general application (Form 1023) pending with it, as long as the general application has not yet been assigned for review. The streamlined application will be treated as a request for withdrawal of the general application. The user fee[60.2] paid in connection with the general application generally will not be refunded. The filing date of the streamlined application will be treated as the date the organization provided the requisite notice.[60.3] Thus, if the filing date of the streamlined application is within the 27-month period, the organization may be recognized as exempt from the date it is organized; otherwise, the exemption will generally be effective from the date the streamlined application was filed.[60.4] If the general application has been assigned for review, the IRS will inform the organization of the nonacceptance of the streamlined application and any user fee that was paid with that application will be refunded.[60.5]

p. 801. *Insert before last paragraph:*

(iii) Application Processing Time Lines. Applications that are properly and completely prepared may result in issuance of a favorable determination letter in a few months. Others will likely entail the gathering of additional information by the IRS, by means of one or more information requests. For many years,

---

[60.1] See § 26.1(h).
[60.2] See § 26.1(d).
[60.3] IRC § 508(a). See § 26.1.
[60.4] Rev. Proc. 2016-5, 2016-1 I.R.B. 188 § 6.02(1).
[60.5] *Id.* § 6.02(2).

EO Determinations gave applicant organizations 21 days to respond to an information request. An organization could obtain a 14-day extension to respond. If a response did not arrive in a timely fashion, EO Determinations placed the case in suspense and notified the applicant that it had 90 days to supply the requested information. Absent a response within that time period, the case would be closed. Because the IRS has increased the timeliness of its processing of these applications, the IRS has revised the procedures, principally by eliminating the suspense period.

The essence of this new approach, which took effect in September 2015,[64.1] is that, if an applicant organization does not respond to an information request by the designated due date, EO Determinations will close the case without making a determination and will not refund any user fee paid. The concept is that an applicant that does not provide the requested information in a timely fashion *fails to establish* that it meets the requirements for tax-exempt status. An organization whose case is closed under this procedure will have to submit a new application package and pay another user fee.

IRS personnel are instructed to issue a letter to an applicant when it is necessary to seek information in addition to that provided in the application. The letter will incorporate "appropriate streamline, pre-written, or individually composed" questions. The applicant will be given 28 calendar days to respond. The applicant organization is to be called and notified about the letter on the day it is mailed. The agent is to emphasize the importance of responding by the due date, to avoid a case closing. Issues in the case may be discussed on this call.

If the organization requests an extension, the case manager must approve it, based on the facts and circumstances. The normal extension period is 14 days at the most. Managers can approve longer extensions as needed (such as for the filing of an amendment to a corporate document). If the response is incomplete, the agent may issue an additional request for information. An agent must consult with his or her manager before a third request for information is issued.

If a response to an information request has not been received by three business days prior to the response due date, the agent is to call the applicant organization. The organization is to be reminded of the due date and the imminent case closing.

If the organization does not respond by the due date, the agent is to close the case as a failure to establish eligibility for recognition of tax exemption.[64.2]

p. 801, last paragraph, first line. *Insert before existing material:*

    (iv) Expedited Processing of Applications.

p. 802, second paragraph, first line. *Delete* (iii) *and insert* (v).

*(b) *Substantially Completed* **Application**

*p. 802, heading. *Delete* **Substantially.**

[64.1] Memorandum from the Director, Rulings and Agreements, Exempt Organizations Division (September 8, 2015 (TEGE-07-0915-0022)).

[64.2] The IRS, in its work plan for fiscal year 2016, attributed this development to its adherence to the Lean Six Sigma management philosophy.

*p. 802, note 65. *Delete* 2015-9, 2015-2 I.R.B. 249 § 4.07 *and substitute* 2016-5, 2016-1 I.R.B. 188 § 4.08.

*p. 802, fourth paragraph, second line. *Delete* at least substantially.

*p. 802, note 66. *Delete* 2015-9, 2015-2 I.R.B. 249 § 3.08 *and substitute* 2016-5, 2016-1 I.R.B. 188 § 3.12.

*p. 802, note 69. *Delete* 2015-9, 2015-2 I.R.B. 249 § 4.05(2) *and substitute* 2016-5, 2016-1 I.R.B. 188 § 4.05(1).

*p. 803, note 75. *Delete* 2015-9, 2015-2 I.R.B. 249 *and substitute* 2016-5, 2016-1 I.R.B. 188 § 3.12.

*p. 803, note 76. *Delete* 2015-9, 2015-2 I.R.B. 249 § 4.06(1) *and substitute* 2016-5, 2016-1 I.R.B. 188 § 4.07(1).

*p. 804, line 2. *Delete* substantially.

*p. 804, line 4. *Delete* substantially.

*p. 804, line 6. *Delete* substantially.

*p. 804, note 78. *Delete* 2015-9, 2015-2 I.R.B. 249 § 4.06(2) *and substitute* 2016-5, 2016-1 I.R.B. 188 § 4.07.

*p. 804, note 79. *Delete* 2015-9, 2015-2 I.R.B. 249 § 4.05(2) *and substitute* 2016-5, 2016-1 I.R.B. 188 § 4.05(1).

*(c) Issuance of Determinations and Rulings

*p. 804, heading. *Delete* and Rulings

*p. 804, note 80, first line. Delete 2015-9, 2015-2 I.R.B. 249 § 5.03 *and substitute* 2016-5, 2016-1 I.R.B. 188 § 5.01.

*p. 804, note 80, second line. *Delete* 2015-4, 2015-1 I.R.B. 144 *and substitute* 2016-4, 2016-1 I.R.B. 142.

*p. 804, third complete paragraph. *Insert as second to fourth sentences:*

In limited circumstances, applications for recognition of exempt status were transferred to the former EO Technical office for processing.[80.1] All of the procedures in these rules apply to pending applications that were transferred to the former Technical office, including the opportunity for the applicant to request consideration by

---

[80.1] Rev. Proc. 2016-5, 2016-1 I.R.B. 188 § 5.02.

Appeals of a proposed adverse determination.[80.2] An applicant receiving a proposed adverse determination with respect to an application that had been transferred to the former EO Technical office may request a conference with EO Rulings and Agreements in addition to requesting appeals office consideration.[80.3]

*p. 804, note 81. *Delete text and substitute:*

Id. § 5.03.

*p. 804, third complete paragraph. *Delete all text following what was second sentence.*

*p. 804, note 86. *Delete* 2015-9, 2015-2 I.R.B. 249 *and substitute* 2016-5, 2016-1 I.R.B. 188.

*p. 805, first complete paragraph. *Insert following existing text:*

Inaccurate material information includes an incorrect representation or attestation as to the organization's organizational documents, the organization's exempt purpose, the organization's conduct of prohibited and restricted activities, or the organization's eligibility to file the streamlined application.[89.1]

*p. 805. *Insert as second and third complete paragraphs, before heading:*

While the procedures for obtaining a determination letter by submitting a general application for recognition of exemption (Form 1023) may differ from those for obtaining a determination letter by submitting a streamlined application (Form 1023-EZ), grantors and contributors may rely on both types of determination letters to the same extent.[89.2]

Determination letters may be reviewed by EO Quality Assurance and Processing to assure uniform application of the statutes or regulations, or rulings, court opinions, or decisions published in the *Internal Revenue Bulletin*.[89.3] If, on post-determination review, EO Quality Assurance and Processing concludes, based on the information contained in the application file, that a determination letter was erroneously issued, the matter will be processed in accordance with the revocation procedures.[89.4]

*(d) User Fees

*p. 805, note 91, first line. *Delete* 2015-9, 2015-2 I.R.B. 249 *and substitute* 2016-5, 2016-1 I.R.B. 188.

*p. 805, note 92. *Delete* 2015-8, 2015-1 I.R.B. 235 § 6.08(1), (2) *and substitute* 2016-8, 2016-1 I.R.B. 243 § 6.09(2).

[80.2] *Id.* § 5.02(1).
[80.3] *Id.* § 5.02(2).
[89.1] Rev. Proc. 2016-5, 2016-1 I.R.B. 188 § 11.02(1).
[89.2] *Id.* § 11.02(2).
[89.3] *Id.* § 9.01.
[89.4] *Id.* § 9.02. As to these procedures, see § 27.2.

*p. 805, second complete paragraph. *Insert as fourth sentence:*

From its inception, the user fee accompanying the streamlined application for recognition of exemption[92.1] was $400[92.2]; effective July 1, 2016, the fee is $275.[92.3]

*p. 805, note 93. *Delete* 2015-8, 2015-1 I.R.B. 235 § 6.08(3) *and substitute* 2016-8, 2016-1 I.R.B. 243 § 6.09(3).

*p. 805, note 95. *Delete* 2015-8, 2015-1 I.R.B. 235 § 6.07(3) *and substitute* 2016-8, 2016-1 I.R.B. 243 § 6.09(4).

(h) Streamlined Application

*p. 805, note 95. *Insert following existing text:*

The list of IRS private letter rulings eligible for reduced user fees has a new addition: "substantially identical letter rulings requested by taxpayers who are parties engaged together in the same transaction affecting all requesting taxpayers" (Notice 2016-59, 2016-42 I.R.B. 457).

*p. 805. *Insert as third complete paragraph:*

In the case of an application that is returned to the applicant because it is not complete, the user fee will be returned or refunded.[95.1]

*p. 811, note 123. *Delete* 2015-5, 2015-1 I.R.B. 186 *and substitute* 2016-5, 2016-1 I.R.B. 188 § 3.05.

*p. 811, second paragraph, fourth sentence. *Delete and substitute:*

A streamlined application filed by an eligible organization is complete if it includes responses for each required line item, an attestation as to completion of the eligibility worksheet, includes the correct employer identification number, is electronically signed by an authorized individual, and is accompanied by the correct user fee.[123.1]

*p. 811, second paragraph, last line. *Insert footnote at end of line:*

[123.2] *Id.* § 4.08(2).

*p. 811, fourth paragraph, last line. *Delete period and insert footnote following information:*

[92.1] See § 26.1(h).

[92.2] E.g., Rev. Proc. 2016-8, 2016-1 I.R.B. 243 § 6.09(1).

[92.3] Rev. Proc. 2016-32, 2016-22 I.R.B. 1019 § 3.01.

[95.1] Rev. Proc. 2016-5, 2016-1 I.R.B. 188 § 4.05(2).

[123.1] Rev. Proc. 2016-5, 2016-1 I.R.B. 188 § 3.13.

[123.3] *Id.* § 4.07(3).

*p. 811, fourth paragraph, last line. *Continue sentence with the following:*

and may result in denial of recognition of exemption.[123.4]

*p. 812, note 139. *Insert following existing text:*

Rev. Proc. 2016-5, 2016-1 I.R.B. 188 § 3.06.

p. 812. *Insert as eleven complete paragraphs, before heading:*

*(iii) Nonacceptance by IRS. A submitted streamlined application that is not complete will not be accepted for processing by the IRS. The IRS may request additional information to validate information presented or to clarify an inconsistency. An organization the application of which is not accepted for processing will be so notified; any user fee paid will be returned or refunded. An eligible organization may then submit a properly completed application with a new user fee or may file the general application (Form 1023).[139.1]

The IRS will not accept for processing a streamlined application if the applicant has an application for recognition of exemption (other than a Form 1023) pending with the IRS. The applicant will be so notified and any user fee paid will be returned or refunded. The same is the case with respect to a pending Form 1023 that has been assigned for review.[139.2]

(iii) Controversies. This streamlined application is generating considerable controversy. The two major complaints are that the application is too skimpy and that it is allowing favorable determination letters to be issued by the IRS to organizations that do not in fact qualify as tax-exempt charitable entities.

Typical of these complaints are the charges made in the National Taxpayer Advocate Mid-Year Report to Congress on Fiscal Year 2016 Objectives, published in July 2015. The Taxpayer Advocate Service (TAS) has endorsed the idea of a shorter application for putative charitable organizations, but, in this report, it asserts that the IRS "has gone too far" in designing and implementing the Form 1023-EZ. The complaint is that this application elicits "only a series of checkmarks in boxes." The TAS expressed its belief that "helping taxpayers meet the requirements for exempt status from inception, prior to granting recognition of exempt status, is the most effective approach for increasing cost effectiveness, reducing taxpayer burden, and enhancing consumer protection."

The TAS also took this occasion to complain about the e-Postcard (Form 990-N),[139.3] stating that the information on the e-Postcard "is insufficient to allow a potential donor or researcher to determine whether the organization actually conducts exempt activities." The TAS concluded: "Thus, Form 1023-EZ and Form 990-N, even taken together, provide almost no transparency."[139.4]

The TAS noted that, since the launch of the Form 1023-EZ, the IRS approval rate in connection with these applications is 95 percent. The TAS projects an error

---

[*123.4] E.g., Priv. Ltr. Rul. 201614038.
[*139.1] Rev. Proc. 2016-5, 2016-1 I.R.B. 188 § 4.06.
[*139.2] *Id.* § 4.06(1), (2).
[139.3] See § 28.4.

rate of over 21 percent in this process.[139.5] This has led the TAS to charge that the IRS is issuing favorable determination letters in response to applications "it would have rejected had the applications been subject to the slightest scrutiny."[139.6]

The Office of the Taxpayer Advocate, in an annual report to Congress dated January 6, 2016, continued its campaign against the streamlined application.[139.7] The Taxpayer Advocate Service stated that it conducted "research" involving a "representative sample" of the articles of incorporation of organizations that received Form 1023-EZ determination letters and found that 37 percent of them do not meet the organizational test. The TAS found it notable that the percentage of Form 1023 applications approved by the IRS is lower than the percentage associated with 1023-EZ applications. (This observation presumably was made to demonstrate unwarranted leniency with use of the Form 1023-EZ. That, however, is not necessarily the case. The streamlined application is only available for the smallest, and thus most simple, applicants. The difference in the percentages is easily attributable to the fact that 1023 applicants are generally more complex, with the potential for more issues.) The TAS report recommended that the IRS revise the Form 1023-EZ to require applicants to submit their organizing documents, a description of actual or planned activities, and past or projected financial information, and that the agency review this information before deciding whether to issue a favorable determination letter.

(iv) First-Year Report. The IRS, on December 2, 2015, issued a report on the first year's use of its streamlined Form 1023-EZ, stating that "[i]nitial analysis indicates that the Form is reducing taxpayer burden and increasing cost effectiveness of the EO operations." From implementation of the form through June 26, 2015, EO has received 43,157 Forms 1023-EZ, this being about 52 percent of the aggregate Forms 1023 and Forms 1023-EZ filed during that period.

The impact of the Form 1023-EZ is reflected in the most recent Customer Satisfaction Survey, administered to a random sample of organizations that have experienced the Exempt Organizations determinations process during the six months ending March 31, 2015. Overall EO customer satisfaction increased to 77 percent from 44 percent in the prior six-month period, while customer dissatisfaction decreased to 7 percent from 29 percent. Further, the average processing time for the form has been 13 days, compared to the average processing time of 191 days for the longer Form 1023 during the same one-year timeframe.

[139.4] In fact, the point of these documents, particularly the Form 1023-EZ, is not transparency but expediency.

[139.5] The TAS noted that TE/GE engaged in a predetermination review of 411 organizations, finding that 301 of them qualified for recognition of exemption. That sample yielded an approval rate of 73 percent. The TAS reported that TE/GE closed, as of the second quarter of fiscal year 2015, 30,601 streamlined cases, approving 29,069 of them (thus, the 95 percent). The TAS then reported that, applying the 73 percent standard, only 22,411 of these applications should have been approved. Comparing 29,069 to 22,411 (a difference of 6,658), the TAS concluded that, in processing all Form 1023-EZ applications, there was an "error rate of more than 21 percent." Consequently, without identifying a single specific case of violation of the operational test (see § 4.5(a)), the TAS charged TE/GE with misapproving applications in more than one-fifth of the instances.

[139.6] The IRS, in its fiscal year 2016 work plan, stated that one of its long-term projects is evaluation of the Form 1023-EZ process to determine if improvements need to be made to the application and review procedures. The agency has largely caught up on its applications inventory backlog (accomplished in large part by utilization of the streamlined application); this may lead to a more detailed Form 1023-EZ and/or enhancement of the predetermination review process.

[*139.7] The portion of this report discussing Form 1023-EZ is captioned "Form 1023-EZ Process Allows Unqualified Entities to Obtain Tax-Exempt Status."

To mitigate the risks associated with the Form 1023-EZ, the EO Division performs pre-determination compliance checks on 3 percent of the EZ applications filed. Based on these checks, 77 percent of the reviewed applications have been approved, while the others have been rejected, primarily due to the applicant's ineligibility to use the form. Overall, 95 percent of all Forms 1023-EZ closed to date have been approved.

EO has continuously analyzed the usage data and has taken steps to correct or mitigate issues. For example, these steps have included researching taxpayer accounts to to resolve rejections caused by an incorrect EIN, referring applications to revenue agents who perform necessary research or request information from the applicant, and calling an applicant if it fails to respond to an initial written inquiry. The current rejection rate for failure to provide additional information is 6 percent of total Form 1023-EZ filers. This rejection rate is comparable to the failure-to-establish closure rate of 4 percent for Form 1023 applications. To reduce the rejection rate based on ineligibility to file, the IRS is pursing changes to the form and its instructions to clarify the application requirements and provide education outreach to practitioners.

EO initiated a post-determination process compliance program for Form 1023-EZ filers in 2016 by conducting correspondence audits of organizations that received a favorable determination letter after filing the Form 1023-EZ. In addition to assessing the level of compliance by these organizations, the IRS will use the findings from this compliance program to identify opportunities to further modify and improve the Form 1023-EZ and its processes.

The IRS issued another report on the Form 1023-EZ, in October 2016. The agency stated that, after two years of its use, this application "continues to reduce taxpayer burden and increase cost effectiveness of the Exempt Organization's operations." The average processing time for the Form 1023-EZ has been 14 days, compared to the average processing time of 97 days for the Form 1023. Due to efficiencies gained through use of the Form 1023-EZ, 31 determination agents have been assigned to Examinations.

(j) Applications Processing Controversy

p. 814. *Insert following existing text:*

The Senate Committee on Finance, on August 5, 2015, released its report on the Committee's bipartisan investigation of the IRS's handling of applications for recognition of tax exemption submitted by political advocacy organizations.[153.1] This investigation found that, from 2010 to 2013, IRS management was "delinquent" in its "responsibility to provide effective control, guidance, and direction over the processing of applications for [recognition of] tax-exempt status filed by Tea Party and other political advocacy organizations." IRS managers were said to fail in their responsibility to "keep informed about the very existence of the applications" or "recognize the sensitivity of these applications." As to the former, IRS management "forfeited the opportunity to shape the IRS's response to the influx of political advocacy applications by simply failing to read reports informing them of the existence of those applications." As to the latter, IRS managers "did not take appropriate steps to ensure that the applications were processed expeditiously and accurately."

[153.1] Senate Committee on Finance, "The Internal Revenue Service's Processing of 501(c)(3) and 501(c)(4) Applications for Tax-Exempt Status Submitted by 'Political Advocacy' Organizations from 2010–2013," S. Rep. No. 114-119 (114th Cong., 1st Sess. 2015).

References to IRS management largely mean those heading the Exempt Organizations Division, the Director of which during the period from 2006 to May 2013 was Lois Lerner. This report states that she first became aware of applications from Tea Party groups in April or May of 2010. The report states, "For the next two years, Lerner failed to adequately manage the EO employees who processed these applications" and "failed to inform upper-level IRS management of the serious delays in processing applications [for recognition of] tax-exempt status from Tea Party and other politically sensitive groups." It is stated that, under the leadership of Ms. Lerner, the Division undertook a number of initiatives to process these applications, with "[e]ach of these initiatives . . . flawed in design and/or mismanaged."

The report discusses the "dysfunctional culture" in the EO Division during this period, stating that it "operated without sufficient regard for the consequences of its actions for the applicant organizations." The brouhaha over the loss of and recovery of some e-mails is related; this was said to delay issuance of this report for more than a year. The report concludes that "[o]verall, the IRS's less than complete response to these circumstances cast[s] doubt about the thoroughness of their efforts to recover all relevant records related to the investigation, as well as their candor to this and other Congressional committees."

This Senate Finance Committee report offered a number of recommendations, including the following: (1) the IRS should publish in the applications' instructions objective criteria that may trigger additional review and the procedures IRS specialists use to process applications involving political campaign activity; (2) the IRS should be prohibited from requesting "individual donor identities" at the application stage, although "generalized donor questions should continue to be allowed"; (3) a position within the Taxpayer Advocate Service should be created, dedicated solely to assisting nonprofit organizations in applying for recognition of exemption; (4) the EO Division should track the age and cycle time of its cases, so that it can detect backlogs early in the process and conduct periodic reviews of over-aged cases to identify the causes of the delays; (5) the standards in the Internal Revenue Manual for timely processing of cases should be enforced, and employees who fail to follow them should be disciplined; (6) IRS employees should be directed to conclude application cases within 270 days of filing; (7) the Sensitive Case Report process should be revised or a more effective way to elevate important issues within the IRS should be developed; (8) there should be "minimum training standards" for all EO Division managers to "ensure that they have adequate technical ability to perform their jobs"; and (9) the IRS should fully implement the recommendations of the Government Accountability Office in its July 2015 report.[153.2]

The majority and minority staff were unable to reach agreement as to these topics: (1) the extent to which, if any, political bias of IRS employees affected the IRS's processing of applications for recognition of tax-exempt status; (2) whether the IRS used improper methods to screen and process applications for recognition

---

[153.2] The GAO report is the subject of § 27.7(a)(v). The Department of Justice, in a letter to the leadership of the House Committee on Ways and Means dated October 23, 2015, stated that it is closing its criminal investigation as to the handling of applications for recognition of exemption filed by political advocacy organizations, without seeking criminal charges. The Department wrote that it "found no evidence that any IRS official acted based on political, discriminatory, corrupt, or other inappropriate motives that would support a criminal prosecution" and "found no evidence that any official involved in the handling of tax-exempt applications [sic] or IRS leadership attempted to obstruct justice." The investigation was said to have "uncovered substantial evidence of mismanagement, poor judgment, and institutional inertia." "But," the Department added, "poor management is not a crime."

of exempt status submitted by "progressive and left-leaning organizations"; and (3) the involvement, if any, of Treasury Department and White House employees, including the President, in directing or approving the actions of the IRS.

In conclusion, the Committee stated that, between 2010 and 2013, the IRS failed to fulfill its obligation to administer the tax law with, in the words of its mission statement, "integrity and fairness to all." The Committee's investigation uncovered "serious shortcomings" as to how the IRS exercises its power when processing the applications at issue—"shortcomings that raise public doubt about whether the IRS is a neutral administrator of the tax laws." The Committee stated, "Immediate and meaningful changes, including increased accountability to Congress and strengthened internal controls, are necessary if diminished public confidence in the IRS is to be restored."

Reforms at the IRS and the findings of congressional committees have not eliminated the likelihood of ongoing litigation in this area. For example, a federal district court certified a class action on behalf of a Tea Party entity and related organizations in connection with a lawsuit by the groups against the IRS for allegedly violating their First Amendment rights during the application-for-recognition-of-exemption process by discriminating against them because of their political views.[153.3]

Debate continues as to whether this applications processing controversy is a true scandal at the IRS or merely a case of lower-level mismanagement. Two appellate courts have adopted the first approach. The U.S. Court of Appeals for the Sixth Circuit issued an opinion that (1) appears to agree with those who assert that the IRS used "inappropriate" criteria in processing Tea Party and similar groups' applications for recognition of exemption and (2) excoriated the IRS for the agency's lack of compliance with the district court's orders in the class action case.[153.4]

Thereafter, the U.S. Court of Appeals for the District of Columbia Circuit held that two cases against the IRS, regarding the controversy, cannot be dismissed as moot because the doctrine of voluntary cessation is inapplicable.[153.5] In its opinion, the appellate court referenced this "unequal treatment" of "victim" applicant organizations by the IRS, the agency's "unconstitutional acts," and the IRS's "discriminatory processing and delay."[153.6]

*§ 26.2   REQUIREMENTS FOR CHARITABLE ORGANIZATIONS

*(a) General Rules

*p. 815. *Insert as third paragraph:*

With respect to streamlined applications,[157.1] an eligible organization that does not submit the application within 27 months from the end of the month in which it was organized will generally be recognized as exempt as of the submission date of its application. For this purpose, the submission date of a streamlined application is determined without regard to the submission date of any previously submitted application for recognition of exemption that has been

---

[153.3] NorCal Tea Party Patriots v. Internal Revenue Service, 2016 WL 223680 (S.D. Ohio).

[153.4] United States v. NorCal Tea Party Patriots, 817 F.3d 953 (6th Cir. 2016).

[153.5] True the Vote, Inc. v. Internal Revenue Service, 831 F.3d 551 (D.C. Cir. 2016).

[153.6] *Id.*

[157.1] See § 26.1(h).

withdrawn by the organization or not accepted for processing by the IRS. Thus, if an eligible organization that has a general application pending with the IRS files a streamlined application outside the 27-month window, it will generally be recognized as exempt from the submission date of its streamlined application, not from the date it submitted its general application.[157.2]

*p. 815, note 162. *Delete* 2014-9, 2014-2 I.R.B. 281 *and substitute* 2016-5, 2016-1 I.R.B. 188.

*(b) Exceptions

*p. 816, last paragraph, first sentence. *Delete* notice; *insert* of filing an application for recognition of exemption *following* requirement.

*p. 817, note 171. *Delete* 26.5 and *insert* 26.10.

p. 819. *Insert following third paragraph, before heading:*

§ 26.3A NOTICE REQUIREMENTS FOR SOCIAL WELFARE ORGANIZATIONS

An organization qualifying as an exempt social welfare organization[197.1] must provide to the IRS notice of its formation and intent to operate as this type of organization.[197.2] This notice, along with a reasonable user fee, must be provided no later than 60 days following establishment of the organization and must include the name, address, and taxpayer identification number of the organization; the date on which, and the state under the laws of which, the organization was organized; and a statement of the purpose of the organization.[197.3] The IRS may extend this 60-day period for reasonable cause.[197.4] Within 60 days of receipt of this notice, the IRS must issue to the organization an acknowledgement of it.[197.5] The notice and acknowledgement are subject to the disclosure requirements.[197.6]

An organization that fails to file this notice in a timely manner is subject to a penalty equal to $20 for each day during which the failure occurs, up to a maximum of $5,000. In the event this penalty is imposed, the IRS may make a written demand on the organization specifying a date by which the notice must be provided. If any person fails to comply with the demand on or before the specified date, a penalty of $20 is imposed for each day the failure continues, up to a maximum of $5,000.[197.7]

[157.2] Rev. Proc. 2016-5, 2016-1 I.R.B. 188 § 11.01(4).

[197.1] See Chapter 13.

[197.2] IRC § 506(a). IRC § 506 was added by the Protecting Americans from Tax Hikes Act of 2015 (Pub. L. No. 114-113, Division Q) § 405; it generally is effective for organizations organized after December 18, 2015.

[197.3] IRC § 506(b).

[197.4] IRC § 506(d).

[197.5] IRC § 506(c).

[197.6] See § 28.12.

With its first annual information return filed or notice submitted after the filing of this notice, the organization must provide such information as the IRS may require in support of its qualification as an exempt social welfare organization.[197.8] The IRS is not required to issue a determination letter following the organization's filing of the expanded first annual information return or notice.

An organization that desires additional certainty regarding its qualification as an exempt social welfare organization may file a request for a determination, together with the requisite user fee, with the IRS. This request for a determination letter must be filed by means of a new application form to be developed by the IRS (that is, other than Form 1024); this application must clearly state that the filing of it is optional. This request for a determination is treated as an application subject to the public inspection and disclosure rules.

Organizations formed on or before December 18, 2015, that have not filed an application for recognition of exemption or annual information return or notice on or before that date must provide this new notice within 180 days of that date.[197.9]

The Department of the Treasury and the IRS extended the due date for submitting this notification until at least 60 days from the date implementing regulations are issued.[197.10] Final and temporary regulations[197.11] and proposed regulations[197.12] were thereafter issued. The IRS developed an electronic form as the notification document.[197.13] Notification is not required in the case of a social welfare organization that, on or before July 8, 2016, applied for recognition of exemption or filed at least one annual information return or submitted a notice.

The IRS published additional and restated guidance as to compliance with these rules, including payment of a user fee ($50) and the process by which the agency will be acknowledging receipt of these notifications.[197.14] A memorandum for Exempt Organizations Rulings and Agreements employees from the function's acting director, dated July 8, 2016, summarizes the manner in which the IRS will be processing this notification form.[197.15]

*§ 26.6 REQUIREMENTS FOR CERTAIN PREPAID TUITION PLANS

p. 820, note 210. *Delete* 519 *and insert* 529.

*§ 26.9 RULES FOR OTHER ORGANIZATIONS

*p. 821, note 221. *Delete* 2015-9, 2015-2 I.R.B. 249 *and substitute* 2016-5, 2016-1 I.R.B. 188.

*p. 822, note 224, second line. *Delete* 2015-9, 2015-2 I.R.B. 249 § 11 *and substitute* 2016-5, 2016-1 I.R.B. 188 § 11.01.

[197.7] IRC § 6652(c)(4).
[197.8] IRC § 6033(f)(2).
[197.9] PATH Act § 506(f)(2).
*[197.10] Notice 2016-09, 2016-6 I.R.B. 306.
*[197.11] T.D. 9775 (Reg. § 1.506-1T).
*[197.12] REG-101689-16.
*[197.13] Form 8976.
*[197.14] Rev. Proc. 2016-41, 2016-30 I.R.B. 165.
*[197.15] TEGE-07-0716-0017.

*§ 26.10   GROUP EXEMPTION RULES

*p. 822, note 229. *Delete* 2015-9, 2015-2 I.R.B. 249 *and substitute* 2016-5, 2016-1 I.R.B. 188.

*p. 823, carryover paragraph, fourth line. *Insert footnote at end of line:*

[230.1] The IRS has reserved the right to decline to issue a group exemption letter when appropriate in the interest of "sound tax administration" (Rev. Proc. 2016-5, 2016-1 I.R.B. 188 § 4.09).

*p. 823, first complete paragraph, first line. *Delete* letter.

*p. 824, carryover paragraph, seventh line. *Delete* letter.

*p. 824, carryover paragraph, eighth line. *Delete* letter.

*p. 824, carryover paragraph, twelfth line. *Delete* letter.

*p. 826, note 241. Delete 2015-9, 2015-2 I.R.B. 249 § 3.09 and substitute 2016-5, 2016-1 I.R.B. 188 § 3.14.

*p. 827, note 253. Delete 2015-9, 2015-2 I.R.B. 249 § 3.07 and substitute 2016-5, 2016-1 I.R.B. 188 § 3.10.

*§ 26.14   FORFEITURE OF TAX EXEMPTION

*p. 833. Delete 2015-4, 2015-1 I.R.B. 144 and substitute 2016-4, 2016-1 I.R.B. 142.

*p. 834. *Insert following carryover paragraph and before heading:*

*§ 26.14A   MODIFICATION OF TAX EXEMPTION

Legislation enacted in 2015 expanded the availability of declaratory judgment rights to nearly all categories of tax-exempt organizations.[308.1] This law revision prompted the IRS to issue revised procedures as to modifications of exempt status.[308.2] Preexisting law, it was said, is "no longer applicable" because of "these expanded rights." This memorandum stated that this legislation requires all revocations to be treated in the same way. Thus, it added, all revocations pertaining to these types of exempt organizations "will follow the same procedures and processes as those previously used for IRC § 501(c)(3) organizations."

Pursuant to this new approach, the IRS will revoke—or treat as a revocation for declaratory judgment purposes—the status of any organization that "no longer qualifies" under the Code section for which tax exemption was recognized or self-declared. A revoked organization is able to apply or reapply for recognition

---

[308.1] See § 27.6(b), text accompanied by note 158.1.
[308.2] Memorandum TEGE-04-0216-0003.

of exemption under a different Code section. An example is given of an organization recognized as an IRC § 501(c)(4) entity that wishes to be recognized as an IRC § 501(c)(7) entity.

This deemed revocation procedure also applies with respect to disqualifications of tax-exempt status on a year-to-year basis for organizations described in IRC § 501(c)(12) or (15) that fail their respective 85 percent-member-income test gross receipts test for a year. These cases will be treated as involving revocations for declaratory judgment purposes for the failed tax years.

This new procedure, however, does not apply in the case of an organization that wants to convert from one category of tax exemption to another, where it continues to qualify for the exemption status it has, such as an organization that wants to forfeit its exemption by reason of IRC § 501(c)(3) and convert to an IRC § 501(c)(4) entity.

§ 26.15 CONSTITUTIONAL LAW ASPECTS OF PROCESS

p. 834, note 313. *Insert following existing text:*

This decision was affirmed, with the appellate court stating that the appellee is not seeking to "restrain 'the assessment or collection' of a tax, but rather to obtain relief from unconstitutional delay, the effects of which it is now suffering" (Z Street v. Koskinen, 791 F.3d 24 (D.C. Cir. 2015)). Likewise, True the Vote, Inc. v. Internal Revenue Service, 831 F.3d 551 (D.C. Cir. 2016); Freedom Path, Inc. v. Lerner, 2016 WL 3015392 (N.D. Tex., May 25, 2016). Z Street's tax exemption was recognized on October 19, 2016.

CHAPTER TWENTY-SEVEN

Administrative and Litigation Procedures

*§ 27.1 ADMINISTRATIVE PROCEDURES WHERE RECOGNITION DENIED

*p. 836, note 3. *Delete* 2014-9, 2014-2 I.R.B. 281 *and substitute* 2016-5, 2016-1 I.R.B. 188.

*p. 836, first complete paragraph, last line. *Insert footnote at end of line:*

3.1 *Id.* § 7.02.

*p. 836, note 4. *Delete* 7.02 *and substitute* 7.03.

*p. 836, note 5. *Insert* § 7.04 *following existing text.*

*p. 836, note 6. *Delete* § 7.05.

*p. 836, note 7. *Insert following existing text:*

Subsequent federal tax law requires the IRS to prescribe procedures pursuant to which a tax-exempt organization may request an appeal to the Appeals Office (IRC § 7123(c), added by enactment of the Protecting Americans from Tax Hikes Act of 2015 (§ 404), Pub. L. No. 114-113 (114th Cong., 2nd Sess.)).

*p. 836, note 9. *Delete* 7.06; *delete* 2014-5, 2014-1 I.R.B. 169 § 4.04 *and substitute* 2016-2, 2016-1 I.R.B. 102.

*p. 836, note 10. *Delete* 7.08 *and substitute* 7.06.

§ 27.2 REVOCATION OR MODIFICATION OF TAX-EXEMPT STATUS: ADMINISTRATIVE PROCEDURES

*p. 837, first complete paragraph. *Move footnote 12 reference to end of last line.*

*p. 837, note 12. *Delete 28.5 and substitute 28.6.*

*p. 837, note 13. *Delete text and substitute:*

Rev. Proc. 2016-5, 2016-1 I.R.B. 188 § 12.02.

*p. 837. *Delete third complete paragraph.*

p. 838. *Insert as second complete paragraph:*

In 2015, Congress required the IRS to prescribe procedures under which a tax-exempt organization may request an administrative appeal (including a conference relating to such an appeal, if requested) to the IRS's Office of Appeals of an adverse determination.[22.1] For this purpose, an *adverse determination* includes a determination adverse to the organization relating to (1) the initial qualification or continuing qualification of the organization for tax-exempt status; (2) the initial qualification or continuing qualification of the organization as an entity that is eligible to receive deductible contributions; (3) the initial or continuing classification of the organization as a private foundation or public charity; or (4) the initial or continuing classification of the organization as a private operating foundation.[22.2]

§ 27.3 RETROACTIVE REVOCATION OF TAX-EXEMPT STATUS

*p. 839, note 30. *Delete 2015-9, 2015-2 I.R.B. 249 and substitute 2016-5, 2016-1 I.R.B. 188.*

*p. 839. *Insert as first complete paragraph:*

A misstatement of material information includes an incorrect representation or attestation as to the organization's organizational documents, the organization's tax-exempt purpose(s), the organization's conduct of prohibited and restrictive activities, or the organization's eligibility to file a streamlined application for recognition of exemption.[31.1] Information provided on an application for recognition of exemption that has been withdrawn will not be considered by the IRS for purposes of limiting the retroactive effect of a revocation or modification of a determination letter.[31.2]

[22.1] IRC § 7123(c)(1).

[22.2] IRC § 7123(c)(2). These law changes were occasioned on the enactment of the Protecting Americans from Tax Hikes Act of 2015 (Pub. L. No. 114-113, Division Q) § 404(a). The changes apply to determinations made on or after May 19, 2014 (PATH Act § 404(b)); this law is a codification of procedures announced by the IRS on that date (IRS Memorandum, "Appeals Office Consideration of All Proposed Adverse Rulings Relating to Tax-Exempt Status from EO Technical by Request").

*[31.1] Rev. Proc. 2016-5, 2016-1 I.R.B. 188 § 12.01(3). As to the last of these items, see § 26.1(h).

*[31.2] *Id.* § 12.01(4).

*p. 839, note 32. Delete 2015-9, 2015-2 I.R.B. 249 and substitute 2016-5, 2016-1 I.R.B. 188.

p. 839, second complete paragraph, note 38. *Insert following existing text:*

In one of these instances, having found that an organization omitted or misstated material facts and has been operating in a manner materially different from that originally represented, thus justifying retroactive revocation of exemption, the IRS observed that the organization "has not turned square corners in dealing with the Federal government" (Priv. Ltr. Rul. 201543019).

§ 27.6   REVOCATION OF TAX-EXEMPT STATUS: LITIGATION PROCEDURES

(b) Declaratory Judgment Rules

p. 851, last paragraph. *Insert as second sentence:*

This procedure was extended, in 2015, to the initial determination of or continuing classification of any other category of tax-exempt organization, including apostolic entities.[158.1]

*p. 851, note 159, first line. *Delete* 2015-9, 2015-2 I.R.B. 249 *and substitute* 2016-5, 2016-1 I.R.B. 188.

*p. 852, second paragraph, ninth line. *Delete* farmers' cooperatives for *and substitute* nonprofit organizations for tax.

*p. 852, note 166, third line. *Delete* 2015-9, 2015-2 I.R.B. 249 *and substitute* 2016-5, 2016-1 I.R.B. 188.

*p. 852, note 167. *Delete text and substitute* IRC § 7848(a).

*p. 852, note 170. *Delete* 2015-9, 2015-2 I.R.B. 249 *and substitute* 2016-5, 2016-1 I.R.B. 188.

*p. 853, carryover paragraph. *Insert as last sentence:*

Moreover, the nonacceptance of an application for recognition of exemption for incompleteness[173.1] is not a final determination for these purposes.[173.2]

*p. 854, note 187, first line. *Delete* (Form 1023).

*p. 854, note 187, second line. *Delete* 2015-9, 2015-2 I.R.B. 249 *and substitute* 2016-5, 2016-1 I.R.B. 188.

*p. 854, note 187. *Insert as second to fourth sentences:*

[158.1] This extension occurred on enactment of the Protecting Americans from Tax Hikes Act of 2015 (Pub. L. No. 114-113, Division Q) § 406.

[173.1] See § 26.1(b).

[173.2] Rev. Proc. 2016-5, 2016-1 I.R.B. 188 § 10.05(1).

Also, the nonacceptance of an incomplete application (see § 26.1(b) is not a failure to make a determination (Rev. Proc. 2016-5, 2016-1 I.R.B. 188 § 10.05(2)). The nonacceptance of an application for recognition of exemption for incompleteness (see § 26.1(b)) is not a final determination (*id.* § 10.05(1)). An organization will not have exhausted its administrative remedies if it was ineligible to submit a streamlined application (see 26.1(h)) (*id.*)).

*p. 856, second complete paragraph, second line. *Delete* substantially.

*p. 856, note 201. *Delete* 2015-9, 2015-2 I.R.B. 249 *and substitute* 2016-5, 2016-1 I.R.B. 188.

*p. 856, third complete paragraph, third line. *Delete* substantially.

*p. 856, third complete paragraph, fourth line. *Delete* a group exemption request (*and accompanying footnote*).

*p. 856, note 207. *Delete* 2015-9, 2015-2 I.R.B. 249 *and substitute* 2016-5, 2016-1 I.R.B. 188.

*p. 856, note 207. *Insert following existing text:*

These steps will not be considered completed by the IRS until the agency has had a reasonable time to act on an appeal or protect (*id.* § 10.04).

§ 27.7   IRS EXAMINATION PROCEDURES AND PRACTICES

(a) General IRS Exempt Organizations Audit Procedures and Practices

*p. 862, second complete paragraph. *Insert as second sentence:*

This initiation of an examination will always be by mail, rather than by telephone.[241.1]

p. 866. *Insert following first paragraph, before heading:*

(*v*) *Government Accountability Office 2015 Report.* The Government Accountability Office (GAO), in a report issued in July 2015, concluded that there are "several areas" where the Exempt Organizations Division's controls intended to enable it to properly select tax-exempt organizations for examination "were not well designed or implemented."[257.1] The GAO stated that the "control deficiencies GAO found increase the risk that [the Division] could select organizations for examination in an unfair manner—for example, based on an organization's religious, educational, political, or other views."[257.2]

[241.1] Memorandum to IRS Division Commissioners from the Deputy Commissioner for Services and Enforcement, May 20, 2016; this change in practice was initiated due to the continuing threat of telephone scams, phishing, and identity theft.

[257.1] "IRS Examination Selection: Internal Controls for Exempt Organization Selection Should Be Strengthened," 33 (GAO-15-514).

[257.2] *Id.*

In other instances, the GAO reported, the Division maintains "well-documented procedures for several examination selection processes" in the Internal Revenue Manual (IRM).[257.3] IRS staff can deviate from the procedures that are part of the IRM only with executive management approval. One of the examples of "internal control deficiencies" the GAO found was that procedures for some audit processes are not included in the IRM, as required by IRS policy. Then, said the GAO, IRS staff can sidestep procedures without approval, increasing the "risk of unfair selection of organization's returns for examination."[257.4]

Another GAO finding was that Division management "does not consistently monitor examinations and database files to ensure that selection decisions are documented and approved, to help ensure fairness."[257.5] The GAO's review of examination files found that "approval of some selection decisions was not documented, as required by [the Division's] procedures."[257.6]

The GAO recommended that the Commissioner of Internal Revenue direct the Division to take nine actions, including the following: (1) develop, document, and implement a process to ensure that IRM sections and other procedures are reviewed and updated annually, and that updates reflect current practice, as required; (2) complete the development of and formally issue the IRM sections on compliance checks and compliance reviews; (3) develop, document, and implement additional monitoring procedures to ensure case selection controls; (4) develop, document, and implement procedures to ensure that all criteria or methods used in projects to select returns for examination are consistently documented and approved; and (5) provide cross-training for IRS employees who process complaints (known as *referrals classifiers*), and prioritizing training for classifiers who process political activity, church, and high-profile referrals.[257.7]

Another set of recommendations pertained to the membership of *referral committees*. These are committees that are composed of a rotating set of senior examination staff or managers who make the final decision about the potential for examinations. According to the IRM, committee members should rotate every 12 months on a staggered schedule to maintain continuity and expertise. The Exempt Organizations Division utilizes three types of committees to review referrals: political activity referral committees, church referral committees, and high-profile referral committees. The GAO recommended that referral committee members rotate every 12 months or that the IRM be revised to require an alternative rotation schedule. Just prior to issuance of the GAO report, however, the Director of the Exempt Organizations Division issued a memorandum stating that referral committee members will serve for two years.[257.8]

The GAO also recommended that the Commissioner determine whether additional controls may be needed to ensure that all closed examination files are tracked and maintained accurately.[257.9]

[257.3] *Id.*, introductory page.
[257.4] *Id.*
[257.5] *Id.*
[257.6] *Id.*
[257.7] *Id.* at 52–53.
[257.8] TEGE-04-0715-0018 (July 21, 2015).
[257.9] GAO report, *supra* note 257.1, at 53.

(vi) IRS Fiscal Year 2016 Work Plan. The EO Division, in its fiscal year 2016 work plan, stated that its "overarching compliance strategy" is to ensure that tax-exempt organizations comply with the requirements for exemption and adhere to all applicable federal tax laws. This strategy is to be implemented by means of "data-driven decisions with the intended goal of identifying and addressing existing and emerging high-risk areas of non-compliance with the optimal use of available resources."

The Division intends to use the "most appropriate, cost-effective and least intrusive compliance treatment." This is to include educational efforts, compliance reviews, compliance checks, and correspondence and field examinations. This strategy is expected to be achieved through (1) determining the coverage of "all major subsections and size[s] of organizations by stratifying the universe of exempt organizations into the major subsections and allocating anticipated new examination cases among each subsection and asset class"; (2) determining issues to focus on through a data-driven approach where the Division will identify the highest risk areas of noncompliance through the use of return data of the exempt organizations' community and historical information; and (3) identifying areas of high noncompliance risk through stakeholder input, reliable outside data, and public information.

The Division will be focusing its resources on these strategic issue areas: (1) nonexempt-purpose activity and private inurement; (2) self-dealing, excess benefit transactions, and loans to disqualified persons; (3) unrelated business income tax and employment tax liability; (4) oversight of funds expended outside the United States; and (5) tax-exempt hospitals and nonexempt charitable trusts.

*(vii) IRS Fiscal Year 2017 Work Plan. The EO Division, in its fiscal year 2017 work plan, stated that, in FY 2016, Exempt Organizations Examinations embarked on an "overarching compliance strategy" to ensure that tax-exempt organizations complied with the requirements for exemption. The agency implemented a "data driven case selection process" with a goal of identifying and addressing existing and emerging high-risk areas of noncompliance. Resources were focused on five issue areas: tax exemption, protection of assets, the tax gap, international spending, and emerging issues.

As of June 30, 2016, EO Examinations had completed 4,984 examinations. The issue areas were filing, organizational, and operational matters, including delinquent returns (2,109); employment tax issues, including worker classification and noncompliance with withholding requirements (1,323); unrelated business income issues (611); discontinued operations, foundation status changes, and revocations (195); private inurement and private benefit matters (192); legislative, political, and governance issues (59); and other matters (495).

Hospitals are being reviewed for compliance with IRC § 501(r).[257.10] As of June 30, 2016, the IRS completed 692 reviews and referred 166 hospitals for field examinations. Issues for which these referrals were made are lack of a community health needs assessment, lack of a financial assistance and/or emergency medical care policies, and noncompliance with billing and collection requirements.

In FY 2016, the IRS continued post-determination compliance examinations of 1,400 exempt organizations that filed Forms 1023 or 1024 and were approved

---

[*257.10] See § 7.6(b).

pursuant to the streamlined process. As of June 30, 2016, the IRS closed 1,051 examined returns, with 61 percent closing as no change and 39 percent having changes ranging from amendments to organizational documents to failure to file returns. In addition, five organizations had their status revoked.

The IRS also began post-determination compliance examinations of exempt organizations that were granted recognition of status through submission of Form 1023-EZ.[257.11] A statistically valid random sample of 1,182 organizations has been selected. As of June 30, 2016, 36 examined returns have been closed, with 34 closed with no change and two requiring amendments to their organizing documents.

The IRS was of the view that both of these processes are "working well." The agency intends to continue both programs in FY 2017.

In FY 2017, the IRS will continue its compliance strategy and utilization of data-driven decisions. It will implement newly developed models for the Forms 5227 and 990-T and the post-determination compliance program. It will work on the referral system, continue in the five strategic issue areas, and continue review of exempt hospitals. The agency will utilize data sources to identify organizations at risk for private inurement and private benefit issues, and to "identify anomalies" on returns filed by private foundations. During FY 2017, the IRS will include 400 returns in the work plan identified for "high risk" of private inurement and private benefit issues, and 100 private foundation returns with anomalies detected.

The IRS will be implementing a statistical sampling methodology to assess compliance by exempt organizations. This statistical sample is intended to assist in the assessment of the overall compliance levels of the exempt organizations community and address the recommendations made by the General Accountability Office in 2015.[257.12]

*(b) IRS Exempt Organizations Examination Guidelines

*p. 867. *Insert as first complete paragraph, before heading:*

In an IRS memorandum dated December 30, 2015, from the director of Exempt Organizations Examinations, reference is made to a then newly renamed "EO Referrals Group," which is to create a "peer review group" that will be responsible for reviewing "high profile referrals" (complaints).[289.1] These referrals are said to include "information items" containing or involving evidence or allegations of financial transactions with, including contributions to, individuals or organizations with known or suspected terrorist connections; evidence or allegations involving a church; high-impact issues (e.g., the decision may result in media attention); sensitive cases (e.g., the information was submitted by an elected official other than those in the congressional or executive branches); items submitted by a member of Congress or congressional staff; and other factors indicating that review by the group would be desirable for reasons of "fairness or integrity."

[257.11] See § 26.1(h).
[257.12] See § 27.7(a)(v).
[289.1] TE/GE-04-1215-0029.

(c) Church Audits

p. 867, note 293, penultimate line. *Delete* 1999 and *substitute* 2009.

*§ 27.10   IRS DISCLOSURE TO STATE OFFICIALS

*p. 874, note 355. *Delete* 2015-9, 2015-2 I.R.B. 249 *and substitute* 2016-5, 2016-1 I.R.B. 188.

CHAPTER TWENTY-EIGHT

Operational Requirements

*§ 28.1 CHANGES IN OPERATIONS OR FORM

*(a) Changes in Form

*p. 880. *Delete first complete paragraph (including footnotes).*

*p. 881. *Insert following second complete paragraph, before heading:*

*(c) Redomestications

Redomestication is a mechanism under state law enabling a nonprofit organization to change its state of domicile. This mechanism typically does not require formation of a new legal entity.[24.1] A nonprofit organization may consider changing its state of domicile for practical reasons that do not involve a change in the organization's character, purposes, or methods of operation. In contrast to a change in legal form, a redomestication, at least under certain circumstances, does not trigger a requirement to file a new application for recognition of exemption and thus allows the nonprofit exempt organization to continue to rely on its determination letter.

The IRS has distinguished a redomestication from circumstances where there is establishment of a new legal entity. In its principal guidance on the point, the IRS ruled that, under certain circumstances, a redomestication does not require the filing of a new application.[24.2] In this instance, the redomestication process

---

[24.1] Cf. § 28.1(b).
[24.2] Priv. Ltr. Rul. 201446025.

required an amendment to the articles of incorporation (as opposed to the filing of new articles of incorporation), the laws of the state of incorporation and the state of redomestication provided that the organization maintained its original date of incorporation and treated the organization as the same entity before and after the redomestication, and the organization maintained the same liabilities following the redomestication. The IRS also ruled that the redomestication did not represent a substantial change in the organization's character, purposes, or methods of operation for purposes of its reliance on the determination letter.[24.3]

The Tax Section of the American Bar Association asked the IRS to issue a revenue ruling to clarify this aspect of the law, observing that "[t]here is no practical or legal reason for the tax laws to impose a burden on a nonprofit organization seeking to redomesticate when the redomestication will not result in the creation of a new legal entity or a substantial change in the character, purposes, or methods of operation of the organization."[24.4]

*§ 28.2 ANNUAL REPORTING RULES

*(d) Group Returns

*p. 891, note 139. *Delete* 26.6 *and substitute* 26.10.

§ 28.3 ANNUAL INFORMATION RETURN

(i) Schedule B

p. 894, note 152, last line. *Delete text following first comma and insert:*

784 F.3d 1307 (9th Cir. 2015).

p. 894, note 152. *Insert following existing text:*

Likewise, Americans for Prosperity Foundation v. Harris, 809 F.3d 536 (9th Cir. 2015); Citizens United v. Schneiderman, 2015 WL 4509717 (S.D.N.Y., July 27, 2015). Nonetheless, a federal district court granted a motion for a permanent injunction enjoining the Attorney General of California from demanding Schedules B in an as-applied challenge (Americans for Prosperity Foundation v. Harris, 115 F. Supp. 3d 457 (C.D. Cal. 2016)). Similarly, Thomas More Law Center v. Harris, 2016 WL 6781090 (C.D. Cal., Nov. 16, 2016).

*§ 28.4 NOTIFICATION REQUIREMENT

*p. 901. *Insert as second complete paragraph, before heading:*

With respect to streamlined applications,[179.1] an eligible organization (other than a private foundation) that normally has gross receipts of $50,000 or less is not

---

[24.3] The IRS ruled that a "conversion" of an exempt corporation, formed by an act of a state legislature, to a nonprofit corporation pursuant to a general state law did not entail creation of a new organization for purposes of the notice requirement and thus that a new application was not required (Priv. Ltr. Rul. 201426028); this ruling appears to be incorrect, in that a new legal entity was established.

[24.4] Letter to the IRS dated June 22, 2016.

[179.1] See § 26.1(h).

required to file an annual information return but must file this notice. An eligible organization (other than a private foundation) that applies for recognition of exempt status is not required to separately notify the IRS that it is excepted from the annual filing requirement if it is claiming a filing exemption solely on the basis that its gross receipts are normally $50,000 or less. If, however, such an organization claims an exception from filing an annual information return on another basis, it must file with the IRS[179.2] and provide a statement of facts on which its claim is based. Alternatively, the organization may file a general application (Form 1023) and submit information supporting its claimed exception from filing annual information returns.[179.3]

§ 28.11   IRS DOCUMENT DISCLOSURE RULES

(a) Federal Tax Law Disclosure Requirements

*p. 909, note 241. *Insert following existing text:*

The U.S. Tax Court ruled that it lacked the jurisdiction to order a properly issued determination letter "un-issued" and thus not disclosable, where the IRS agreed to withdraw the letter as part of a settlement of litigation (Anonymous v. Comm'r, 145 T.C.M. 246 (2015).

p. 910, last complete paragraph, first sentence. *Insert footnote at end of sentence:*

[252.1] The federal tax law generally protects the confidentiality of tax returns and tax-return information (IRC § 6103(a)); these terms are broadly defined. Wrongful disclosure of returns and return information is punishable criminally or civilly (IRC §§ 7213, 7431).

p. 911. *Delete last sentence (including footnote) and substitute:*

One of the exceptions to this nondisclosure rule is that return information may be disclosed in a federal judicial proceeding related to tax administration if treatment of an item reflected on a return is directly related to resolution of an issue in the proceeding.[255]

*p. 911, note 256, first line. *Delete* 2015-9, 2015-2 I.R.B. 249 *and substitute* 2016-5, 2016-1 I.R.B. 188.

*p. 911, note 256, first paragraph. *Insert as first sentence and convert the balance of the text to a separatev paragraph:*

These documents may be requested by submitting Form 4506-A. The IRS states that "[o]rganizations should ensure that applications and supporting documents do not include unnecessary personal identifying information (such as bank account numbers or social security numbers) that could result in identity theft or other adverse consequences if publicly disclosed" (*id.* § 8.01(1)).

[*179.2] Form 8940.

[*179.3] Rev. Proc. 2016-5, 2016-1 I.R.B. 188 § 11.01(5).

[255] IRC § 6103(h)(4)(B). Applying this *item test*, a court concluded that a list of applicants for recognition of exemption provided by the IRS to the Treasury Department must be disclosed (even though it is return information) to plaintiffs seeking it because it is directly related to the issue of certification of a class of entities allegedly mistreated during their application processes (NorCal Tea Party Patriots v. IRS, 2015 WL 1487112, April 1, 2015 (S.D. Ohio 2015)). On appeal, the appellate court excoriated the IRS for its delays in this case and instructed the IRS to begin complying with the district court's orders, and refused to issue a writ of mandamus overriding the lower court (United States v. NorCal Tea Party Patriots, 817 F.3d 953 (6th Cir. 2016)).

p. 911. *Insert as second complete paragraph:*

The law does not permit an exempt organization's written determination letter from being considered "un-issued" and thus nondisclosable, nor does the U.S. Tax Court have jurisdiction to restrain the IRS from disclosing portions of an examination report. These points were illustrated in a situation where the IRS issued an exempt organization a final adverse determination letter, accompanied by an examination report, retroactively revoking exemption, and then agreed as part of a settlement to reconsider exempt status; the agency recognized the entity's exemption and revoked the exemption retroactively in a second revocation letter, which did not include the examination report. The second determination letter was made available for public inspection. The organization brought an action to restrain disclosure of the first determination letter and report or, alternatively, to order the IRS to not disclose a portion of the report. The Tax Court held that the first determination letter and report were properly issued and had to be made public, rejecting the notion that there is any legal basis for "un-issuing" a properly issued determination letter.[258.1] The court also declined to restrain the IRS from disclosing a portion of the examination report, ruling that such an excision is outside the scope of the required redactions[258.2] and that the relief sought was beyond the scope of its jurisdiction.[258.3]

*p. 912, note 277, third line. *Delete* **2015-9, 2015-2 I.R.B. 249** *and substitute* **2016-5, 2016-1 I.R.B. 188.**

*§ 28.12 DOCUMENT DISCLOSURE OBLIGATIONS OF EXEMPT ORGANIZATIONS

*(a) General Rules

*p. 915, note 294, first line. *Delete* **2015-9, 2015-2 I.R.B. 249** *and substitute* **2016-5, 2016-1 I.R.B. 188.**

§ 28.18 TAX-EXEMPT ORGANIZATIONS AND TAX SHELTERS

(e) Tax Shelters in Exempt Organizations Context

p. 939. *Insert as third complete paragraph, before heading:*

Two individuals devised and promoted a plan or arrangement involving the use of trusts, limited liability companies, and corporations sole. The corporations sole plan, the couple claimed, could reduce an individual's federal income tax liability. They told their "customers" that they could assign their personal income to a corporation sole, thereby transforming otherwise taxable income into

---

[258.1] Anonymous v. Comm'r, 145 T.C. 246 (2015).

[258.2] See the text accompanied by *supra* note 244.

[258.3] IRC § 6110(f)(3)(A). Earlier, the court held that it lacked the authority to restrain disclosure of an IRS private letter ruling "in its entirety" (Anonymous v. Comm'r, 134 T.C. 13, 19 (2010)).

nontaxable income of the corporation sole. They advised customers who earned income by means of a business to operate their ministries through a corporation sole and form an LLC to operate the business. Customers were further advised to create a trust as the ministry entity, with the trust also serving as the majority member of the LLC. The customer was to hold a minority interest in the LLC and function as the LLC's managing member. The couple claimed that the income flowing to the trust would be tax-free and that customers could have a charitable deduction if they contributed up to 50 percent of the income of the LLC allocated to them to the church. A federal district court enjoined the promotion, having found that these two individuals had the educational and business background to know that the statements they made in connection with the ostensible tax benefits of their corporation sole plan were false.[513.1] Another court found that the penalty for promoting an abusive tax shelter[513.2] existed, and the amount of the penalty was imposed on each individual.[513.3]

§ 28.19   INTERNATIONAL GRANTMAKING REQUIREMENTS

(a) Charitable Organizations Generally

p. 942. *Insert as fourth complete paragraph:*

This body of law was detailed, by means of a ruling concerning an organization, classified as a charitable entity, which received contributions from families and transferred the funds, as tuition payments, to foreign schools it supports. This activity was ruled to provide an improper private benefit to the parents of students[544.1] and to cause the organization to be a mere conduit of funds (for tuition) to the schools, resulting in revocation of exemption.[544.2] The organization was seen by the IRS as operating as a conduit because it failed to exercise any discretion and control over the funds it provides to the schools. The entity was so faulted for a variety of reasons, including failure to have a grant application, failure to approve grants in amounts that vary from the amount requested, failure to require grant recipients to provide written reports, and lack of a system by which it can pursue an accounting of funds and seek to recover any misspent funds.

[513.1] United States v. Gardner, 2008 WL 906696 (D. Ariz. 2008), *aff'd*, 457 Fed. Appx. 611 (9th Cir. 2011).

[513.2] See text accompanying and *supra* note 496.

[513.3] Gardner v. Comm'r, 145 T.C. 161 (2015).

[544.1] See § 20.12.

[544.2] Priv. Ltr. Rul. 201539032.

CHAPTER TWENTY-NINE

Tax-Exempt Organizations and Exempt Subsidiaries

§ 29.6 Revenue from Tax-Exempt
Subsidiary

§ 29.6 REVENUE FROM TAX-EXEMPT SUBSIDIARY

p. 964, note 128. *Delete sentence and substitute:*

Congress, in 2006, enacted a special rule whereby certain items of revenue paid from a subsidiary to a controlling tax-exempt organization are not treated as forms of unrelated business income as long as they are reasonable and other criteria are met (see § 30.7(d)).

CHAPTER THIRTY

Tax-Exempt Organizations and For-Profit Subsidiaries

§ 30.2 Potential of Attribution to Parent   § 30.7 Revenue from For-Profit Subsidiary

§ 30.2 POTENTIAL OF ATTRIBUTION TO PARENT

p. 972, note 50. *Delete appellate court citation and insert* **486 Fed. Appx. 655 (6th Cir. 2012).**

*****p. 973, second paragraph.** *Insert as second sentence:*

Likewise, an exempt university that formed a for-profit subsidiary to conduct on-line educational programs for adults received a ruling from the IRS holding that the subsidiary is a separate legal entity with its own "activities and management," having a "real and substantial business purpose," so that its operations will not be attributed to its parent.[60.1]

§ 30.7 REVENUE FROM FOR-PROFIT SUBSIDIARY

(d) Temporary Rule

p. 982, second heading. *Delete* **Temporary** *and substitute* **Special.**

p. 982, last paragraph. *Delete first sentence (including footnote) and substitute:*

Notwithstanding the foregoing, a special rule applies with respect to certain payments to tax-exempt controlling organizations by their subsidiaries.[127]

p. 983, carryover paragraph, sixth line. *Delete* **Temporary** *and insert* **Special.**

[60.1] Priv. Ltr. Rul. 201503018.

[127] IRC § 512(b)(13)(E). This rule, having most recently expired at the close of 2014, was reinstated and made permanent by the Protecting Americans from Tax Hikes Act of 2015 (Pub. L. No. 114-113, Division Q) § 114.

CHAPTER THIRTY-TWO

Tax-Exempt Organizations: Other Operations and Restructuring

§ 32.7 SINGLE-MEMBER LIMITED LIABILITY COMPANIES

p. 1035, note 146. *Insert following existing text:*

Uses of SMLLCs in the exempt organizations context are illustrated by two other developments: The IRS stated that a private foundation may make a grant directly to a SMLLC and treat that transfer as a qualifying distribution (IRC § 4942) where the sole member of the LLC is a U.S. public charity (INFO-2010-0052) and that a donor may make a deductible charitable contribution directly to a SMLLC in like circumstances (Notice 2012-52, 2012-35 I.R.B. 317).

§ 32.10 CONVERSION FROM NONEXEMPT TO EXEMPT STATUS

(b) Federal Tax Law

p. 1045. *Insert following existing text:*

The IRS is hostile to these types of conversions, adhering to a nearly immutable policy that tax exemption as a charitable organization is not available where the entity is a successor to a for-profit business. For example, an entity whose principal functions are healing services for individuals and animals was denied recognition of exemption as a charitable organization, with the IRS ruling that the intent of the proprietors of the activities to obtain contributions and grants is a form of private inurement.[209.1] Often, the IRS will also rule that exemption is unavailable because the organization is operating in a commercial manner.[209.2] The IRS is aided in this regard by a Tax Court decision holding that

---

[209.1] Priv. Ltr. Rul. 201540019.
[209.2] E.g., Priv. Ltr. Rul. 201540016.

an entity is ineligible for exemption if its activities amount to the same operations as those conducted by its for-profit predecessor.[209.3]

*§ 32.11 CONVERSION FROM ONE EXEMPT STATUS TO ANOTHER

A change in the federal tax law expanded declaratory judgment rights to nearly all categories of tax-exempt organizations.[209.4] This expansion of declaratory judgment rights applied retroactively to final adverse determination letters issued on or after December 18, 2015. This law revision prompted the IRS to issue revised procedures as to modifications of exempt status.[209.5]

The IRS guidance is predicated on the fact that this law revision generally mandates that all revocations of exempt status are to be treated in the same manner. Pursuant to this approach, the IRS will revoke — or treat as a revocation for declaratory judgment purposes — the status of any organization that "no longer qualifies" under the Internal Revenue Code provision for which tax exemption was recognized or self-declared. A revoked organization is able to apply or reapply for recognition of exemption under a different Code section. A conversion of an organization's exempt status is thus regarded as commencing with a *deemed revocation.*

This revised approach apparently does not contemplate situations where an exempt organization continues to qualify for the exemption classification it has but nonetheless wants to switch to another category of exemption.

[209.3] Asmark Institute, Inc. v. Comm'r, 101 T.C.M. 1067 (2011), *aff'd*, 486 Fed. Appx. 566 (6th Cir. 2012). This issue was bizarrely highlighted when, on October 23, 2015, seven members of the U.S. Senate wrote to the IRS and the Department of Education, asserting that conversions of for-profit schools to tax-exempt schools are "superficial" and resulting in "sham non-profits"; one of these senators, in an accompanying press release, charged that these conversions constitute fraud and tax evasion.

*[209.4] See § 26.14A.

*[209.5] Memorandum TEGE-04-0216-0003.

APPENDIX A

Sources of Tax-Exempt Organizations Law

*p. 1057, note 24. *Insert following existing text:*

In general, Cummings, Jr., "The Supreme Court's Deference to Tax Administrative Interpretation," 69 *Tax Law.* (No. 2) 419 (Winter 2016).

*p. 1062. *Insert following third paragraph, before heading:*

Level-of-Guidance Controversy. For more than 100 years, the Department of the Treasury and the IRS have issued guidance documents to help taxpayers comply with the federal tax law. These documents include, as discussed, tax regulations, revenue rulings and revenue procedures, notices, announcements, technical advice memoranda, and private letter rulings. This guidance is based on the statutory authorization extended to the Secretary of the Treasury to "prescribe all needful rules and regulations for the enforcement of" the federal tax law.[53.1]

Some of this tax law guidance is published in the weekly *Internal Revenue Bulletin.* The U.S. General Accountability Office estimated that annually about 2,000 pages of regulations and other forms of guidance are published in the *Bulletin.*[53.2] Indeed, "Treasury and IRS are among the largest generators of federal agency regulations and they issue thousands of other forms of taxpayer guidance."[53.3] It is the view of the IRS that only guidance published in the *Bulletin* states the IRS's authoritative interpretation of the law.[53.4]

In addition to the guidance published in the *Internal Revenue Bulletin,* thousands of other documents that provide information to taxpayers are available on the IRS's website. Some IRS guidance written by its Office of Chief Counsel provides detailed and technical explanations of the federal tax law for professional return preparers as well as taxpayers generally. Other IRS sources of information that explain the tax law in "plain language" include (1) forms, instructions, and publications for taxpayers to use in preparing their returns; (2) news releases, fact sheets, and tax tips to the news media; (3) online interactive tools by means of which taxpayers can receive answers after asking general or taxpayer-specific questions; and (4) instructional audio and visual presentations.[53.5]

[53.1] IRC § 7805(a).
[53.2] GAO, "Regulatory Guidance Processes: Treasury and OMB Need to Reevaluate Long-Standing Exemptions of Tax Regulations and Guidance" (GAO-16-720), issued in September 2016 (Regulatory Guidance Processes Report), at 3.
[53.3] *Id.* at 2.
[53.4] *Id.* at 7.
[53.5] *Id.* at 3.

There are five statutory authorities for the IRS to follow when drafting and issuing regulations: the Administrative Procedure Act (APA),[53.6] the Paperwork Reduction Act,[53.7] the Regulatory Flexibility Act,[53.8] the Congressional Review Act (CRA),[53.9] and a section of the Internal Revenue Code.[53.10] The APA generally requires federal agencies to notify the public about, and solicit comments on, proposed regulations via a notice of proposed rulemaking published in the *Federal Register*. The CRA requires agencies to submit each rule to Congress and to the Comptroller General before it can take effect. All agencies are required by the CRA to specify whether the rule is *major*, yet the Office of Information and Regulatory Affairs (OIRA), within the Office of Management and Budget (OMB), is responsible for determining whether a rule is major based on certain criteria.[53.11] The Government Accountability Office (GAO) issues reports to Congress on major rules, summarizing and assessing the agency's compliance with required procedural steps.

Presidents have issued executive orders to centralize review of executive branch agency rulemaking within the OMB, and to require executive branch agencies to prepare additional assessments and analyses of the potential costs and benefits of rules that are *significant* and *economically significant*.[53.12] The OIRA is responsible for the coordinated review of regulatory actions by federal executive agencies. This coordinated review is necessary to ensure that, among other outcomes, regulations are consistent with applicable laws, the President's priorities, and the principles set forth in executive orders, and that decisions made by one agency do not conflict with the policies or actions taken or planned by another agency. Executive agencies provide the OIRA with lists of planned regulatory actions when drafting rules, including assessments about whether the rules are significant, to determine if additional OIRA review is required. If so, agencies provide the text of the draft regulation and any required analyses (including information on estimated costs and benefits) to the OIRA before issuing the rule. The OIRA staff reviews the rule

---

[53.6] 5 U.S.C. §§ 551–559.

[53.7] 44 U.S.C. §§ 3501–3520. This Act requires federal agencies to minimize the paperwork burden they impose on the public and submit certain proposed information collections to the OMB for approval.

[53.8] 5 U.S.C. §§ 601–608. This Act generally requires federal agencies to consider the impact of their regulatory proposals on small businesses and other small entities, analyze effective alternatives that minimize the impact on small entities, and make their analyses available for public comment.

[53.9] 5 U.S.C. §§ 801–808.

[53.10] IRC § 7805.

[53.11] The CRA defines a *major* rule as one that the OIRA determines has resulted in or is likely to result in (1) an annual effect on the nation's economy of at least $100 million; (2) a major increase in costs or prices for consumers, individual industries, federal, state, or local government agencies, or geographic regions; or (3) significant adverse effects on competition, employment, investment, productivity, innovation, or the ability of U.S.-based enterprises to compete with foreign-based enterprises in domestic and export markets.

[53.12] Pursuant to Executive Order No. 12866 (Oct. 4, 1993), a regulatory action is *significant* if it is likely to result in a rule that (1) has an annual effect on the economy of at least $100 million or adversely affects the nation's economy, a sector of the economy, productivity, competition, jobs, the environment, public health or safety, or state, local, or tribal governments or communities; (2) creates a serious inconsistency or otherwise interferes with another agency's actions taken or planned; (3) materially alters the budgetary impact of entitlements, grants, user fees, or loan programs or the rights and obligations of recipients thereof; or (4) raises novel legal or policy issues. A rule that meets the first of these criteria is colloquially referred to as "economically significant" and further assessments of the rule's costs and benefits are required.

and related documents and may request changes or additional analyses. The OIRA can notify the agency that it has separately determined that a planned regulation is a significant regulatory action.[53.13]

The OIRA is also responsible for reviewing certain non-regulatory guidance issued by executive branch agencies. The OMB issued a bulletin in 2007 to establish policies and procedures for the development, issuance, and use of significant guidance documents by executive branch agencies.[53.14] This bulletin's definition of a *significant* guidance document is similar to the definition of a significant regulatory action under the executive order.[53.15] The bulletin requires that agencies establish procedures to allow the public to view and comment on significant guidance documents after they are released and, for any economically significant guidance documents, also to make a draft available for public comment and announce its availability in the *Federal Register*. Consistent with an OMB memorandum implementing the bulletin, the OIRA has the opportunity to review some significant guidance documents prior to issuance.[53.16] Guidance that is not significant, as defined by the OMB bulletin, is not subject to policies and procedures in the bulletin; guidance procedures are, in these circumstances, left to agency discretion.[53.17]

Tax regulations are Treasury's and the IRS's official interpretation of the federal tax laws. These regulations are the most authoritative source of published guidance, inasmuch as they are binding on the IRS and taxpayers, having the force and effect of law. Other guidance in the *Internal Revenue Bulletin*—revenue rulings, revenue procedures, notices, and announcements—do not have the same "force and effect" as Treasury regulations, but taxpayers can still rely on it as authoritative. Written determinations are Chief Counsel letters to, or memoranda regarding, individual taxpayers; the IRS cautions that only the taxpayer addressed by the guidance can rely on it as precedent. Again, the weekly *Internal Revenue Bulletin* is the "authoritative instrument" for publishing official IRS rulings and procedures, and tax regulations.[53.18]

The GAO discovered an anomaly: The IRS has extensive policies and procedures for producing guidance, but these procedures do not include selection of a type of guidance. The IRS's detailed procedures for identifying guidance projects, designating guidance projects as priorities, and issuing guidance are in the *Internal Revenue Manual*, in a section of it known as the Chief Counsel Directives Manual. The IRS also has detailed policies and procedures to determine when to add a guidance topic to each year's Priority Guidance Plan and designate it as a priority for the year.[53.19] By contrast, according to the GAO, the IRS "does not have documented procedures for selecting the type of guidance product to issue."[53.20]

Treasury and IRS officials told the GAO that it may not be "practical or feasible" to develop clear-cut procedures for selecting guidance types because "determining the appropriate type is not always a straightforward process." That is, "sometimes

---

[53.13] Regulatory Guidance Processes Report at 4–5.
[53.14] OMB Bulletin No. 07-02 (Jan. 18, 2007).
[53.15] The bulletin's definition of *guidance document* does not include many types of documents, including speeches.
[53.16] OMB Memorandum No. M-07-13 (April 25, 2007).
[53.17] Regulatory Guidance Processes Report at 5–6.
[53.18] *Id.* at 9.
[53.19] *Internal Revenue Manual* §§ 32.1.1.4.3 and 32.2.2.6.4.
[53.20] Regulatory Guidance Processes Report at 16-17.

the most appropriate type of guidance may not be known at the start of a project, and the choice of guidance type may change as the project develops." The GAO did not relent on this point, observing: "According to internal control standards, agencies should use techniques and processes to identify and manage risk."[53.21]

The GAO concluded that "few" tax regulations are deemed significant by the OIRA, and subject to additional rulemaking requirements and analysis under the executive order. For example, between 2013 and 2015, merely one of more than 200 tax regulations issued was determined to be significant; this rule was determined to not be economically significant. Likewise, few tax regulations have been deemed by the OIRA to be major under the CRA.[53.22]

Treasury and IRS policies and procedures state that the notice and comment procedures under the APA do not apply to most tax regulations because these regulations are almost always *interpretative*, as opposed to *legislative*, in nature. The thought behind this is that the underlying tax code' provision being implemented by the regulation contains the necessary legal authority for the action taken; that is, any effect of the regulation flows directly from the code. Nonetheless, according to Treasury and IRS officials, the IRS provides for notice and comment on nearly every tax regulation.[53.23]

Treasury and IRS officials told the GAO that they rarely recommend to the OIRA that tax regulations are *major* under the CRA or *economically significant* under the executive order because of their view that any economic impact of a tax regulation generally is derived from the underlying statute, not the regulation.[53.24] Also, some tax regulations are exempt from OIRA review that would otherwise be required under the executive order based on a long-standing agreement between Treasury and the OMB. This agreement, entered into in 1983, exempts regulations issued by the IRS from further analysis and review unless the regulations are legislative in nature and major under an executive order. This agreement also exempts from OMB review documents such as revenue rulings and revenue procedures. The effect of this agreement has been that few tax regulations and none of other types of tax guidance are subject to OMB review. This agreement was reworked in 1993.[53.25]

[53.21] *Id.* at 17.

[53.22] *Id.* at 18–21.

[53.23] *Id.* at 21. This attitude on the part of the Treasury Department and the IRS was dubbed *tax exceptionalism* by two commentators who observed that the tax law, being "complex and its impact pervasive," has evolved to the point that "[n]o other field of law is thought to be so complex or to compel so many to regularly bare their financial souls to the government just to be in compliance with the law" (Abreu and Greenstein, "Tax as Everylaw: Interpretation, Enforcement, and the Legitimacy of the IRS," 69 *Tax Law.* (No. 3) 493, 497 (Spring 2016)). They quoted another commentator as to the idea that "tax law is somehow deeply different from other law, with the result that many of the rules that apply trans-substantively across the rest of the legal landscape do not, or should not, apply to tax" law (Zelenak, "Maybe Just a Little Bit Special, After All?," 63 *Duke L.J.* 1897, 1901 (2014)). They also quoted former Treasury officials on the point: "Federal tax statutes and the legislative process that produces them differ from other legislation in such degree that the difference is tantamount to a difference in kind. The unique nature of the Internal Revenue Code is widely acknowledged" (Ferguson, Hickman, and Lubick, "Reexamining the Nature and Role of Tax Legislative History in Light of the Changing Realities of the Process," 67 *Taxes* 804, 806 (1989)).

[53.24] Regulatory Guidance Processes Report at 24–25.

[53.25] *Id.* at 25–27. This agreement was made public on September 26, 2016, pursuant to a Freedom of Information Act request.

The GAO is of the view that this agreement should be reconsidered. One historical rationale for the agreement has been to insulate the Executive Office of the President from a charge that it was using the OMB's review of the IRS for political purposes. Another such reason was that historically the OMB lacked staff expertise on tax policy. One reason for the GAO's view is the "importance of increasing the transparency of the rulemaking process." Another reason lies in the nature of tax regulations subsequently being issued, namely, that the tax regulations are "related to social and economic objectives rather than traditional tax collection or administration issues." For example, recently, 20 percent of the tax regulations were related to the implementation of the Patient Protection and Affordable Care Act.[53.26]

The OMB's 2007 bulletin on agency good guidance practices and the accompanying memorandum establish executive branch policies and procedures for federal agencies to follow when they develop and issue significant guidance documents. This bulletin excludes tax guidance documents from the definition of *economically significant* guidance. The effect is that non-regulatory tax guidance is exempted from centralized review and additional analysis. Nonetheless, the IRS "routinely provides opportunities for the public to comment on non-regulatory guidance documents that address topics that are likely to be covered by future regulations."[53.27]

The GAO recommended that the Commissioner of Internal Revenue take the following actions: (1) "Communicate more clearly the limitations of information not published in the IRB to taxpayers," (2) amend current policies and procedures for drafting guidance to include factors to consider when deciding what type of guidance to issue and procedures for documenting those decisions internally,[53.28] (3) develop policies and procedures to help guidance-drafting teams assess whether non-regulatory guidance should be considered a rule for purposes of the CRA, and (4) take action to ensure that required steps are consistently documented during key phases of the non-regulatory guidance process.

The GAO recommended that the Director of the Office of Management and Budget and the Secretary of the Treasury examine the relevance of the long-standing agreement that exempts certain IRS regulations from executive order requirements and OIRA oversight, and, if relevant, make publicly available any reaffirmation of the agreement and the reasons for it. Another recommendation was that these two officials develop a process to ensure that the OIRA has the information necessary to determine whether IRS rules are major under the CRA

[53.26] Regulatory Guidance Processes Report at 26–28.

[53.27] *Id.* at 28–31.

[53.28] A revised approach along this line could have an immense impact on the nature of the law of tax-exempt organizations. Much of the guidance issued by the IRS in the exempt organizations context is issued at too lowly a level, such as notices and announcements, and some is not authoritative at all, such as private letter rulings. As to the latter, the most egregious example pertains to the IRS's decision to embark on its efforts to regulate nonprofit governance, coupled with the document guidance approach selected by the agency. This was a decision with enormous economic and other significance to public charities and other types of tax-exempt organizations, affecting the composition and functioning of their governing boards, the management of these entities (including adoption of various governance policies), and their use (and need for use) of legal counsel, accountants, management consultants, and others. Yet none of the guidance issued by the IRS at that time and since is authoritative. All the exempt community has seen to date is the text of a few speeches by IRS officials and dozens of private letter rulings.

and significant under the executive order. Consideration should be given to ways to solicit public comments on the potential effects of proposed regulations and non-regulatory guidance, including measures of economic impacts, and on how to document internally the consideration of significant comments by both the IRS and the OIRA.[53.29]

[*53.29] Regulatory Guidance Processes Report at 34–35.

Table of Tax-Exempt Organizations Law Tax Reform Proposals

The principal source of specific tax reform proposals at the present is the proposed Tax Reform Act of 2014, introduced by the then-Chairman of the House Committee on Ways and Means Dave Camp (who has since retired from Congress). This proposal (Camp Proposal) was never introduced as a bill; it was published, on February 26, 2014, as a discussion draft. Tax reform proposals are also in the Administration's proposed budget for fiscal year 2016, in items of tax law revision legislation that are pending in the current (114th) Congress, and in the July 2015 Report of the Business Income Tax Working Group to the Senate Committee on Finance (Working Group Report).

Tax reform proposals directly affecting the tax law pertaining to tax-exempt organizations are inventoried in the following list. (Proposals concerning the tax law of charitable giving are in a table that is part of the 2016 Cumulative Supplement accompanying *The Tax Law of Charitable Giving, Fifth Edition*.)

I. Tax Reform Proposals Affecting Public Charity Law

    A. Type II and Type III Supporting Organizations

        1. Present law: One of the several ways a tax-exempt charitable (IRC § 501(c)(3)) organization can be a public charity (IRC § 509(a)) is to qualify as a supporting organization (IRC § 509(a)(3)). Four basic tests must be satisfied for supporting organization status, one of which is the *relationship test*. Pursuant to this test, an organization must be (1) operated, supervised, or controlled by one or more qualified supported organizations (usually a form of public charity) (known as a Type I supporting organization); (2) supervised or controlled in connection with one or more qualified supported organizations (Type II supporting organization); or (3) operated in connection with one or more qualified supported organizations (Type III supporting organization). The classification of a supporting organization depends on how close its relationship is to the supported organization(s), with Type I supporting organizations having the closest relationship (being akin to a parent–subsidiary arrangement).

        2. Proposal: Federal tax law authorizing Type II and Type III supporting organizations would be repealed (Camp Proposal § 5304). Thus, these entities would be required to either qualify as a public charity on another basis or be private foundations.

    B. Intermediate Sanctions Rules

        1. Present law: Penalty excise taxes may be imposed on disqualified persons who improperly benefited from excess benefit transactions with applicable tax-exempt organizations and on managers of the organization who participated in the transactions knowing they were improper

(IRC § 4958). A rebuttable presumption of reasonableness arises under certain circumstances with respect to these transactions (Reg. § 53.4958-6). Participation of an organization manager in a transaction is ordinarily not considered *knowing* for these purposes to the extent that, after making full disclosure of the factual situation to an appropriate professional, the organization manager relies on a reasoned written opinion of that professional with respect to elements of the transaction that are within the scope of the professional's expertise (Reg. § 53.4 958-1(d)(4)).

2. Proposal: Rebuttable presumption of reasonableness and professional advice reliance safe harbor rule for managers would be eliminated.

C. Definition of Disqualified Person

1. Present law: For purposes of the intermediate sanctions rules, the term *disqualified person* means (1) any person who was, at any time during the five-year period ending on the date of the transaction involved, in a position to exercise substantial influence over the affairs of the organization; (2) a member of the family of an individual in the foregoing category; and (3) an entity in which individuals described in the preceding two categories own more than a 35 percent interest (IRC § 4958(f)(1)(C)).

2. Proposal: This definition of *disqualified person* would be expanded to include athletic coaches and investment advisors (Camp Proposal § 5201).

D. Donor-Advised Funds

1. Present law: A donor-advised fund is a fund or account (1) that is separately identified by reference to contributions of one or more donors; (2) that is owned and controlled by a sponsoring organization; and (3) as to which a donor or donor advisor has, or reasonably expects to have, advisory privileges with respect to the distribution or investment of amounts held in the fund by reason of the donor's status as a donor (IRC § 4966(d)(2)(A)).

2. Proposal: Donor-advised funds would be required to distribute contributions within five years of receipt; penalty would be imposed for failure to meet this payout rule (Camp Proposal § 5203).

E. Private Colleges and Universities Investment Income Tax

1. Present law: No category of public charity is required to pay tax on its net investment income. A few other types of tax-exempt organizations, such as social clubs (IRC § 501(c)(7) entities) and political organizations (IRC § 527 entities) are subject to such a tax, as are private foundations (see II A).

2. Proposal: Large private colleges and universities would be subject to 1 percent excise tax on their net investment income (Camp Proposal § 5206).

F. Proposed Agricultural Research Organizations

1. Present law: There is no existing law for agricultural research organizations. They would be modeled on present law providing for medical research organizations (IRC § 170(b)(1)(A)(iii)), and thus would be public charities (IRC § 509(a)(1)) and be eligible for charitable contributions at the higher percentage limitations.

2. Proposal: Provision for these organizations would be created (proposed Charitable Agriculture Research Act (S. 908)). To qualify, an agricultural research organization would have to be engaged in the continuous active conduct of agricultural research (as defined in the Agricultural Research, Extension, and Teaching Policy Act of 1977) in conjunction with a land-grant college or university or a non-land-grant college or university. For a contribution to this type of organization to qualify for the 50 percent limitation, during the calendar year in which a contribution is made to the organization it must be committed to spend the contribution for this type of research before January 1 of the fifth calendar year that begins after the date of enactment. An agricultural research organization would be permitted to use the expenditure test (IRC § 501(h)) for purposes of determining whether a substantial part of its activities consist of carrying on propaganda or otherwise attempting to influence legislation.

II. Tax Reform Proposals Directly Affecting Private Foundation Law

A. Tax on Net Investment Income

1. Present law: Private foundations and certain charitable trusts are subject to a 2 percent excise tax on their net investment income (Internal Revenue Code of 1986, as amended, IRC § 4940(a)). An organization may reduce the excise tax rate to 1 percent by meeting certain requirements regarding distributions to qualifying tax-exempt organizations during a tax year (IRC § 4940(e)).

2. Proposal: This excise tax on net investment income would be reduced to a single rate of 1 percent (Camp Proposal § 5204).

3. The proposed America Gives More Act (H.R. 644), which was passed by the House of Representatives on February 12, 2015, would reduce this tax to 1 percent.

4. The Administration's budget for fiscal year 2016 proposes reduction of this tax to a single rate of 1.35 percent (a budget-neutral percentage).

5. A proposal in the Working Group Report would reduce this tax to 1 percent.

B. Exempt Operating Foundations Excise Tax Exemption

1. Present law: Exempt operating foundations (IRC § 4940(d)(2)) are exempt from this excise tax on net investment income (IRC § 4940(d)(1)).

2. Proposal: This exemption would be repealed (Camp Proposal § 5204).

C. Expansion of Self-Dealing Tax Regime

1. Present law: Disqualified persons and managers who engage in self-dealing transactions with private foundations (IRC § 4941(d)) are subject to excise tax (IRC § 4941(a), (b)).

2. Proposal: An excise tax of 2.5 percent would be imposed on a private foundation when a self-dealing tax is imposed on a disqualified person. This tax rate would be increased to 10 percent in cases where the self-dealing involves the payment of compensation (Camp Proposal § 5202).

D. Foundation Managers' Reliance on Professional Advice

1. Present law: A private foundation manager may avoid excise tax for knowingly participating in a self-dealing transaction (IRC § 4941(a)(2)) if the manager relies on advice provided by an appropriate professional, including lawyers, certified public accountants, and independent valuation experts (Treas. Reg. § 53.4941(a)-1(b)(6)).

2. Proposal: Foundation managers would no longer be able to rely on this professional advice safe harbor (Camp Proposal § 5202).

E. Private Operating Foundations' Distribution Exception

1. Present law: Private foundations generally are required to pay out a minimum amount each year to accomplish one or more exempt purposes or for reasonable and necessary administrative expenses; there are excise tax penalties for failure to distribute (IRC § 4942). Private operating foundations (IRC § 4940(j)(3)) are not subject to these payout requirements; they have a different payout regime.

2. Proposal: Private operating foundations would be required to distribute income in accordance with rules for private foundations generally or be taxed (Camp Proposal § 5205).

F. Excess Business Holdings

1. Present law: A private foundation's ability to own a business—one that is not conducted as an exempt function—is limited by rules concerning "excess business holdings" (IRC § 4943). The basic rule is that the combined ownership of a business enterprise, by a private foundation and those who are disqualified persons with respect to it, may not exceed 20 percent.

2. Proposal: An exception to these excess business holdings rules would be created for philanthropic business holdings (proposed Philanthropic Enterprise Act of 2015 (S. 909)). This pertains to a business enterprise that meets requirements relating to exclusive ownership, minimum distribution of net operating income for charitable purposes, and independent operation (i.e., enterprise not controlled by substantial contributors or family members).

G. Electronic Filing

1. Present law: Private foundations (including split-interest charitable trusts) that file at least 250 returns must file their annual information returns (Form 990-PF) electronically.

2. Proposal: All private foundations would be required to file Form 990-PF electronically (Camp Proposal § 6004).

3. A proposal in the Working Group Report would require all tax-exempt organizations to file all returns and the like in the Form 990 series electronically.

4. A proposal in the Working Group Report would require the IRS to make all information provided in this series available to the public in machine-readable format as soon as practicable.

H. Executive Compensation (see III)

I. Harmonization of Deduction Limitations (see IV B)

III. Tax Reform Proposals Affecting Executive Compensation

A. Present for-profit law: Deduction allowed to publicly traded C corporations for compensation paid with respect to chief executive officers and certain highly paid officers is limited to $1 million annually. Current law limits deductibility of certain severance-pay arrangements (*parachute payments*).

B. Present nonprofit law: Generally, the rule under private inurement doctrine is that compensation paid to insiders must be reasonable; penalty is loss of payor's tax exemption. In the private foundation context, generally compensation to disqualified persons must be for personal services and be reasonable (IRC § 4941(d)(1)(D), (2)(E)); penalty is one or more self-dealing taxes (see I C 1). In public charity, social welfare organization, and health insurance issuer contexts, excessive compensation is subject to penalty taxes and other intermediate sanctions rules (IRC § 4958).

C. Proposal: A tax-exempt organization would be subject to 25 percent excise tax on compensation in excess of $1 million paid to any of its five highest-paid employees for the tax year. This tax would apply to all remuneration paid to a covered person for services, including money and cash value of all remuneration (including benefits) paid in a medium other than cash, except for payments to a tax-qualified retirement plan and amounts that are excludable from the executive's gross income. Once an employee qualifies as a covered person, excise tax would apply to compensation in excess of $1 million paid to that person as long as the exempt organization pays the person compensation (Camp Proposal § 3803).

D. Proposal: An excise tax would apply to excess parachute payments paid by exempt organizations to covered persons. An excess parachute payment generally would be defined as a payment contingent on the employee's separation from employment with an aggregate present value of three times the employee's base compensation or more (*id.*).

IV. Other Tax Extender

A. Modification of tax treatment of certain payments to controlling tax-exempt organizations. In general, interest, rent, royalties, and annuities paid to an exempt organization from a controlled entity are treated as forms of unrelated business income of the exempt organization (IRC § 512(b)(13)). A special rule (that expired at the close of 2014) provided that, if these payments are no more than at fair market value, the payment is excludable from the exempt organization's unrelated business income (IRC § 512(b)(13)(E)).

B. This special provision would be extended for two years (through 2016) by tax extenders legislation approved by the Senate Committee on Finance on July 23, 2015.

V. Other Working Group Reform Proposals

A. Extension of declaratory judgment procedure (IRC § 7428) to the initial determination or continuing classification of organizations as tax-exempt to all categories of tax-exempt organizations (IRC § 501(c), (d) entities).

B. An organization may seek a declaratory judgment from the U.S. Tax Court in the case of any type of determination or failure to which the declaratory judgment rules currently apply.

C. An organization could seek a declaratory judgment from the U.S. District Court for the District of Columbia or the U.S. Court of Federal Claims only in the case of determinations or failures relating to the following:

1. Initial qualification or continuing classification of an organization as a charitable entity (IRC §§ 501(c)(3), 170(c)(2)).

2. Initial qualification or continuing classification of an organization as a private foundation or private operating foundation.

3. Initial qualification or continuing classification as a farmers' cooperative (IRC § 521(b)).

Cumulative Table of Cases

Cumulative Table of IRS Revenue Rulings

Revenue Rulings	Book Sections	Revenue Rulings	Book Sections
53-44	15.1	56-185	7.6(a), 7.6(e)
54-12	19.12	56-245	16.2
54-73	24.5(l), 25.1(l)	56-249	18.4
54-134	28.1(b)	56-304	21.5(f)
54-170	31.1(a)	56-305	15.1(b)
54-243	4.1(a), 27.6(c), 32.1(a)	56-403	6.3(a)
54-282	16.2	56-475	15.1(b)
54-296	7.15	56-486	7.8
54-369	31.1(a)	56-511	24.2(g)
54-394	13.1(a)	57-128	7.15, 19.21(c), 19.21(d)
55-133	19.1, 19.7	57-187	7.15
55-156	13.1(b)	57-297	13.1(b), 13.5
55-189	19.13	57-313	24.4(g)
55-192	29.5	57-420	19.5(b)
55-230	16.2	57-449	6.3(a)
55-261	7.6(j)	57-453	14.2(c)(ii)
55-311	13.1(a), 19.3, 19.5(b)	57-466	16.2, 24.4(g), 24.5(f)
55-319	7.15	57-467	6.3(c), 7.6(e)
55-406	7.1	57-493	13.5
55-439	13.5	57-494	19.3
55-449	24.2(h), 24.4(g)	57-574	10.8
55-495	13.1(a), 19.4(a)	57-588	16.2
55-516	13.1(a)	58-117	13.1(b)
55-558	19.12	58-143	16.1, 29.2
55-587	7.8, 8.4	58-147	7.13(a)
55-611	19.12	58-190	17.9, 19.6
55-656	7.6(j)	58-194	7.8, 8.6, 24.5(a)
55-676	25.2(b)	58-209	3.6
55-715	14.2(c)(ii), 14.4	58-224	14.1(d)
55-716	13.1(a), 15.1(b), 19.5(b)	58-265	7.15
56-65	14.1(f), 14.2(c)(i), 14.2(c)(ii), 13.4	58-293	4.1(a)

Revenue Rulings	Book Sections	Revenue Rulings	Book Sections
56-84	13.4, 14.2(c)(ii),	58-294	13.2, 14.1(c)(ii)
56-138	6.3(a), 20.5(q)	58-328	10.8
56-152	20.9	58-482	24.4(g)
58-483	19.12	63-252	29.2(e)
58-501	15.6, 32.9(b)	64-108	4.6
58-502	20.9, 24.5(e)(iv)	64-109	19.6
58-566	19.2(a)	64-117	7.8
58-588	15.2	64-118	7.8, 15.1(b)
58-589	15.1(b), 20.10	64-128	8.3(a)(i)
59-6	8.4, 16.1	64-174	7.12
59-41	7.15	64-175	7.12
59-151	19.11(a)	64-182	4.5(a), 4.7, 7.13(a), 7.14(b)
59-152	7.15		24.5(d)
59-234	14.2(c)(ii)	64-187	13.5
59-310	6.3(a), 7.7	64-192	8.5
59-330	16.1, 24.2(c), 24.5(d), 24.5(f)	64-193	19.5(a)
		64-194	19.4(a)
59-391	14.1(a)(iii), 14.1(b), 14.3	64-195	8.4, 20.3(c)(iii)
60-86	16.2, 24.4(g), 24.5(f)	64-217	19.6
60-143	7.8	64-231	7.6(e)
60-193	4.3(c), 20.3(c)(iii), 23.2(c), 23.5(b)	64-246	19.12
		64-274	7.8
60-228	24.4(g) 24.5(e)(ii)	64-275	8.4
60-243	7.15	64-286	7.13(a)
60-323	15.2, 20.10	64-313	13.1(b)
60-324	15.2	65-1	6.3(e), 9.2, 20.5(i)
60-351	8.5, 8.6	65-2	7.11, 8.4
60-367	29.5	65-5	19.12
60-384	4.1(a), 7.15	65-6	19.6
61-72	7.6(e)	65-60	9.2
61-87	7.8, 8.6	65-61	11.3
61-137	19.6	65-63	15.2
61-153	13.1(a)	65-64	15.6
61-158	13.1(b)	65-99	19.5(a), 19.5(b), 26.13
61-170	14.2(c)(ii), 20.5(i), 24.5(e)(iv)	65-164	14.1(d)
		65-174	19.5(b)
61-177	14.1(c)(ii), 14.1(d), 22.6	65-191	7.8, 8.4

Revenue Rulings	Book Sections	Revenue Rulings	Book Sections
62-17	16.1	65-195	13.1(a)
62-23	8.3(a)(i)	65-201	13.2(a), 19.5(a), 19.5(b)
62-66	7.15	65-219	15.2
62-71	20.3(c)(iii)	65-244	14.2(c)(ii)
62-113	29.2(e)	65-270	7.12, 8.4
62-156	23.2(b)(iv)	65-271	7.12
62-167	13.1(a), 15.1(b)	65-298	6.3(a), 8.4, 9.2, 9.4
62-191	16.1, 24.4(g), 24.5(f)	65-299	7.3(a), 13.1(a)
63-15	7.13(a)	66-46	7.12
63-20	7.15	66-47	24.4(g)
63-190	13.1(a), 15.1(b)	66-59	19.3
63-208	7.13(a)	66-79	29.2(e)
63-209	7.13(a)	66-102	19.2(a)
63-220	7.8, 8.6	66-103	7.8, 7.12
63-234	8.6	66-104	6.3(e), 8.6
63-235	7.8, 8.6, 26.11(a)	66-105	16.2
66-108	19.12	67-149	7.8, 7.13(a), 7.14(a)
66-146	7.7, 7.11	67-150	7.1, 8.4
66-147	8.5, 9.4	67-151	11.1
66-148	13.1(a)	67-152	19.12
66-149	15.2	67-170	6.3(d), 19.6
66-150	13.1(b), 15.1(b), 19.2(a)	67-175	14.1(d)
66-151	13.1, 13.2, 24.4(g), 24.5(e)(i), 24.5(e)(ii), 24.5(e)(iv)	67-176	24.5(e)(ii)
		67-182	14.2(c)(ii)
66-152	19.12	67-216	8.5, 16.2
66-177	4.1(a)	67-217	7.8, 8.6
66-178	7.12	67-219	14.1(d), 24.5(d)
66-179	7.7, 8.5, 11.1(a), 13.1(a), 15.1(b), 16.3	67-223	19.12
		67-249	15.1(b)
66-180	19.3	67-250	7.11, 8.5
66-212	18.3	67-251	20.9
66-219	4.1(a)	67-252	16.2
66-220	7.10, 8.5, 8.6	67-253	19.12
66-221	24.1	67-264	14.1(b)
66-222	20.9	67-265	19.5(a), 19.5(b)
66-223	14.1(d)	67-284	19.22
66-225	20.10	67-290	7.15

Revenue Rulings	Book Sections	Revenue Rulings	Book Sections
66-255	8.5	67-291	7.8
66-256	8.5, 23.2(c)	67-292	7.7, 7.16(a), 8.3(c)
66-257	6.3(a), 7.1	67-293	22.3, 22.5
66-258	20.3(c)(iii), 23.2(c), 23.5(b)	67-294	13.1(a)
		67-295	14.1(d)
66-259	20.3, 20.5(l)	67-296	20.9, 24.5(d), 24.5(e)(iv)
66-260	14.1(d)	67-302	15.2
66-273	13.1(a)	67-325	6.2(b)(ii), 6.3, 6.3(a)
66-295	19.2(a), 28.15	67-327	8.4
66-296	28.15	67-342	8.5
66-323	7.6(j), 24.2(e), 24.2(f), 26.4(g)	67-343	14.1(b)
		67-344	14.1(d)
66-338	14.2(c)(ii), 24.5(e)(i)	67-346	19.12
66-354	13.1(a), 14.2(c)(ii), 16.1, 18.3	67-367	6.3(a), 20.5(i)
66-358	6.3(b), 7.7, 20.7	67-368	23.5(b)
66-359	11.1	67-390	28.1(b)
66-360	13.1(b)	67-391	7.7, 8.5
67-4	6.3(b), 7.8, 7.13(a), 8.5	67-392	7.12, 8.4
67-5	20.5(b)	67-394	14.1(f)
67-6	7.4, 7.11, 13.2(a), 22.5	67-422	19.12
67-7	16.1	67-428	15.1(b), 15.2
67-8	15.1(b), 20.5(i)	67-429	19.12
67-71	23.2(b)(iv), 23.5(b)	67-430	19.12
67-72	7.8, 8.4, 20.12(a)	68-14	7.7, 8.5, 13.2(a), 20.12(a)
67-77	14.1(c)(ii)	68-15	7.7, 7.11, 8.5
67-109	13.1(a), 24.4(a)	68-16	7.8, 8.4
67-128	19.12	68-17	7.4, 7.11, 8.5
67-138	7.4, 7.11, 8.5	68-534	16.1
67-139	8.5, 15.1(b)	68-535	20.10
67-148	8.4	68-538	8.6
68-26	4.5(a), 7.10, 10.2(a), 10.2(b), 28.15	68-550	24.4(d)
		68-563	7.10, 10.2(a)
68-27	22.1(c), 7.6(f)	68-564	19.5(b)
68-45	13.1(b)	68-581	24.5(a)
68-46	14.1(b), 24.4(g)	68-609	32.10(b)
68-70	7.11, 8.5	68-638	15.2, 15.4
68-71	8.4, 8.5	68-655	7.4, 7.11

CUMULATIVE TABLE OF IRS REVENUE RULINGS

Revenue Rulings	Book Sections	Revenue Rulings	Book Sections
68-72	7.10, 8.4	68-656	22.5
68-73	7.6(j)	68-657	14.1(d)
68-75	19.5(b)	69-51	24.5(f)
68-76	19.12	69-52	19.12
68-104	24.5(n)	69-66	20.5(h)
68-117	7.1, 29.2(c)	69-68	15.1(b)
68-118	13.1(a)	69-69	24.4(g), 27.1(a), 27.1(h)
68-119	20.10	69-80	29.2(e)
68-123	10.9, 24.4(g)	69-96	3.6
68-164	8.5	69-106	14.1(d)
68-165	7.1, 8.4, 29.2(e)	69-144	18.3
68-166	7.1	69-160	11.4
68-167	4.4, 7.1, 8.6	69-161	7.1, 7.16(d)
68-168	20.10	69-162	25.1(g)
68-175	8.3(a)(i)	69-174	7.1
68-182	14.1(c)(ii)	69-175	20.5(i)
68-217	28.0	69-176	20.5(l)
68-222	19.2(a)	69-177	8.6
68-224	13.1(a)	69-217	15.2
68-225	24.5(d)	69-219	15.2
68-263	20.3(c)(iii), 23.2(c)	69-220	15.2, 15.5, 24.1
68-264	14.2(c)(ii), 14.2(c)(iv)	69-222	19.12
68-265	14.1(d), 14.2(c)(iv)	69-232	15.5, 15.6
68-266	15.1(b)	69-247	21.5, 21.16
68-267	24.4(g)	69-256	4.3(a), 4.3(b), 20.5(i)
68-296	30.1(a), 31.7	69-257	7.8
68-306	7.10	69-266	4.6, 7.6(j), 19.4(j)
68-307	8.5	69-267	24.5(b)(i)
68-371	19.2	69-268	24.5(b)(i), 24.5(c), 25.2(b)
68-372	8.3(b)	69-269	24.5(b)(i)
68-373	9.2, 11.3, 20.5(i), 25.1(l)	69-278	19.2(a)
68-374	24.5(b)(ii), 26.4(b)(ii)	69-279	4.3(a), 4.3(b)
68-375	24.5(b)(ii)	69-280	13.2(a)
68-376	24.5(b)(i)	69-281	13.2(a), 15.1(b)
68-422	6.3(a), 20.5(g)	69-282	19.7
68-438	7.4, 7.11, 8.5	69-283	19.1, 19.7
68-455	13.1(b)	69-381	19.2(a)

Revenue Rulings	Book Sections	Revenue Rulings	Book Sections
68-489	4.7, 6.3(b), 28.19	69-383	20.3
68-490	19.2(a)	69-384	13.1(a)
68-496	19.12	69-385	13.1(b), 13.5
68-504	6.3(a), 8.4, 20.12(a)	69-386	16.1
68-505	24.3(b), 24.4(g), 25.2(e)	70-583	7.1, 7.7, 8.4
69-387	14.1(f)	70-584	7.7, 7.8, 8.4, 23.5(b)
69-400	7.8, 8.4	70-585	7.1, 7.4, 7.11
69-417	19.12	70-590	7.6(j), 8.5, 24.2(e)
69-441	7.1, 7.3(a), 8.5	70-591	14.1(d)
69-459	7.15	70-604	13.2(a)
69-463	24.5(b)(ii)	70-640	4.6, 8.5
69-492	8.3(a)(i)	70-641	7.6(h), 8.5, 14.1(b), 14.1(e)
69-526	7.6(j), 9.1, 9.2	71-29	7.7
69-527	15.1(b)	71-97	7.8
69-528	7.13(a), 28.15	71-99	7.7
69-538	7.8	71-100	19.12
69-545	7.6, 7.6(a), 7.6(f), 32.9(b)	71-131	7.15, 19.21(c)
69-572	6.3(b), 7.13(a), 23.2(g)	71-132	7.15
69-573	7.8, 15.1(b)	71-155	14.1(d), 14.2(c)(ii), 24.5(e)(ii)
69-574	24.2(g)		
69-575	19.12, 30.2	71-156	18.4
69-632	6.3(e), 9.1, 14.1(c)(iii), 14.1(f), 20.5(i)	71-276	28.1(b)
		71-300	19.6
69-633	3.6, 7.13(c), 11.4, 24.4(g), 25.2(f)	71-311	29.3
		71-395	7.12, 20.5(i)
69-634	14.1(f)	71-413	7.8
69-635	15.1(b)	71-421	8.4, 15.1(b)
69-636	20.10	71-447	6.2(b)(ii)
69-637	19.6	71-460	4.1(a), 29.2(e)
69-651	19.12	71-504	14.1(e)
70-4	7.11, 13.1(a)	71-505	14.1(e)
70-31	14.1(a)(ii)	71-506	8.5, 9.4, 14.1(e)
70-32	15.1(b)	71-529	7.8, 7.13(a), 8.6, 24.2(e), 28.14(b)
70-48	20.10		
70-79	7.7, 7.11, 8.5, 20.3(c)(iii)	71-544	19.2(a)
70-81	14.3	71-545	8.3(c)
70-129	7.8	71-553	7.13(a)

CUMULATIVE TABLE OF IRS REVENUE RULINGS

Revenue Rulings	Book Sections	Revenue Rulings	Book Sections
70-130	19.5(b)	71-580	7.10, 20.5(h)
70-186	6.3(b), 7.7, 7.16(a), 20.5(i), 20.12(a)	71-581	25.2(c), 28.15
		72-16	7.6(j), 8.4, 24.5(b)(v)
70-188	18.4	72-17	19.6
70-189	18.4	72-36	19.5(b)
70-202	19.3	72-37	19.7
70-244	14.1(b)	72-50	19.12
70-270	12.1(g)	72-51	19.12
70-321	7.8, 8.5, 23.2(c)	72-52	19.12
70-372	16.2	72-101	7.8, 8.3(a)(i), 20.12(a)
70-411	18.3	72-102	13.2(a), 19.14
70-449	22.3(c)(iii)	72-124	6.3(a), 6.3(c), 7.6(e), 24.2(e)
70-533	4.5(d), 7.1, 8.3(a), 20.7	72-147	20.5(i)
70-534	8.4, 24.5(j)	72-209	7.6(j)
70-535	13.1(b)	72-211	14.1(f), 14.2(c)(i)
70-536	18.4	72-228	7.11, 8.5
70-562	7.15	72-355	3.6, 17.0
70-566	19.13	72-369	4.4, 4.5(a), 4.6, 7.13(a), 24.5(k)
72-391	16.1, 16.2, 20.5(i)	73-570	19.12
72-430	8.3(a)(i)	73-587	24.4(g)
72-431	24.4(g), 24.5(i)(iii), 25.2(k)	74-13	19.22
72-512	23.2(b)(i), 23.2(b)(iv)	74-14	7.15
72-513	22.3(c)(i), 23.2(b)(iv)	74-15	7.15
72-542	28.15	74-16	8.4
72-559	4.6, 6.3(b), 7.1	74-17	13.2(a), 19.14
72-560	7.7, 8.5	74-18	18.3
72-589	19.12	74-21	3.6, 17.0
73-45	7.12, 24.2(e)	74-23	17.0
73-59	19.12	74-30	15.1(b)
73-93	19.12	74-38	24.5(h)
73-104	24.5(c)	74-81	14.2(c)(ii), 24.5(e)(i), 24.5(e)(ii)
73-105	4.4, 4.5(a), 24.5(c)		
73-124	24.3(a)	74-99	13.2(a)
73-126	20.5(g)	74-116	14.1(c)(iii)
73-127	8.6, 24.4(b)	74-117	23.2(b)(iv)
73-128	6.3(b), 7.1, 8.4, 8.6, 24.2(b)	74-118	16.2

CUMULATIVE TABLE OF IRS REVENUE RULINGS

Revenue Rulings	Book Sections	Revenue Rulings	Book Sections
73-148	19.12	74-146	6.3(e), 7.8, 7.13(a), 20.7
73-164	28.15	74-147	14.1(c)(iii), 14.1(f)
73-165	19.4(a)	74-148	15.1(b), 20.10
73-192	19.4(a)	74-167	16.1
73-193	25.1(g)	74-168	15.2
73-247	19.12	74-194	11.1
73-248	19.12	74-195	16.2
73-285	7.10, 7.11	74-199	3.6, 17.0, 19.14
73-306	13.1(b)	74-224	10.4
73-307	18.4	74-228	14.2(c)(ii)
73-308	19.12	74-246	7.7
73-313	4.6, 6.3(e), 7.6(h), 7.6(j)	74-281	19.3
73-349	13.1(b)	74-287	12.2(b)
73-364	28.2(b)(ii)	74-308	14.2(c)(ii)
73-370	19.4(b)	74-318	3.6
73-386	24.4(b)	74-319	3.6
73-407	21.7	74-327	19.12
73-411	4.6, 14.3, 14.4	74-361	7.7, 13.1(a), 13.5, 24.5(d)
73-422	26.3(b), 28.1(b)		25.2(a)
73-424	24.3(a), 24.5(h)(ii)	74-362	19.5(b)
73-434	8.3(a)(i)	74-368	12.1(g)
73-439	20.5(k)	74-399	24.2(d), 24.5(c)
73-440	22.2(a)	74-443	11.4
73-452	14.1(f)	74-450	12.1(b)
73-453	19.5(b)	74-475	17.0
73-454	19.6	74-488	16.2
73-455	12.2(a)	74-489	15.2
73-504	26.3(a)	74-490	28.1(b)
73-520	15.1(b)	74-493	11.4
73-543	8.3(a)(i)	74-518	16.2
73-567	7.6(h), 8.7, 14.1(g)	74-523	29.2(e)
73-569	8.5	74-553	7.6(h), 9.2, 14.1(g)
74-567	19.12	74-563	13.2(a)
74-572	7.6(a)	75-473	16.1
74-574	23.2(b)(iv), 23.2(c)	75-492	8.3(a)(i)
74-575	7.10, 20.7	75-494	13.2(a), 15.1(b), 20.10
74-587	7.11, 7.16(e)	75-516	25.2(f)

Revenue Rulings	Book Sections	Revenue Rulings	Book Sections
74-595	8.5	76-4	8.5, 20.7
74-596	16.1	76-18	12.4(a)
74-600	8.3(b)	76-21	7.1
74-614	7.8, 7.13(a), 7.13(c), 24.2(e)	76-22	7.1
		76-31	16.1
74-615	8.5	76-33	24.5(a), 24.5(b)(v)
75-4	19.12	76-37	7.8
75-5	19.12	76-38	14.2(c)(ii)
75-38	4.3(a), 12.1(g)	76-81	22.5, 24.5(e)(ii)
75-42	21.7	76-91	32.10(b)
75-65	29.2(e)	76-93	24.5(h)(ii)
75-74	7.16(d)	76-94	24.4(b)
75-75	7.16(d)	76-147	7.11, 13.2(a)
75-76	7.16(d)	76-152	7.3(b), 7.12
75-97	19.12	76-167	8.3(a)(i), 8.3(b)
75-110	19.12	76-204	7.8, 7.9, 7.16(a), 16.2
75-196	6.3(a), 6.3(e), 8.3(c), 8.4, 20.12(a)	76-205	7.10, 7.11, 8.5
		76-206	7.12, 20.1, 20.9, 20.12(b)
75-197	7.6(j)	76-207	14.1(d), 14.3
75-198	6.3(a), 7.1, 7.6(e), 7.6(j)	76-233	19.12
75-199	13.1(a), 19.4(a)	76-241	16.2
75-200	20.5(h)(ii)	76-244	6.3(a), 7.1
75-201	24.5(h)(ii), 24.5(i)(iv)	76-296	9.3, 25.1(g), 25.1(l)
75-207	7.16(a)	76-297	25.1(g)
75-215	8.3(a)(i)	76-298	19.12
75-228	19.12	76-323	10.9, 24.4(g)
75-231	6.2(b)(ii)	76-335	19.2(a)
75-258	3.6, 6.6	76-336	7.8
75-282	7.6(c), 7.10, 7.13(a), 26.12(a)	76-337	25.3
		76-354	24.9(c)
75-283	7.1	76-366	8.6
75-284	7.4, 7.8, 8.4	76-384	8.3(a)(i)
75-285	7.11, 8.5	76-388	19.12
75-286	7.7, 13.2(a), 20.12(a)	76-399	16.2
75-287	14.1(f), 16.2	76-400	14.1(c)(ii), 14.1(d)
75-288	16.1	76-402	24.4(d)
75-290	26.2(a)	76-408	7.11
75-359	7.13(a), 7.15		

CUMULATIVE TABLE OF IRS REVENUE RULINGS

Revenue Rulings	Book Sections	Revenue Rulings	Book Sections
75-384	6.3(i), 7.7, 13.1(a)	76-409	14.2(c)(ii)
75-385	6.3(a), 7.1	76-410	14.1(f)
75-387	12.3(b)(iv)	76-417	8.3(a)(i)
75-388	19.12	76-418	7.7
75-434	7.10, 29.2(e)	76-419	7.11
75-436	7.15	76-420	16.1
75-470	7.11, 8.3(b)	76-440	12.3(b)(i), 12.3(b)(iv)
75-471	6.3(e), 7.12	76-441	20.5, 32.9(b), 32.10(b)
75-472	7.6(j), 8.4, 24.4(f), 24.5(b)(v)	76-442	6.3(e)
76-443	8.5	77-416	32.9(b)
76-452	7.6(a)	77-429	19.2, 19.2(a)
76-455	9.2	77-430	7.10
76-456	23.2(c)	77-436	24.4(g)
76-457	19.4(b)	77-440	19.12
76-495	19.14	77-469	28.1(b)
76-549	19.21(b)	78-41	7.6(c), 7.13(a), 26.12(a), 29.2(d)
76-550	19.21(b)		
77-3	7.1	78-42	7.8, 16.1
77-4	8.5	78-43	24.5(j)
77-5	16.1	78-50	13.1(a)
77-42	7.1	78-51	24.5(e)(i)
77-43	18.4	78-52	24.5(e)(i)
77-46	16.1	78-68	7.7, 13.1(a)
77-68	7.6(j), 7.8, 8.4	78-69	7.7, 13.1(a)
77-69	7.6(h)	78-70	14.4
77-70	19.6	78-82	8.3(a)(i)
77-71	24.9(b)	78-84	7.16(b)
77-72	24.9(c)	78-85	6.3(e), 13.2(a)
77-111	4.6, 7.11, 7.16(e)	78-86	4.6, 13.1(a)
77-112	14.1(a)(i)	78-87	19.4(a)
77-114	26.2(a)	78-88	24.2(g)
77-116	26.3(b)	78-95	12.3(b)(i)
77-121	28.15	78-98	24.4(d)
77-124	28.15	78-99	8.5
77-153	16.2	78-100	10.8
77-154	16.1	78-131	7.12, 13.1(a)
77-159	28.1(b)	78-132	13.1(b)

CUMULATIVE TABLE OF IRS REVENUE RULINGS

Revenue Rulings	Book Sections	Revenue Rulings	Book Sections
77-160	21.7	78-143	19.6
77-162	28.2(a)(v)	78-145	7.6(j), 24.2(e), 24.2(f), 26.4(g)
77-165	7.15, 19.21(b)		
77-206	20.9	78-160	23.2(c)
77-207	26.3(a)	78-188	10.2(a)
77-208	26.3(a), 28.1(b)	78-189	10.2(a)
77-214	3.6	78-190	10.2(a)
77-232	7.15, 14.1(e)	78-225	14.3
77-246	6.3(a), 7.1	78-232	10.2(c), 20.5(h)
77-258	19.4(b)	78-238	19.5(b)
77-261	19.21(b)	78-239	19.11(a)
77-272	6.2(e), 7.8, 8.4	78-240	25.2(f)
77-283	23.2(b)(iv)	78-248	23.2(b)(iii), 23.2(c)
77-290	24.4(g)	78-276	19.21(b)
77-295	10.8	78-287	16.1
77-331	21.7	78-288	16.1
77-365	6.2(d), 8.4, 24.4(d)	78-289	28.0
77-366	4.4, 7.10, 8.4	78-305	8.2
77-367	8.3(b), 20.7	78-309	8.3(a)(i)
77-381	10.5	78-310	7.8, 7.13(a), 8.4
77-384	19.12	78-315	12.1(b)
77-407	25.3(b)	78-316	19.21(b), 28.2(b)(iii)
78-385	7.10, 8.5, 10.2(a), 24.4(g)	78-384	7.8, 7.9, 7.16(a)
78-426	9.2, 11.3	80-295	24.5(a)
78-427	7.6(j)	80-296	24.5(a)
78-428	7.1, 7.16(d), 24.2(e)	80-297	24.4(d)
78-434	19.10	80-298	24.4(d)
78-435	24.5(b)(i)	80-301	20.5(i)
79-9	27.4(b)	80-302	20.5(i)
79-11	17.1(a)	80-309	7.6(j)
79-12	17.1(a)	80-316	11.4
79-13	17.1(a)	81-19	25.2(b), 26.12(a)
79-17	7.1, 7.2(a), 24.2(e)	81-27	24.5(e)(iv)
79-18	6.3(a), 7.1, 7.2(a), 24.2(e), 24.2(e)	81-28	7.1, 7.6(j)
		81-29	6.3(b), 6.3(e), 7.8, 7.13(a), 20.7, 24.2(e), 24.5(b)(i)
79-19	7.1, 7.2(a), 24.2(e), 24.5(b)(v)	81-58	13.1(b), 19.4(a)

CUMULATIVE TABLE OF IRS REVENUE RULINGS

Revenue Rulings	Book Sections	Revenue Rulings	Book Sections
79-26	7.8, 8.2	80-301	20.5(i)
79-31	24.2(f)	80-302	20.5(i)
79-99	6.2(b)(ii)	80-309	7.6(j)
79-128	19.3	80-316	11.4
79-130	8.3(a)(i)	81-19	25.2(b), 26.12(a)
79-222	24.7	81-27	24.5(e)(iv)
79-316	13.1(b), 13.2(b)	81-28	7.1, 7.6(j)
79-323	7.15	81-29	6.3(b), 6.3(e), 7.8, 7.13(a), 20.7, 24.2(e), 24.5(b)(i)
79-358	7.1, 7.6(j)		
79-359	7.10	81-58	13.1(b), 19.4(a)
79-360	7.6(i), 24.5(b)(iv)	81-59	16.2
79-361	24.4(g), 24.5(b)(v)	81-60	16.0, 20.9
79-369	7.12, 8.5	81-61	24.4(f)
79-370	24.5(h)(iii), 26.5(h)	81-62	24.4(g)
80-21	8.3(a)(i)	81-68	18.4
80-63	13.2(a)	81-69	15.5
80-86	19.5(b)	81-75	24.5(e)(i)
80-103	17.5	81-94	10.2(c), 20.5(h)
80-106	20.7, 28.15	81-95	17.6, 23.5(a)
80-107	13.1(b)	81-96	19.12
80-108	3.2, 23.3(a), 26.2(a),	81-101	24.5(h)(ii), 26.5(g)
80-113	26.3(a)	81-108	19.2(b)
80-114	7.6(j)	81-109	19.5(b)
80-124	18.4	81-116	4.6, 13.1(a)
80-130	20.10	81-117	19.4(b)
80-200	7.16(f)	81-138	14.3
80-205	13.1(a)	81-174	14.2(b)(i), 14.2(c)(ii)
80-206	13.1(b)	81-175	14.2(b)(i), 14.2(c)(ii)
80-215	7.11	81-177	26.2(b)
80-259	26.2(b)	81-209	7.15
80-278	6.3(b), 7.16(a), 7.16(d), 23.2(g)	81-276	6.3(e), 7.6(h), 7.7, 12.3(b)(i)
80-279	6.3(b), 7.16(a), 23.2(g)	81-284	7.11, 7.16(e)
80-282	23.2(b)(iii), 23.2(c)	81-291	19.5(b)
80-286	7.8, 7.16(f), 8.4, 29.2(e)	81-295	19.22
80-287	14.2(c)(ii)	82-138	14.1(a)(ii), 24.5(e)(iv)
80-294	20.9, 24.5(a), 24.5(e)(iv)		

CUMULATIVE TABLE OF IRS REVENUE RULINGS

Revenue Rulings	Book Sections	Revenue Rulings	Book Sections
82-139	24.5(e)(i)	86-98	13.1(a), 13.1(b), 14.2(c)(ii)
82-148	19.3	87-2	7.15, 19.21(c)
82-216	17.0	87-119	17.1(a)
83-43	19.5(a)	87-126	13.1(b)
83-74	19.14	88-56	19.14
83-104	6.2(b)(i)	88-115	17.3(a)
83-131	19.21(b)	89-74	10.2(c)
83-140	8.3(a)(i)	89-94	19.1, 28.2(b)(ii)
83-153	12.3(b)(i), 12.3(b)(iv)	90-36	19.24
83-157	7.6(a)	90-42	19.12
83-164	14.1(c)(iii)	90-74	18.17, 19.21(b)
83-166	11.4, 19.8	90-100	26.3(a), 26.9
83-170	13.1(a), 15.1(b), 19.5(b)	93-73	10.2(a)
84-48	19.4(a)	94-16	19.22
84-49	19.4(a)	94-65	19.22
84-55	24.5(j)	94-81	19.22
84-81	19.12	95-8	24.9(c)
84-140	19.11(a)	97-21	20.4(c)
85-1	7.7	98-15	4.5(e), 20.12(c), 31.3(b)
85-2	7.7	2000-44	28.7(a)
85-109	24.5(b)(iii), 25.2(b)	2002-43	12.4(a)
85-110	24.5(b)(iii)	2002-55	19.5(b), 30.2
85-115	17.5	2003-38	24.5(o)
85-160	4.3(a)	2003-49	26.11, 28.7(a)
85-173	26.2(b)	2003-64	15.5, 25.3
85-184	29.5	2004-6	17.4, 23.2(b)(iv), 23.5(a)
85-199	18.3	2004-51	31.4
86-49	7.11	2004-112	24.5(o), 25.2(f)
86-75	19.4(a)	2006-27	6.3(b), 7.5
86-95	23.2(c)	2007-41	23.2(b)(iii)

Cumulative Table of
IRS Revenue Procedures

Revenue Procedures	Book Sections	Revenue Procedures	Book Sections
59-31	29.2(e)	85-58	28.2(a)(vi)
67-37	19.12	86-43	8.2
68-14	26.1(b)	90-29	19.12
71-17	15.2	91-20	10.7
71.39	7.16(d)	92-59	7.16(d)
72-5	26.1	92-85	19.14, 27.6(b)(ii)
72-16	19.12	94-17	28.2(b)(iii)
72-17	19.12	95-21	24.5(e)(iii)
72-54	6.2(b)(ii)	95-35	22.6(c)
73-29	28.2	95-48	28.2(b)(iii)
73-39	19.12	96-32	7.4, 31.5
75-13	7.16(d)	96-40	26.9
75-50	6.2(b)(ii), 6.2(d)	97-12	24.5(e)(iii)
76-9	28.2(a)(vi)	2003-40	27.9
76-34	27.6(b)(ii)	2003-21	28.2(b)(iii)
78-9	27.6(a)	2004-51	4.5(e)
79-2	28.2(a)(vi)	2007-27	28.7(a)
79-6	27.8	2010-40	22.6(a), 25.2(j), 25.2(l)
79-8	27.2(a)(v)	2011-14	27.13(b)
79-63	26.2(b)(ii)	2011-15	28.4
80-27	26.1, 26.9	2011-33	28.6
80-28	27.6(c)	2011-36	26.1(d)
80-30	25.1	2012-4	26.13
81-7	12.3(b)(iv)	2012-11	26.7
82-2	4.1(a), 4.3(b)	2013-35	24.7(j), 24.7(l)
82-39	27.4	2014-11	26.1(d), 28.5
83-23	28.2(b)(iii)	*2016-2	26.1, 27.1
84-47	26.2(a)	*2016-4	26.1, 26.14
84-86	27.4		

Revenue Procedures	Book Sections
*2016-5	3.2, 26.1, 26.1(a), 26.1(a)(i), 26.1(a)(ii), 26.1(b), 26.1(c), 26.1(d), 26.2, 26.3(a), 26.7, 26.8, 26.9, 26.10, 26.11, 26.13, 27.1, 27.2, 27.3, 27.5, 27.5(b), 27.5(b)(i), 27.5(b)(ii), 27.6, 27.7, 27.8, 27.10, 28.1(a), 28.4, 28.9(a)(ii), 28.10(a), 28.11, 28.12
*2016-6	26.1
*2016-8	26.1
*2016-32	26.1
*2016-41	26.3A
*2016-44	20.12(c)
*2016-55	22.6(a), 25.2(j), 25.2(l)

Cumulative Table of IRS Private Determinations Cited in Text

PRIVATE LETTER RULINGS, TECHNICAL ADVICE MEMORANDA, EXEMPTION DENIAL AND REVOCATION LETTERS, GENERAL COUNSEL MEMORANDA, AND CHIEF COUNSEL ADVICE MEMORANDA

Private Determinations	Book Sections	Private Determinations	Book Sections
7740009	10.8	7946001	24.5(i)(i)
7741004	25.1(g)	7946009	17.7
7742008	17.1(a)	7948113	24.5(a), 24.5(h)
7806039	25.2(a)	7951134	7.13(c), 20.7
7816061	24.4(f)	7952002	20.12(c), 31.2(a)
7820007	11.3	8004011	24.5(b)(i)
7820057	31.7	8018073	19.3
7820058	20.12(c), 31.2(a)	8020010	24.4(d)
7823062	26.4(e)	8024001	24.4(d)
7826003	24.4(d)	8025222	24.5(a)
7833055	24.9(b)	8032039	7.13(c)
7838028	10.9	8037103	11.2
7838108	15.4	8040014	8.3(b), 25.2(a)
7840072	24.4(d)	8041007	25.2(c)
7845029	24.5(a)	8107006	24.4(f)
7847001	24.5(e)(ii)	8109002	19.5(b)
7851003	24.5(a)	8112013	24.5(e)(i)
7851004	24.5(a)	8116095	25.2(c)
7902006	24.5(e)(i)	8119061	19.21(b)
7903079	29.5	8120006	24.4(f)
7905129	24.3(a)	8122007	25.2(c)
7908009	24.4(d)	8127019	24.5(i)(iii)
7919053	24.5(a)	8128072	21.7
7921018	20.12(c)	8141019	15.3
7922001	14.1(d), 24.4(f), 24.5(a)	8145011	19.2(a)
		8147008	17.7
7924009	25.1(1)		

Private Determinations	Book Sections	Private Determinations	Book Sections
7926003	25.1(g)	8147009	17.1(a)
7930005	11.3	8202019	17.7
7930043	24.5(a)	8203134	24.3(b), 24.5(i)(i)
7935043	7.15	8204057	32.9(b)
7936006	25.1(l)	8211002	25.2(a)
7937002	19.4(a), 24.5(e)(ii)	8216009	24.5(i)(iii)
7944018	16.1	8226019	24.4(g)

PRIVATE LETTER RULINGS AND TECHNICAL ADVICE MEMORANDA

Private Determinations	Book Sections	Private Determinations	Book Sections
8232011	24.5(i)(i)	8516001	17.7
8234084	20.5(c), 32.9(b)	8518067	26.2(a)
8234085	32.9(b)	8518090	24.4(f)
8242003	15.3	8519069	32.9(b)
8244114	32.1(b)	8521055	31.1(b)
8303001	24.4(g)	8523072	24.4(f)
8303078	24.5(a)	8524006	14.2(c)(i), 14.2(c)(iv),
8304112	30.1(a)		24.5(e)(i)
8306006	9.5	8539091	19.11(a)
8309092	10.4	8541008	15.3
8317004	4.9(d)	8541108	31.2(b)(i)
8326008	24.5(c)	8542003	15.3, 15.4
8337092	15.6	8602001	25.2(h)
8338127	31.2(a)	8605002	24.5(c)
8347010	31.7	8606056	9.5, 30.2
8349051	24.4(f)	8606074	24.4(f)
8349072	24.4(f)	8621059	31.1(b)
8351160	24.4(f)	8626080	24.4(f), 24.5(b)(v)
8402014	10.5	8628001	17.7
8409055	11.3	8628049	24.4(f)
8416065	10.5	8633034	24.4(f)
8417003	24.5(e)(i)	8634001	8.3(b)
8418003	24.5(e)(iv)	8638131	30.5
8422170	14.1(f)	8640007	24.4(f)
8426001	15.3, 15.4	8640052	32.2(b)
8427105	24.5(b)(i)	8650001	17.1(a)

CUMULATIVE TABLE OF IRS PRIVATE DETERMINATIONS CITED IN TEXT

Private Determinations	Book Sections	Private Determinations	Book Sections
8429010	16.2, 24.5(f)	8705041	19.2(a), 29.5
8429049	19.14	8706012	30.1(a)
8432004	24.5(c)	8709051	30.3(a)
8433010	25.2(a)	8709072	24.4(f)
8433077	19.14	8715055	31.7
8437014	24.4(g)	8719004	21.7
8442064	4.10	8725056	24.5(i)(i)
8442092	24.5(d)	8730060	24.5(e)(iv)
8443009	24.5(d)	8736046	24.5(b)(viii)
8444097	8.3(b)	8737090	19.21(b)
8446008	15.3	8739055	29.2(c)
8446047	28.1(b)	8747066	24.5(i)(ii)
8450006	24.4(f)	8749085	24.4(f), 24.5(b)(viii)
8452011	24.5(b)(vii)	8802079	24.5(e)(iv)
8452012	24.5(b)(vii)	8814004	24.4(g)
8452099	24.5(b)(vii)	8817039	31.1(b)
8502003	17.5	8818008	31.1(b)
8503103	24.5(e)(iv)	8819034	25.1(n)
8505002	7.6(i), 24.4(f), 24.5(b)(iv)	8820093	20.6
		8822065	25.5(b)(viii)
8505044	30.3(a)	8823109	24.5(i)(ii)
8505047	24.5(e)(iv)	8824018	24.4(f)
8512058	18.3	8826012	29.5
8512084	9.5	8939002	30.5
8828011	24.5(e)(ii)	8942099	20.6
8833038	30.1(g)	8944007	21.7
8836037	25.1(n)	9003045	14.1(f)
8836038	28.14(b)	9010073	32.9(b)
8836040	29.5	9012045	32.2(a)
8842071	19.21(a)	9014061	7.8
8851039	32.1(a)	9016003	21.7
8910001	6.2(b)(iii)	9016072	30.1(a)
8922047	25.1(n)	9017003	29.2(a)
8925092	31.6	9019004	29.2(d)
8936002	23.2(d)(iv), 23.2(g)	9023081	24.5(e)(i)
8938001	31.2	9024026	25.1(n)
8938072	32.9(b)	9024086	25.1(n)

CUMULATIVE TABLE OF IRS PRIVATE DETERMINATIONS CITED IN TEXT

Private Determinations	Book Sections	Private Determinations	Book Sections
9027003	8.4	9245031	29.2, 29.3(a)
9027051	25.1(n)	9246004	28.14(b)
9029047	24.5(e)(ii)	9246032	29.3
9032005	14.1(f)	9252037	24.4(f)
9036025	24.5(a)	9302023	25.2(a)
9042004	17.7	9303030	32.3, 32.4
9042036	19.14	9305026	30.3(a), 30.6(b)
9042038	25.1(i)	9308047	30.1(a), 30.3(c)
9043001	24.4(g)	9309037	32.3
9043039	25.1(n)	9314058	7.2(b)
9050002	14.1(f)	9314059	32.3
9105001	17.7	9315001	28.13
9105002	17.7	9316032	24.2(h), 24.2(i)
9110041	19.5(b)	9316052	9.5, 20.4(c)
9111001	19.5(b)	9317054	32.3
9114025	21.7	9320042	24.4(c)
9128003	14.2(c)(iv), 24.4(g)	9325062	24.4(f)
9130002	20.1, 20.5(c), 31.2, 32.9(b)	9329041	7.6(i), 24.5(b)(iv)
		9335001	31.2
9130008	17.1(a)	9335061	24.5(b)(v), 24.5(b)(viii)
9141050	26.13		
9145002	24.4(g)	9345004	24.5(e)(iii)
9147007	24.3(d), 24.5(a)	9346015	32.3
9217001	7.12	9352030	30.5
9220010	13.1(a)	9401031	24.4(f)
9231047	20.6	9401035	19.5(b)
9233037	20.6	9404029	24.5(b)(i)
9237034	6.3(e)	9405004	24.5(b)(i)
9237090	24.5(b)(viii)	9407007	25.1(n)
9241055	24.5(b)(v), 24.5(b)(viii)	9408002	24.5(e)(i)
9242002	19.2(a), 29.2(d)	9414002	19.2
9242035	24.4(f)	9414044	18.3
9242038	30.3(b)	9416002	24.5(e)(iii)
9242039	30.3(g)	9417003	32.1(b)
9243008	9.5	9425030	24.3(a)
9244003	17.3	9425032	17.5

Private Determinations	Book Sections	Private Determinations	Book Sections
9426040	32.1(b)	9545014	32.9(a), 32.9(b)
9428029	18.5	9548019	32.3
9428030	18.5	9550001	14.1(d), 14.2(c)(i), 24.4(g), 24.5(e)(i), 24.5(k)
9429016	22.6(a)		
9434041	7.6(c)		
9438029	30.8	9550003	26.5(c)
9438030	31.2(b)(i), 32.1(b)	9551009	32.3
9440001	24.5(e)(i)	9603019	24.9(g)
9441001	24.5(e)(ii)	9608003	24.5(k)
9442013	25.2(e)	9608039	12.3(b)(i), 12.3(b)(iv), 31.2(a)
9442025	7.6(c)		
9448036	20.9	9609007	23.2(b)(iv)
9451001	20.4(b), 32.1(b)	9610032	21.7
9451067	12.4(d)	9612003	24.2(g)
9502009	25.2(k)	9615030	6.3(b), 20.12(b)
9509002	25.1(g)	9615045	25.1(h)(iii)
9516006	17.1(a)	9619069	25.1(j)
9522022	32.3	9627001	21.7
9522039	18.17	9629030	25.1(j)
9527031	9.5	9631004	6.3(a)
9527043	29.1, 32.2(a)	9633044	24.5(e)(iv)
9530008	32.3	9635003	23.2(c), 23.3
9530024	7.7	9637050	30.1(b)
9530036	32.3	9637051	30.6(b)
9533015	15.3, 15.4, 32.3	9641011	24.5(k)
9534021	22.6(c)	9645004	24.2(f), 24.4(d), 25.2(b)
9535023	24.4(b), 24.5(b)(vii), 26.5(b)(vi), 25.2(b)		
		9645007	28.14(b)
9535043	12.2(b)	9645017	30.6(b), 30.8
9538026	32.9(b)	9646002	8.3(b)
9538031	32.9(b)	9651046	24.4(f)
9539015	24.4(f)	9651047	7.6(g), 24.5(k)
9539016	20.4(a)	9652026	17.1(a), 17.7, 22.3(b)
9540002	4.6, 24.5(j)	9702004	8.4, 24.2(f), 24.5(j)
9540042	21.7	9703020	21.7
9542002	11.4	9703028	29.2(e), 32.10(b)
9544029	25.2(a)	9709014	31.3(a)

CUMULATIVE TABLE OF IRS PRIVATE DETERMINATIONS CITED IN TEXT

Private Determinations	Book Sections	Private Determinations	Book Sections
9711002	24.5(k)	9837031	24.5(b)(i)
9711003	4.7, 24.1	9839039	24.5(k), 24.7, 31.7, 32.6
9711004	26.9		
9712001	24.3(d)	9839040	24.5(b)(viii)
9715031	30.2, 31.3(a)	9840049	29.4
9719002	24.2(b)	9840050	16.8
9720002	24.5(c)	9840051	29.4
9722006	19.5(b), 30.2	9840053	32.3
9726006	21.7	9840054	32.3
9728004	27.2	9841049	25.2(b)
9732022	16.2	9847002	24.5(b)(i), 24.5(k)
9732032	7.6(i), 8.5, 24.5(a), 24.5(b)(iv)	9847006	17.5
		9848002	24.5(e)(iv)
9733015	29.5	9849027	24.5(k), 28.15
9736047	7.6(i), 24.5(b)(iv)	9850025	17.6
9738055	32.3	9851054	24.5(b)(iii)
9738056	32.3	199905031	24.5(e)(i)
9739043	24.5(b)(iii)	199910060	24.5(k)
9740032	25.1(h)(i)	199912033	13.1(b), 15.3, 15.4
9802045	21.4(a)	199914040	7.2(b)
9808037	17.1(a)	199914051	32.3
9809054	29.4	199916053	32.3
9809055	19.5(b)	199920041	24.4(f)
9810038	24.4(f)	199925051	17.1(a)
9811001	24.5(k)	199929049	24.4(f)
9812001	23.2(b)(iv)	199938041	30.1(a)
9812037	19.19(c)	199939049	21.7
9814051	24.4(f)	199943053	24.5(b)(viii)
9821049	24.4(f)	199945062	24.4(f)
9821063	24.5(b)(viii)	199946036	24.5(b)(viii)
9821067	24.4(g)	199946037	24.5(b)(viii)
9822004	24.5(k)	199952088	32.4
9822006	24.4(g)	200003053	18.3
9822039	24.5(b)(viii)	200009051	18.3
9825001	21.7	200011063	25.3
9825030	24.4(f)	200020056	14.1(a)(iii)
9835003	20.7, 26.1(f), 28.1(a)	200020060	20.4(b)

CUMULATIVE TABLE OF IRS PRIVATE DETERMINATIONS CITED IN TEXT

Private Determinations	Book Sections	Private Determinations	Book Sections
200021056	4.4, 4.5(c), 4.7, 4.11(a) (ii), 4.11(d), 7.1, 8.6, 24.1, 24.2(d), 24.2(f), 24.4(a), 24.5(c)	200131034	24.2(g), 24.5(n), 26.4(g)
		200132040	30.2, 32.1(d)
		200133036	15.3
200022056	24.5(k)	200134025	4.1(b)(ii), 26.2(c), 28.2(c), 32.7
200030028	32.3		
200033046	22.1(c)	200147058	24.7
200033049	24.2(f), 26.4(f), 26.4(g)	200149043	30.2
		200151045	11.4, 31.2, 31.2(b)(ii)
200037050	24.5(k)	200151047	24.4(f)
200037053	11.8(d)	200151060	23.2(b)(iv), 29.3
200041034	29.3	200151061	24.4
200044038	23.2(b)(iv)	200152048	19.6
200044039	28.10(b)	200201024	32.7
200044040	32.6	200202077	32.7
200047049	24.2(b), 24.2(h), 24.2(i), 24.4(g)	200203069	30
		200204045	18.3
200051046	15.6	200204051	24.4(f)
200051049	7.6(i), 24.1	200206056	18.4
200101034	24.5(k)	200210024	19.21(c)
200101036	24.5(b)(iv)	200211051	24.5(b)(i)
200102051	24.5(h)(i)	200211053	18.3
200102052	32.6	200213027	24.4(f)
200102056	18.5	200217044	32.10(c)
200103083	20.12(b)	200222030	8.3(b), 8.6, 24.5(c)
200103084	23.2(b)(iv), 32.1(d)	200222031	29.5(b)(viii)
200108045	24.5(k)	200223067	14.1(b)
200111046	18.3	200223068	25.3
200114040	20.12(a)	200225041	18.3
200117043	32.6	200225044	24.4(f)
200118054	31.1(b), 31.4, 32.6	200225046	30
200119061	24.2(f), 24.2(h), 25.1(j)	200227007	30.3(a)
		200230005	25.2(c), 29.5
200124022	32.7	200233024	7.6(i)
200126033	24.4(f)	200234071	29.3, 32.3
200126034	18.3	200238001	19.21(a)
200128059	24.5(i)(iv)	200243057	28.17(e)

CUMULATIVE TABLE OF IRS PRIVATE DETERMINATIONS CITED IN TEXT

Private Determinations	Book Sections	Private Determinations	Book Sections
200244028	21.4(a), 21.9(b)	200402003	32.10(c)
200245064	7.6(f)	200404057	25.1(h)(iii)
200246032	25.1(j)	200405016	30.2
200247055	21.4(a)	200411044	32.6
200249014	24.5(a), 32.7	200413014	21.9(b)
200251016	25.1(n)	200421010	21.4(a)
200251017	25.1(n)	200425050	30
200251018	25.1(n)	200425052	32.3
200301047	18.3	200427016	19.21(c)
200301048	24.4(f)	200428021	19.21(d)
200302052	18.3	200431018	32.7
200303051	32.10(c)	200432026	24.9(b)
200303062	24.5(h)(i), 24.5(o), 24.6	200435005	30.8
		200435018	21.4(c)
200304036	24.5(a), 32.7	200436022	31.4, 32.6
200304041	31.1(b), 32.6	200437040	5.2, 10.3(b), 21.16, 23.3, 30.4
200305032	32.3		
200307065	19.21(c)	200439043	7.6(h), 8.7, 24.5(q)
200307094	24.5(o)	200444024	7.4, 7.5
200311034	19.19(c), 32.6	200444044	30
200313024	19.19(c), 24.5(a)	200446025	20.1
200314024	19.19(d)	200446033	23.2(b)(iv), 23.3, 29.3
200314030	15.6		
200314031	24.5(k), 25.1(h)(iii)	200447038	6.2(b)(i)
200316043	32.4	200447046	7.3(d)
200325003	32.6	200447050	20.11(d)
200326035	9.5, 30.0	200450037	7.3(c)
200328042	24.2(i)	200450038	7.4
200332018	21.4(a), 21.5(f)	200450041	4.1(a), 4.3, 4.3(e), 4.4, 15.1(b)
200333008	32.10(c)		
200333031	32.6	200451031	15.6
200335037	21.4(a), 21.7	200452036	3.4(h), 7.3(c)
200341023	32.7	200501020	13.5
200343027	4.5(a)	200502044	10.3(b)
200345041	24.4(f)	200503027	18.3
200348029	32.3	200504035	19.5(b)
200351033	31.1(b), 31.4, 32.7	200505024	14.1(c)(iii)
		200506024	4.5(a)

CUMULATIVE TABLE OF IRS PRIVATE DETERMINATIONS CITED IN TEXT

Private Determinations	Book Sections	Private Determinations	Book Sections
200506025	24.4(f)	200540012	19.11(a)
200508016	14.2(d)	200541042	32.3
200508019	4.3	200544020	13.2(a)
200509027	20.1	200552021	19.9
200510030	32.7	200602035	19.5(b)
200511019	4.11(d)	200602039	30.2, 30.7(c)
200511022	16.0	200602042	23.2(b)(iii), 23.2(b)(iv), 23.3
200512023	13.5		
200512027	4.11(d)	200603029	6.2(e)
200519084	19.11(a)	200606042	6.3(b), 19.12(b)
200520035	19.9	200607027	4.1(a)
200522022	14.2(c)(ii), 14.2(c)(iii)	200611033	7.7
		200614030	19.12(b)
200524024	28.19	200619024	24.2(h)
200525020	4.11(d)	200620036	8.3(a)
200528008	19.24	200621023	4.4
200528029	4.5(e), 31.1(b)	200621025	6.3(a)
200530016	19.21(d)	200622055	5.6(f), 6.3(h), 8.2, 31.1(c)
200530028	10.3(b)		
200530030	19.7	200623068	12.3(b)(ii)
200531024	28.2(a)(vi)	200623069	25.1(n)
200531025	13.1(a)	200623072	15.2
200532052	29.2(c)	200623075	7.5
200532056	15.6	200624068	7.7
200532058	7.7	200625033	19.5(b)
200534022	7.4	200625035	24.5(a)
200534023	15.3	200631028	4.5(a)
200535029	5.2, 20.1, 26.1(a)(i)	200634016	7.2(b)
200536021	26.1(a)(i)	200723030	24.5(b)(ii), 32.7
200536023	14.2(c)(ii)	200724034	7.7
200536024	7.16(c)	200727020	7.7
200536025	19.16(a)	200727021	10.3(b)
200536026	14.1(c)(iii)	200728044	24.2(h)
200537038	7.16(e), 24.9(b)	200731034	12.3(c)
200538026	8.3(a)(i)	200733030	24.4(f)
200538027	24.9(b), 25.1(h)(iii)	200736037	5.7(c)
200539027	4.11(d)	200737044	5.7(c)

CUMULATIVE TABLE OF IRS PRIVATE DETERMINATIONS CITED IN TEXT

Private Determinations	Book Sections	Private Determinations	Book Sections
200739012	7.7	200849018	4.4, 7.16(c)
200742022	13.1(b), 14.2(c)(ii)	200851033	26.1(a)(i)
200752043	27.3	200851040	4.4
200810025	27.3	200852036	9.2
200815035	4.11(d), 26.1(a)(i)	200902013	31.1(b)
200819017	21.14	200903080	23.5(a)
200825046	4.7	200904026	26.1(a)(i)
200826038	15.6	200905028	4.4
200826043	6.2(a)	200905029	4.4
200828029	5.7(c)	200905033	20.12(b)
200829029	13.2(b)	200906057	4.4, 15.1(b)
200830025	19.9	200908050	23.1
200830028	1.2, 5.7(c), 20.11(d)	200909064	6.2(a), 6.2(b)(iii)
200832027	4.11(e), 24.2(e), 24.2(f), 24.5(k)	200909072	4.4
		200910060	11.3
200833021	23.5(a), 23.5(b)	200911037	18.3
200837035	14.1(c)(iii), 14.2(a)	200912039	10.3(b)
200839034	6.3(a), 7.2(b), 7.2A	200915053	15.1(b)
200839037	7.8	200916035	5.7(c), 20.11(d)
200841038	19.12	200917042	20.9
200842047	4.3(b)	200926033	7.2(b)
200842050	30.2	200926036	10.3(b)
200842051	20.4(h)	200926037	5.7(c)
200842055	11.2	200926049	10.3(b)
200843032	5.7(c)	200928045	23.1
200843033	23.5(a)	200929019	7.7
200843035	14.2(a)	200930049	4.4
200843036	24.9(b)	200931059	29.2(e)
200843040	32.3	200931064	24.4(a), 24.5(g)
200843051	20.4(i)	200941038	11.6
200843052	5.6(n)	200943042	22.3(d)(iv)
200844022	27.3	200944053	20.12(b), 24.2(e)
200844029	8.6	200944055	20.1, 20.4(b)
200845053	5.7(c), 20.11(d)	200947064	7.6(a)
200845054	14.2(a)	200950047	4.11(e)
200846040	5.7(c)	200950049	18.3
200849017	20.12(g)	200952069	4.5(d), 22.1

Private Determinations	Book Sections	Private Determinations	Book Sections
200953029	18.3	201042040	20.12(a)
201002040	19.4(b)	201043041	25.1(n), 30.2, 32.4
201002042	19.5(b)	201043042	15.1(b)
201002043	15.6	201044015	32.1(c)
201003022	15.6	201044016	30.2
201004046	26.1(a)	201044019	10.3(b)
201005061	14.2(c)(iii), 14.2(c)(iv)	201044025	20.12(d)
		201045034	14.2(a), 14.2(c)(ii)
201007060	24.2(e)	201046016	4.11(e)
201012051	14.2(c)(ii)	201048045	7.16(a)
201012052	24.5(b)(vi)	201049046	32.7
201013060	20.8	201049047	24.2(h)
201014068	7.11, 13.2(a)	201050017	19.21(b)
201015037	24.3(a)	201051024	4.11(e)
201016088	5.7(b)	201103057	4.7, 7.14(b), 24.5(i)(i)
201017067	6.3(a)		
201019033	4.10(c), 6.3(h), 24.2(e)	201103062	4.4
		201105043	24.5(e)(iv)
201020021	8.2, 23.2(b)(v)	201105045	19.5(b)
201024066	14.1(a)(ii), 14.2(a)	201105048	14.2(c)(ii)
201024069	24.3(a)	201106019	24.5(a)
201025078	15.1(b), 20.10, 20.12(d)	201107028	14.2(a)
		201108041	20.11(d)
201027058	22.7	201109030	7.16(a)
201028042	20.3, 20.10	201113041	5.7(c)
201029031	4.11(e)	201114035	9.1, 9.2
201031033	4.6	201115026	30.2
201032045	15.6	201119036	7.4
201035034	11.2	201120036	8.2
201035035	19.11(a), 32.1(a)	201121021	20.4(b), 20.5(j)
201037029	11.2	201121027	16.1
201038015	14.1(c)(iii), 14.2(a)	201122022	4.11(e)
201038020	8.3(a)(i)	201122028	4.11(e)
201039035	7.4	201123035	26.13
201039046	20.5(j)	201123041	26.9
201039048	7.4	201123045	7.6(i), 24.5(b)(iv)
201040020	14.2(a)	201123046	28.11(f)
201041045	4.11(d)		

CUMULATIVE TABLE OF IRS PRIVATE DETERMINATIONS CITED IN TEXT

Private Determinations	Book Sections	Private Determinations	Book Sections
201125043	30.3(c), 32.4	201209010	7.7
201127013	23.2(b)(iv), 29.3, 30.2	201209011	5.7(c)
		201210044	7.16(a)
201128027	24.5(l)	201213029	7.7
201128028	7.6	201213030	7.3(d)
201128030	20.12(d)	201213033	20.1
201128032	20.12(d)	201213034	15.6
201128034	20.12(d)	201213035	15.6
201128035	20.12(d)	201213036	15.1(b)
201131029	24.9(b)	201214034	7.7
201133011	19.2(b)	201214035	23.5(a)
201134023	32.7	201216040	30.2
201135032	7.15(e)	201217022	32.2(a), 32.4
201136027	4.3(b)	201217026	20.12(d)
201138031	28.16(g)	201218041	5.7(c), 6.3(a)
201140013	28.16(g)	201219024	32.4
201141021	20.4(b)	201219030	32.4
201142026	24.9(c), 25.1(g)	201219032	20.1
201142027	20.12(d)	201221022	5.7(c)
201143020	4.4, 20.12(a)	201221023	7.16(a)
201144030	20.12(b)	201221025	20.12(d)
201144032	20.4(a)	201221026	20.12(d)
201145025	7.6(m)(iii), 20.12(b)	201221027	20.12(d)
201146022	29.1	201221028	20.12(d)
201147034	14.2(a)	201221029	20.12(d)
201147035	29.1	201221030	18.3
201148008	20.5(i)	201222040	24.2(b)
201149032	4.3(b)	201222043	24.4(f), 32.7
201150027	28.16(g)	201222050	14.1(a)(ii)
201150034	4.11(d)	201224034	23.5(a)
201151028	20.12(b)	201224036	6.3(i)
201203018	14.2(a)	201224037	18.3
201203025	5.7(c)	201225019	25.3
201204016	10.6	201228026	19.1
201205011	6.3(a), 20.5(h)	201231012	4.11(d)
201205012	7.3(d)	201231013	14.1(c)(iii)
201205013	4.11(d)	201232034	5.7(c), 10.3(b)

CUMULATIVE TABLE OF IRS PRIVATE DETERMINATIONS CITED IN TEXT

Private Determinations	Book Sections	Private Determinations	Book Sections
201233017	5.7(c)	201325017	5.7(c), 10.3(b)
201235024	15.6	201327014	24.5(q)
201236033	5.7(c)	201332013	4.3(f)(ii)
201239012	22.3(d)(v)	201332015	4.7, 7.14(b)
201242014	5.7(c)	201333014	4.1(a), 6.3(i)
201242016	5.7(c), 14.1(a)(ii), 14.2(c)(iii), 20.9	201336020	21.3
		201338059	29.2(b)
201244020	5.7(c)	201340017	19.5(b)
201245025	7.14(c)	201340020	7.2(a)
201246039	20.9	201344009	7.6(i)
201249016	8.4	201345031	28.18(a)
201250025	4.11(e), 7.6(k), 20.3, 20.12(b)	201347022	14.2(a)
		201347023	20.1
201251018	10.3(b)	201347024	22.3(d)(v)
201251019	24.3(d)	201349019	4.5(c), 14.2(a)
201252021	5.7(c)	201349021	14.1(a)(ii)
201301014	8.4	201351024	13.2(a)
201301015	21.7	201403016	12.3(b)(iii)
201302040	5.7(c)	201403017	4.11(d)
201303018	8.4	201403019	23.5(a)
201307008	12.3(b)(iii)	201403020	23.5(a)
201309014	19.2(a)	201405018	4.3(f)(ii), 7.16(a), 20.12(d)
201309016	7.14(c)		
201310046	7.14(c)	201405022	4.5(c), 7.11
201310047	6.2(a), 6.3(i)	201405029	24.5(h)(ii), 24.6
201311035	11.8(b)	201406019	30.2
201313034	11.8(b)	201406020	24.4(f)
201314044	12.3(a)	201407014	7.14(c)
201315027	4.11(d)	201407022	24.2(h)
201315028	7.6(m)(iii)	201407024	4.5(c), 24.9(c)
201317013	20.2, 20.3	201408030	30.2
201318034	27.3	201408031	7.7, 24.4(f)
201320023	24.4(g)	201409009	30.1(a)
201321026	14.2(e)	201409012	4.11(d), 7.6
201321036	28.14(b)	201410035	4.11(d), 7.14(c)
201322046	12.3(b)(iii)	201411037	20.5(a)
201323037	7.14(c)	201411038	4.11(d)
201325016	13.3	201411039	20.8

CUMULATIVE TABLE OF IRS PRIVATE DETERMINATIONS CITED IN TEXT

Private Determinations	Book Sections	Private Determinations	Book Sections
201411040	14.2(a)	201444013	24.9(c)
201411041	18.4	201446025	28.1(c)
201413012	7.7	201446028	4.11(e)
201414029	15.2	201448026	4.5(a)
201415003	4.7	201503018	30.2
201415008	18.3	201503019	21.1
201415009	26.12(b)	201505040	7.16(f)
201415011	18.3	201507026	5.7(c), 7.14(c)
201416009	19.7	201512006	25.3
201416011	23.2(b)(iv)	201514011	20.12(b)
201417017	20.5(c), 26.1(a)(i)	201515035	15.1(b)
201419015	20.12(b)	201515036	18.3
201421022	5.7(c)	201518018	13.1(b)
201422025	18.3	201519027	19.22(d)
201424023	14.1(e)	201519034	6.3(a)
201424028	23.5(a)	201519035	6.3(a)
201425016	15.6	201523021	23.2(c)
201426028	28.1(c)	201523022	20.5(n)
201426029	14.1(g)	201528010	19.22(b)
201427018	5.7(c)	201528038	18.3
201428009	15.2	201531022	7.7
201428011	20.11	201534020	7.4
201428026	20.5(b)	201537025	10.5
201428030	24.5(b)(iii)	201538027	7.6(b)
201429027	5.7(c), 7.14(c)	201539032	28.19(a)
201429029	24.5(c)	201540016	32.10(b)
201430017	25.1(b)	201540017	14.2(c)
201430019	4.5(b), 15.1(b)	201540019	4.11(d), 5.7(c), 32.10(b)
201431031	4.5(b)		
201431032	14.2(c)(iii), 16.1	201541013	5.7(c)
201434022	15.1(b)	201543019	5.7(c), 27.3
201436050	5.7(c)	201544025	24.5(a), 24.5(i)(i), 25.1(h)(i)
201438032	30.3(c)		
201440020	5.7(c)	201544028	20.5(h)
201440023	20.12(b)	201545026	18.3
201442066	20.12(b)	201545029	4.11(d), 20.12(a)
201443021	5.7(c)	201548021	4.11(d), 20.1
		201548025	4.11(d)

Private Determinations	Book Sections	Private Determinations	Book Sections
201605019	19.6	201623013	13.2(b)
201605021	15.1(b)	201626004	24.1
201614038	26.1(h)	201633032	24.5(l)
201615014	4.5(c)	201636042	24.2(b)
201615022	7.7	201639016	4.5(c), 14.2(c)
201616002	23.7	201640022	20.5(e)
201617012	20.12(a)		

EXEMPTION DENIAL AND REVOCATION LETTERS

Ex. Den. and Rev. Ltrs.	Book Sections	Ex. Den. and Rev. Ltrs.	Book Sections
20042701E	15.1(b)	20044018E	31.1(c)
20042702E	14.2(d)	20042708E	7.16(c)
20042704E	18.3	20044001E	14.3
20042705E	7.6(a)(i)	20044002E	4.5(a)
20044008E	13.5, 20, 20.12(d), 23.5(b)	20044006E	4.11(e)
		20044044E	7.3(c)
20044010E	23.1	20044045E	7.3(c)
20044016E	15.2	20044275E	7.6(a)

GENERAL COUNSEL MEMORANDA

GCM	Book Sections	GCM	Book Sections
14407	19.21(b), 19.21(c)	35921	19.5(b)
31433	7.6(j)	36078	26.2(b)
32287	27.5	36918	20.4(c)
32453	20.4(c)	37126	4.3(b)
32583	27.5	37158	32.9(b)
33207	4.3(b)	37257	24.2(e)
33912	23.2(b)(vi), 30.2, 31.4	37351	19.2(a)
34608	14.2(c)(ii)	37458	26.2(b)
34631	23.2(b)(vi)	37726	16.1
35719	27.5, 30.2, 31.4	37783	32.9(b)
35811	24.5(a)	37789	20.12(c), 31.2(b)(ii), 32.9(b)
35855	20.7	37858	6.2(a), 23.2(g)
35862	16.1	379v42	16.1
35869	20.5(g)	38104	24.5(g), 24.5(h)(ii)

GCM	Book Sections		GCM	Book Sections
38168	24.5(g), 24.5(h)(ii)		38444	23.2(c)
38205	24.5(g), 24.5(h)(ii)		38458	14.2(c)(ii)
38248	10.1(b)		38459	6.3(b), 7.9, 8.4, 20.1, 24.2(e)
38283	4.10, 21.4(b)		38497	7.16(e)
38437	8.3(a)(i)		38577	11.3

GENERAL COUNSEL MEMORANDA

GCM	Book Sections		GCM	Book Sections
38735	7.6(f)		39674	20.4(c), 20.5(g), 21.4(c)
38827	10.8, 10.9		39692	11.4
38878	30.7(b)		39694	23.2(a), 23.4
38881	7.3(a)		39703	28.14(b)
38905	21.4(b)		39717	24.5(n)
38949	24.5(c)		39721	14.1(e)
38954	21.5(f)		39727	24.5(i)(ii)
39005	20.12(c), 31.2, 31.2(a), 31.2(b)(i), 31.2(b)(ii)		39732	20.12(c), 31.2(b)(ii), 33.3(b)
			39744	24.5(n)
39063	15.1(b)		39757	6.2(b)(ii), 8.8
39082	6.2(e)		39762	32.9(b)
39105	14.2(c)(ii)		39775	11.2
39107	21.7		39776	11.5
39108	24.1		39792	6.2(e)
39115	15.4		39806	24.5(n)
39212	19.4(a)		39809	28.2(a)(vi)
39288	6.3(b)		39811	17.6, 23.2(f),28.0
39326	30.2, 31.4		39813	27.4(a), 27.4(b)
39341	19.2(a)		39817	18.3
39343	15.2		39828	7.6(f), 28.14(b)
39524	6.2(b)(iii)		39830	26.11(a)
39525	6.2(b)(iii)		39837	17.7
39546	20.12(c), 31.2, 31.2(b)(i)		39862	20.1, 20.6, 20.7, 20.12(c), 31.1(b), 31.2(b)(ii)
39574	6.2(b)(ii)			
39598	30.2, 30.5		39865	24.3(b)
39612	6.3(b)		39872	8.8
39613	8.8		39873	18.3
39622	8.8		39877	17.5
39633	4.3(a)		39891	24.3(b)
39670	20.3, 20.4(c)			

CHIEF COUNSEL ADVICE MEMORANDA

CCAM	Book Sections	CCAM	Book Sections
39357	19.3	39510	19.4(a)
39389	28.2(a)(vi)	200431023	7.3(c), 21.4(a), 21.11
39411	14.2(c)(ii)	200504031	7.2(b), 28.18
39444	20.12(c), 31.2(b)(i), 31.2(b)(ii)	200620001	7.3(c), 8.2
		200819017	21.15
39498	20.3, 20.4(c)	200936027	19.11(a)
39508	7.6(j)		

Cumulative Table of IRS Private Letter Rulings, Technical Advice Memoranda, and Counsel Memoranda

The following citations, to pronouncements from the Internal Revenue Service issued in the context of specific cases, are coordinated to the appropriate footnotes (FN) in the suitable chapters.

Citations are to IRS private letter rulings, technical advice memoranda, general counsel memoranda, and chief counsel advice memoranda, other than those specifically referenced in footnotes, directly pertinent to the material discussed in the text. Seven-number and nine-number items are either private letter rulings, technical advice memoranda, or general counsel memoranda; five-number items are chief counsel memoranda.

While these pronouncements are not to be cited as precedent (IRC § 6110(k)(3)), they are useful in understanding the position of the IRS on the subjects involved.

FN	Private Letter Rulings, etc.
Chapter 3	
102	39782
110	8337006
Chapter 4	
13	8705078, 8709069, 8810048
17	9014063, 9629020
45	200150027
56	200740012
58	201249016
61	200508020, 200508022, 200508031, 200509028, 200509031
62	8936050, 9526033
63	201615016, 201619010, 201620012
64	201031034
91	30808
92	200151045
94	39736
134	200634041
153	200447047, 20044015E, 20055035E
169	20044041E
179	201040036, 201220035
183	9132005
187	8142024, 8204016, 32689, 34682, 36130, 37596, 38686

188	39684
210	20044002E, 20044003E, 20044011E, 20044012E, 20044015E, 20044035E, 20044039E, 20044047E, 200443033, 200447048, 200447049, 200449035, 200449044, 200452035, 200503028, 200505023, 200508017, 200511018, 200511020, 200511021, 200511025, 200516017, 200519088, 200520030, 200520032, 200531021, 200535029, 200536021, 200549010, 200646019, 200646020, 200717018, 200724035, 200726032, 200728046, 200728047, 200732030, 200739013–200742030, 200742023, 200742025, 200744022, 200748019, 200748022, 200748023, 200802036, 200803025, 200804028, 200805024, 200810033, 200810034, 200812025, 200814027, 200814028, 200817045, 200817055, 200817057, 200822029, 200824025, 200825046, 200829033–200829035, 200829038, 200829043–200829046, 200829049–200849051, 200829054, 200829056, 200837033, 200837043, 200837050, 200850036, 200903081, 200936040, 201011037, 201021029, 201031033–201031035, 201032046–201032053, 201040024, 201040030, 201115025, 201116028, 201116046, 201129054–201129056, 201142028, 201148007, 201149035, 201149044, 201203021, 201203025, 201222044, 201222048, 201237020, 201240026, 201241009, 201244021, 201245021, 201245027, 201246016, 201251005, 201252022, 201252024, 201307015, 201309015, 201309029, 201310045, 201311028, 201314047, 201317011, 201318012, 201318017, 201318027, 201329018, 201329021, 201329026, 201334045, 201335015, 201335016, 201335024, 201335025, 201337018, 201338053, 201341037, 201349022, 201350044, 201402016, 201435027, 201405017, 201405021, 201405022, 201409014, 201411042, 201414021, 201414025, 201415007, 201433018, 201451037, 201514014, 201517008, 201517012, 201517015, 201524026, 201534016, 201544028, 201544030, 201603036, 201603039, 201615017, 201632022, 201635006, 201640021, 201640025
212	200728047, 200748023, 200749024, 200803029, 200807020, 200808032, 200810029, 200811024–200811027, 200817044, 200817046, 200817060, 200829037, 200834023, 200837040, 200837052, 200840047, 200842045, 200844027, 200846026, 200844027, 200846026, 200846036, 201011037, 201013056, 201020034, 201021029, 201021030, 201023057, 201023060, 201023062, 201035026, 201035028–201035030, 201035032, 201037032, 201037034, 201040027, 201040028, 201040033, 201040037, 201044020, 201044025, 201045024, 201045027, 201101024, 201101028, 201108038, 201121022, 201121024, 201124029, 201202040, 201209007, 201218019, 201222045, 201222046, 201225017, 201245024, 201252023, 201309018, 201318009, 201327012, 201327013, 201333015, 201349017, 201350045, 201402017, 201406013, 201414026, 201414032, 201418058, 201435015, 201442057, 201445012, 201449001, 201451034, 201509040, 201514010, 201514012, 201517009, 201517011, 201518021, 201534015, 201552031, 201603037, 201603038, 201603040, 201609007, 201611019, 201615015, 201620013, 201623011, 201631013, 201631015, 201637016, 201640023, 201647009, 201647010, 201648018, 201649015
227	201020021
229	39288, 39716
254	9036001, 200606045
265	201032046–201032053, 201128029, 201129054–201129056, 201138050, 201146023
267	200634046

292	9243008, 9316052
487	9243008, 9316052
499	20044033E
511	201204021
518	201645017
519	20044006E, 20044038E, 200502046, 200505023, 200508017, 200511019, 200520032, 200534021, 200636105, 200651037, 200702042, 200709064, 200724035, 200732034, 200733027, 200743038, 200802036, 200807022, 200809037, 200809040, 200815035, 200817042, 200821037, 200824025, 200824027, 200825051, 200827041, 200837033, 200844029, 200845053, 200847016, 200847019, 200944053, 201008050, 201019033, 201023059, 201023074, 201025078, 201025079, 201029031, 201031032, 201037035, 201503016, 201525011, 201525012, 201526020, 201535019, 201538025, 201544031, 201545030, 201545031, 201548021, 201548025, 201550043, 201550044, 201037037, 201039034, 201039035, 201039037–201039039, 201039048, 201040034, 201044018, 201051024, 201109029, 201114036, 201115025, 201117036, 201122022, 201122028, 201123040, 201124025, 201124026, 201125042, 201126039, 201128029, 201128031, 201130009, 201131025, 201143023, 201149045, 201150035, 201152020, 201202038, 201202039, 201203020, 201203025, 201209009, 201210041, 201215012, 201215019, 201218016, 201218017, 201218023, 201221023, 201226029, 201230024, 201230025, 201231012, 201232036, 201233017, 201234029, 201234030, 201237019, 201238032, 201242017, 201244021, 201245021, 201247017, 201252021, 201252025, 201252026, 201302041, 201303018–201303020, 201305011–201305013, 201307009, 201307014, 201309016, 201310046, 201311028, 201311030, 201313032, 201315027–201315029, 201322045, 201322053, 201322054, 201323024, 201323028, 201323034, 201325014, 201330038, 201331006, 201345030, 201349023, 201350042, 201350043, 201351025, 201403017, 201404012, 201405022, 201407015, 201409012, 201410035, 201414025, 201415006, 201416010, 201419016, 201420021, 201424027, 201428022, 201433016, 201434023, 201438034, 201445018, 201446028, 201450022, 201450042, 201452020, 201503016, 201510059, 201511023, 201514013, 201525011, 201525012, 201526020, 201535019, 201538025, 201540016, 201544031, 201545030, 201545031, 201548021, 201609006, 201632021, 201634029, 201641025
530	20044038E
531	200534021

Chapter 5

96	201252021
103	201023058
107	201332013

Chapter 6

43	200826043, 200829048
57	200527021
79	35986, 37462
84	7851096, 8327066, 33752, 37462, 39082, 39117

CUMULATIVE TABLE OF IRS PRIVATE LETTER RULINGS

95	8910001, 39792
99	201033039, 201036024, 201041046
110	37858
139	8024109
141	200838035, 200839036, 200839038
144	9307027
148	8736046
149	8405083
150	8827074
153	9631004, 200851037
160	9351027, 38050
161	9718034, 20044035E
163	9214031
172	37257, 37787, 38459
182	9408026
217	201620015
220	201323025, 201325015
221	201615018

Chapter 7

8	9718034
9	9752064
16	8801067, 9311034, 9411037
20	8637141
24	9325061
28	201219026
29	201646007
36	9516047
40	199917079
51	200839035, 201221024
53	201217018, 201217021
60	20044045E, 20044046E
73	201249016, 201301014
79	20044044E–20044046E, 200447046, 200450037, 200450039, 200450042–200450045, 200452306, 200506038, 200510031, 200510044, 200514021, 200523024, 200528028, 200536022, 200538028, 200538040, 200549010, 200611035, 200614031, 200625043
82	201152019, 201226029, 201228040, 201309019, 201311029, 201314045

91	200450037, 200450039, 200450042, 200450045, 200452036, 200506038, 200510031, 200510044, 200514021, 200523024, 200528028, 200536022, 200538028, 200538040, 200549010, 200601034, 200602036, 200605012, 200606041, 200606044, 200611035, 200614031, 200625043, 200628041, 200631026, 200634045, 200637039, 200642010, 200642012, 200649033, 200649035, 200649036, 200733034, 200808036, 200808038, 200825047, 200835037, 200837036, 200837047, 200846023, 200851024, 200915059, 200919053, 200936038, 200936043, 200941039, 201005060, 201009015, 201013061, 201013075, 201017060, 201017077, 201021030, 201029036, 201029037, 201033042, 20044044E, 20044045E, 20044046E, 201005060, 201009015, 201013061, 201013075, 201017060, 201017077, 201021030, 201029036, 201029037, 201133042, 201040025, 201040025, 201043052, 201103063, 201119034, 201127014, 201128038, 201132030, 201139013, 201146023, 201149031, 201202041, 201203024, 201213031, 201216051, 201217019, 201217028, 201219040, 201232035, 201250027–201250029, 201307015, 201309019, 201310049, 201314048, 201314049, 201314058, 201318014, 201321041, 201323028, 201335027, 201345032, 201351028, 201405023, 201410043, 201410044, 201412022, 201414033, 201417023, 201419018, 201419019, 201422027, 201422033, 201426035, 201445014, 201503017, 201515034, 201519034, 201541012
92	201218021
93	201445014, 201519034
97	9411037, 20044048E
101	20044048E
105	200721025
107	201624023
117	200534021, 200540013, 200545013, 200610021, 200610029, 200623071, 200623074, 200625036, 200634042, 200643007, 200645025, 200704041, 200711040, 200718034, 200718035, 200732020, 200733031, 200736034, 200739014, 200743034, 200743035, 200747024, 200749025, 200807021, 200809039, 200817051, 200817058, 200819022, 200821038, 200833024, 200842044, 200842053, 200844020, 200844030, 200846025, 200846029, 200851027, 200901034, 200911043, 200915060, 200920062, 200921042, 200940033, 200941039, 201007069, 201009018, 201015044, 201017066, 201018020, 201021036, 201023054, 201025080, 201025081, 201039042, 201039049, 201044022, 201050039, 201102064, 201140031, 201418055, 201428021, 201428023, 201428028, 201452019, 201418055, 201428021, 201428023, 201428028, 201452019, 201506011, 201521016, 201526023
119	9204433
123	9043059, 9535023, 20042706E
136	200233024
139	8633038
141	8251089, 8251096, 8736046, 8936045, 8936046, 9241055, 9242002, 9527035
173	201433016
177	9307027
183	9412002

184	9246004, 38735, 39057, 39487, 39799, 39828, 39829, 39830
187	9714011, 9716021, 9721031, 9722042, 9738038–9738054, 200819023
195	201412018
209	38686, 38894, 39120
210	8237052, 8509044, 8509073, 8511082, 8625081, 9408026, 39340
219	32896, 36827
220	9325061
227	9210032, 9735048
231	9001011
242	9411037, 9541003, 9629002
243	8723052, 9243008, 9246032, 9246033, 9629002, 200606047, 200611033,
244	200634036, 38693, 39347, 39348, 39682, 39685, 39852
245	9047049, 39348
280	200724034
285	9249026
287	9530025, 9530026, 9537035–9537053
291	9408026
294	39733
295	7823052
300	9731038
304	201213029, 201219031
305	199932052
311	8629045, 9802045
312	8429102, 8629045, 9048046, 9237027
324	201140028
330	39562
332	9118012
343	9539013
348	9247030
350	9002036, 9025073, 9306034
351	9002036, 9306034
352	39360
358	38050
359	9407005, 9526033
387	9014063
398	8705078
399	37518
400	37518
405	8536099, 9014063, 35936, 35966, 37180, 38401, 38322
410	201110012

420	9210026
428	8334001, 8849072
429	20044014E, 20044037E
431	8734007
433	8906062, 35945
436	7816061, 7905129, 7951134
437	7902019, 8920084, 201125044, 201210043
446	7816061
452	8753049, 9242002, 9635037, 39562
478	8351103
481	8448020, 8717020, 8721022, 8921061, 9347001
482	7909026, 7935043, 8347031, 8348025, 8944068
520	8630021
522	201641021
525	8349017, 8438027, 8511032
534	8836056
538	8425019, 8425031, 8425032, 8425038, 8425064, 8426029, 8429012, 8429028, 8430026, 8430044, 8431024, 8431025, 8432038, 8432050, 8435027, 8435028, 8435080, 8435089, 8435102, 8436042, 8437021, 8437038, 8437040, 8437041, 8437068, 8437082, 8437095, 8438019, 8441014, 8442081, 8443031, 8443077, 8444019, 8444053, 8445027, 8447013, 8447059, 8447084, 8447102, 8448020, 8448021, 8450009, 8452018, 8501077, 8502026, 8502037, 8502071, 8503031, 8505010, 8506035, 8506048, 8507018, 8507034, 8514019, 8516027, 8516048, 8516093, 8517026, 8517027, 8518072, 8522024, 8524111, 8534020, 8534056, 8536027, 8536037, 8537014, 8537040, 8541025, 8542010, 8543014, 8544015, 8544027, 8546060, 8603034, 8607010, 8607040, 8609020, 8609033, 8610025, 8611036, 8620036, 8621085, 8622034, 8639024, 8639039, 8650008, 201338029, 201338034, 34704
539	8342022, 8412064
540	7823052, 9526033
542	39055
552	200505032
556	201110020
561	8429051, 9240001, 39047, 39883
563	9048046, 9539015
565	39633
578	200521029
589	201505041

Chapter 8

12	201117035
83	8705078
87	8823088

88	201417018
92	9325061
105	9211002, 9211004
106	201117035
108	8645017
110	200333034
111	200333034
126	8909004
128	8846002
137	9414003
144	9019046
168	8751007, 8811021, 9036025, 9851052
169	9210026
180	9048046, 9237027
207	20044015E
210	8930052
212	9638001
228	200939033
230	9335061, 39622

Chapter 9

14	8723061–8723064, 200714026
15	9240001, 39883
18	7852997, 8028004
19	9627023
29	9346006
50	8512084
51	9017052
52	9311032, 9722032

Chapter 10

126	37622, 37503, 37391, 37247
139	8626100, 8626101, 8627044, 8628077, 8629051, 8641069–8641072, 8643055
141	8422171, 8422174, 8423078, 8423079, 8424056, 8424098, 8425058, 8425076, 8425115, 8425118, 8425123, 8425130–8425135, 8426022, 8426023, 8426045, 8426047, 8426068, 8426091, 8426107–8426109, 8427096–8427099, 8427103, 8427104, 8428108, 8428115, 8428110–8428113, 8429065–8429068, 8429106, 8429107, 8429110, 8430073, 8431067–8431069, 8431075, 8431081–8431083, 8432068–8432070, 8432076–8432078, 8432110, 8433053, 8433054, 8433111, 8434064–843067, 8435047, 8435086, 8435158–8435161, 8435168, 8435171–8435174, 8435090–8435098, 8436036, 8436037, 8436039, 8436040, 8436050, 8437070, 8437076, 8437090, 8437101, 8437102, 8437104, 8437112, 8437114, 8438045, 8438061, 8438062, 8438066, 8439014, 8439015, 8439081, 8439097, 8439102, 8439103, 8440092, 8440093, 8440097–8440100, 8441046,

8441065, 8442065–8442073, 8442075, 8442093, 8442097–8442101, 8442110, 8442132, 8442134–8442141, 8443049–3443051, 8443081, 8443090–8443092, 8444085, 8444087–8444089, 8444095, 8444096, 8445074–8445078, 8445080, 8445101–8445107, 8446033, 8446037, 8447066, 8447067, 8447088–8447090, 8448041–8448043, 8448045, 8448049, 8448055–8448058, 8448070, 8449068, 8450072–8450074, 8451051, 8452070–8452073, 8452075, 8452081–8452084, 8453096–8453101, 8501061, 8501062, 8502062, 8502063, 8502076–8502078, 8502085–8502090, 8502096, 8502101, 8503040, 8503042, 8503071, 8503078–8503082, 8504052, 8504057, 8504081, 8505061–8505064, 8505077, 8506067, 8506078–8506080, 8506084, 8506101 8506103, 8506119, 8508082–8508085, 8508100, 8508104, 8509068, 8509101, 8510041, 8510042, 8510058–8510060, 8510090, 8510091, 8511051–8511053, 8511069, 8511070, 8512075, 8512076, 8512080, 8512091, 8512092, 8514056–8514059, 8514061, 8514062, 8514078, 8514083, 8514084, 8514086, 8514096, 8514097, 8515065, 8516059, 8516097, 8516102, 8516108, 8516109, 8516115, 8516136, 8516137, 8517059–8517061, 8517065, 8518055, 8510856, 8518081–8518086, 8518091, 8518092, 8519035, 8519036, 8520047, 8520052, 8520064, 8520067, 8520071, 8520118, 8520119, 8521013, 8521100, 8521104, 8521105, 8522080–8522083, 8522085, 8523082, 8523087, 8523091, 8523094, 8523095, 8523101, 8523104, 8523106–8523111, 8524065–8524069, 8525076, 8525088–8525090, 8526083, 8527045, 8527049, 8527067, 8529051, 8529052, 8529098, 8529105, 8530054–8530058, 8530134, 8531051, 8531066, 8531067, 8532014, 8532015, 8532024, 8532044, 8532047, 8532060, 8532069, 8532095–8532097, 8533020, 8533079, 8534062, 8534086, 8534087, 8535060, 8535061, 8535119, 8536089, 8536090–8536094, 8537059, 8537060, 8537102–8537107, 8538067, 8539090, 8540032, 8540083, 8540089, 8541106, 8541109, 8541110, 8542059, 8542066, 8542096, 8542097, 8543048, 8543057–8543063, 8543090, 8544087, 8546100–8546106, 8546113, 8546114, 8546116, 8546124, 8546130, 8546132, 8546136, 8546137, 8547059, 8547060, 8547068–8547073, 8548081, 8549064, 8550048, 8550049, 8550052, 8550054–8550056 8550074–8550076, 8551048–8551050, 8551052–8551059, 8551067–8551070, 8551078–8551080, 8551081, 8552108, 8601056, 8601057, 8601059–8601062, 8601064, 8601065, 8601068–8601072, 8602048, 8602065, 8603089–8603095, 8603097, 8603107–8603109, 8603122–8603124, 8604081, 8604083, 8604084, 8604090, 8604091, 8604094, 8605048, 8605050, 8606070, 8606071, 8606073, 8606076, 8608081, 8608082, 8609070, 8609071, 8610079, 8610080, 8610084, 8611047, 8611049, 8611080–8611083, 8614045, 8615045, 8615047, 8615049, 8615058–8615062, 8615088–8615090, 8616057, 8616062–8616065, 8616096, 8618045, 8618046, 8618066, 8619048–8619050, 8619054–8619060, 8619063– 8619066, 8620059–8620063, 8620081, 8620083, 8621102, 8621114, 8622046–8622048, 8622052–8622054, 8622057, 8622061, 8623045, 8623052, 8624080–8624083, 8624091, 8624093, 8624094, 8624128, 8624152, 8624166 8624168, 8625089, 8625102–8625105, 8626100, 8626101, 8627044, 8628077, 8629051, 8631061, 8631072, 8631073, 8631080, 8631083, 8631092, 8631093, 8631097–8631099, 8631107, 8631108, 8631110, 8631111, 8631113– 8631117, 8633037, 8634061, 8634064, 8635056, 8635057, 8638124, 8641069– 8641072, 8833001, 9624001, 36078, 36993, 37116

172	9448017, 39614
181	201420020
197	9518021

208	200437040, 200712046, 200712047, 200830028, 201221022, 201232034, 201235022, 201242014, 201251018, 201325017, 201321036, 201321037, 201321039, 201327018, 201329022, 201333017, 201333018 , 201420020, 201609006
216	9518021
224	9434002
237	7838029–7838036
238	33574, 36254, 36787, 37503

Chapter 11

7	9851001
15	9211004, 201110012, 39459, 39560, 39775
18	9129040, 39459, 39560
32	39799, 9851054, 201218016
38	20044009E
54	201433018
57	36738, 39598
67	201047024
74	201313034

Chapter 12

170	201322046
198	200731035, 200807019

Chapter 13

1	9149004, 9201039, 39574, 39866
6	201414028
9	200531025
24	8923001
27	201219030
34	20042708E, 37518
37	200511024, 200714027, 201313031, 21313035, 21318010, 213018016, 21318020-21318024, 201319031, 201321032, 201321033, 201321035, 201321036, 201321037, 21021039, 201323032, 201323036, 201325016, 201329022, 201333017, 201333018, 201338053, 201338055, 201349018, 201351024, 201409013, 201411039, 201414028, 201425013, 201429030, 201431032, 201450023, 201630016, 201640021
39	201215014
46	201313035, 201318021
49	201318010
57	201116030
59	9044060
62	9811003, 9815061
67	201213032, 201215014, 201224035, 201234028
71	200720026

77	201204017
80	200809035, 201252029, 201313031, 201318016, 201318020, 201318022–201318024
87	201409013, 201443020, 201548020
90	200716035, 201636044
92	201040019
115	39763
119	200511024
126	8829072
132	8828058, 8838052

Chapter 14

5	200020056
8	9517036
51	20044041E
53	200601035
72	9029035
88	201329023
93	39721
108	9349022
118	201213032, 201215014, 201321026, 201329024, 201338047, 201347022, 201347023, 201349019, 201349021, 201411040, 201424023, 201425014, 201432026, 201431032, 201502015, 201605020, 201633035, 201633037
122	201621017
124	201622033
133	201639016
142	20044043E, 20044007E, 20044031E, 20044042E, 201605020, 201617010
177	20044043E
186.1	201649017
190	37853
192	9124004, 200528008
199	201150032
200	200833031, 200843034, 200843043, 200844025, 200916036, 201012051, 201050040, 201203018, 201205014, 201205015, 201220034, 201321026, 201347022, 201411040, 201424023, 201432026, 201451038, 201502015
202	201222050, 201639016, 201646005
203	201431032
206	8826004
210	20044007E, 20044031E, 20044043E
211	200505024, 200536025, 200538039, 200601032
212	20042707E, 200606046, 200827040
222	20044001E, 200444024

Chapter 15

2	201615021
12	200728048, 200817064, 200837042, 200846033, 201451030, 201642036
13	201451030
13.1	201551010, 201638028, 201640020
17	39773
36	200449045, 200531026, 200540018
37	20042701E, 200449045, 200519085, 200520031, 200520033, 200531026, 200531027, 201317014, 201323033, 201337017, 201338044, 201338050, 201450023, 201644021
42	9533015, 201313035
43	200919052
47	201635008
49	20044016E, 20044017E, 20044019E, 200511023, 200534023, 200540011, 201111015, 201138054, 201222049, 201225018, 201240025, 201240027, 201240030, 201241018, 201306027, 201317015, 201317016, 201318026, 201322043, 201322044, 201329025, 201330041, 201333019, 201342014, 201343024, 201343025, 201344010, 201344011, 201405026, 201405027, 201406016 201408035, 201428020, 201428027, 201429028, 201445027, 201448021, 201448022, 201450023, 201451039, 201501015, 201517016, 201517017, 201544026, 201612014, 201615019, 201623012, 201635007, 201636045
66	9043019
67	201615021
69	200540011, 200623072, 200624069, 200625042, 200628040, 200631027, 200636106, 200735028, 200735030, EDRLs 20044016E, 20044017E, 20044019E, 200702044, 200729040, 200729041, 200732024, 200735028, 200735030, 200811023, 200825048, 200829041, 200846034, 200850035, 200915055, 200915061, 201007071, 200919072, 201013055, 201023063, 201025082, 201029038, 201038021, 201039036, 201107029, 201107030, 201108039, 201111015, 201138054, 201448022
70	200133037, 200134021
80	200507014
81	200910067
84	200723032
91	9212002
92	201615021, 39688
97	8809087, 8812006, 9043003, 9044022, 39717
99	8729001
108	39658
109	8816004
116	8905002, 8920002, 8922067, 8943009, 9043019, 200625034, 39773
117	8728002, 9246043
125	200451031

126	8737060, 8738075, 8919062, 8951062, 9025001, 9027044, 9040018, 9307004, 9608002, 9629032, 9630001, 9824045, 9844012, 200427031, 200451035, 200638026, 200826038, 200837045, 200916036
127	8724045, 8740002
131	201302043
134	9225001

Chapter 16

6	200649029, 39698
11	200921041
61	201104066
81	8739066, 39672

Chapter 17

13	8850014
17	8650001, 9249002, 9652026, 9725036, 39694
19	9320002
37	200511003
49	9622002
63	9409003
69	9603017
75	201640024
76	9433001
89	7903079, 9042004, 9245001
91	8901050
92	39694
93	8852037

Chapter 18

31	9802038
32	9507009
33	9413042
36	9147059, 9325041, 9332044, 9438017, 9641034, 20042704E, 200651036
37	9437016, 200511003, 201251023, 201251024
39	9145031, 9145032, 200537036, 201221030, 39834
40	201422025
46	39817
51	200549008
52	200602037, 200602038
53	199930040
55	9641034, 200028007, 39879
60	9139003, 200451032, 39621, 39879

65	8822089, 8925091, 8936070, 9006051, 9014065, 9115035, 9252038, 9446036, 9720034, 200023052, 200024054, 200503027, 39801
66	200638027
68	9505019, 9551007, 200038054
69	9401033, 9438017
70	200203073–200203075, 200338023, 200431020, 200450040, 201625018, 201625019
71	200111047, 200111048
72	201450028, 201625004, 201625005
73	200225041
74	200413013, 200450040
76	200126035, 201410037, 201410038
77.1	201545027
78	200327063, 200327066
79	20006056
80	9410048, 9413042
81	201022023
82	9213029
84	8936070, 200003054
88	9214032, 9216033, 9233027, 9242014, 9325054, 9351042, 9401033, 9410048, 9508032, 9640024, 9640025, 9646034, 9649037, 200003053, 200308055
89	200609025, 201406018
91	8717062, 8833039, 8937038
102	8937038
103	9402034, 200006056
107	8951061, 9645022
108	8721092
114	9522023
117	9402034, 9403023
118	8629086, 8929087, 9403023
119	9403023

Chapter 19

3	39859
19	201338045, 201552033
20	8038024, 8207007, 8217023, 8312127, 8534101, 9605001, 9642054, 200003038
25	9213027, 200449034
28	8751006, 9130008
31	200214035, 200214036
37	9308047
39	200449304

43	200449034
45	200615026
55	9721034, 200503029, 200509026, 200705036
75	201640024
77	9113038, 200519087, 200520034, 200808039, 39735
79	201108040, 201126040
85	200818022
87	201332014
96	39575
104	200847017, 201620014
111	200634044, 200907040, 201246038, 201309017
113	9539003, 9542039, 9551010, 9551036
125	201247019
126	200602043, 200721020, 200721021, 200806014, 200806017, 200806018, 200907040, 201246038, 201309017
127	8812016, 9149007, 9715045, 200644039, 200803021, 200842046
128	201016090
130	200504035
131	200601031, 201002042, 201007067, 201016081
135	200849016
137	201246038
141	199908001
142	9110041, 9111001
147	8816004, 39724
149	9510066
151	9510066, 9722006
154	9111001
170	200805025, 200806022
171	8639074, 9231045
174	39865
179	8902003, 9626021
185	200834022
186	9102015
214	39885
219	200837044, 200851026, 200851035, 200903082, 200903089, 200903093, 200903094, 200910066, 200911044, 200913069, 200915054, 200915058, 200915062, 200919051, 200952060, 200952061, 201021034, 201021035, 201021047, 201023063–201023065, 201039040, 201045031, 201133016, 201331005, 201334042, 201338046, 201341035, 201341036, 201342012, 201342013, 201343026, 201405028, 201445016, 201447040–201447042
220	201331005, 201334042

221	200810031, 200829053, 200831028, 200842052, 200842058
225	200529008, 200531019, 200531022, 200531023, 200531028, 200550044, 200550045, 200644047, 200705030, 200715012, 200723027, 200724036, 200736033, 200803022, 200807018, 200808034, 200809034, 200809045, 200822040, 200824024, 200824028, 200824029, 200837041, 200842049, 200850040, 200909062, 200952060, 200952061, 201015043, 201025077, 201101029, 201121029, 201338051, 201428025, 201445016, 201450021, 201517018, 201525013, 201609008, 201613016, 201645019
227	201333014
230	9747003, 199924057–199924059, 200011050, 200850037
231	201013054, 201104046, 201218020, 201414027
232	201335017
236	200519084, 200531018, 201252027, 201450020, 201451041, 201451042
237	9315002
244	8807025, 8811003, 9034043, 9229011
271	8626002
273	9310031
277	9217003, 9314001
282	8750002
287	39522
294	39819
309	9309012
311	9132038
313	200728045
315	9021013
327	201642037
329	8627011, 8644065, 8729071, 8801003, 8804009, 8815019, 8824029, 8827054, 8831043, 8910024, 8934038, 8940025, 8944029, 9003091, 9007022, 9035045,9030014, 9042045, 9045019, 9102008, 9133024, 9201022, 9201022, 9214020, 9233025, 9242018, 9250023, 9315020, 9348018, 9406032, 9413046, 9735021, 9816008, 9850011, 199931045, 200034006, 200203027, 200344017, 200511001, 200652004, 200701009, 200752004, 201126001, 201223011, 201244005, 201327008
341	8524011, 9038018
356	200538039
394	9825035, 200030030, 200024055, 200123065, 200134032, 200214032, 200231020, 200232035
401	9130026
406	7821037, 8107117, 8147094, 8313060, 8314050, 8342022, 8425032, 8453038, 8603034, 8609020, 8621085, 8633034, 8650008, 8721061, 8728057, 8728058, 8728073, 200008024, 200008039
419	9130026
423	9130036, 9611044

427.1	201635004
427	9348021, 9515014, 200428021, 200430008
428	9244003, 200428021, 200430008
429	8719023, 9109030, 9149007
442	8639024, 8645036, 8705015, 8705038, 8705054, 8710016, 8713030, 8719023, 8721022, 8721061, 8722030, 8725010, 8725024, 8725033, 8728057, 8728058, 8729038, 8733018, 8737090, 8738036, 8740015, 8743032, 8747010, 8748017, 8748031, 8748024, 8749030, 8751017, 8752011, 8752022, 8753008, 8803020, 8803022, 8803033, 8803035, 8803057, 8804028, 8804058, 8806028, 8806062, 8809038, 8809047, 8809051, 8810060, 8810062, 8810084, 8814018, 8815009, 8815010, 8815027, 8816022, 8816040, 8819046, 8819055, 8820030, 8821030, 8821046 8823034, 8823035, 8824015, 8825034, 8825081, 8825087, 8825096, 8825100, 8826026, 8826037, 8826048, 8829041, 8829062, 8831047, 8832020, 8832047, 8832056, 8832066, 8832067, 8834031, 8835034, 8836056, 8836038, 8839014, 8839024, 8839039, 8839083, 8842070, 8842071, 8847032, 8849023, 8850037, 8850038, 8850063, 8920056, 8920023, 8920037, 8921024, 8921055, 8923024, 8925010, 8925014, 8925015, 8925028, 8926078, 8927058, 8928061, 8929039, 8930036, 8931008, 8931061, 8931068, 8931069, 8932031, 8933011, 8934009, 8934026, 8934052, 8935012, 8936028, 8938018, 8938044, 8939047, 8940032, 8940034, 8941052, 8942037, 8943051, 8943053, 8944008, 8944031, 8944032, 8944068, 8948057, 8948060, 8950050, 8951048, 8951057, 8951012, 8952016, 8952036, 9002016, 9004034, 9012031, 9015057, 9017052, 9025062, 9026015, 9026054, 9026055, 9027025, 9027028, 9027038, 9028033, 9032012, 9033062, 9034041, 9035013, 9035024, 9037019, 9037046, 9038036, 9041054, 9041070, 9042059, 9042060, 9043017, 9043035, 9043047, 9043067, 9045021, 9046039, 9046042, 9046060, 9049025, 9050052, 9050055, 9103009, 9106007, 9106023, 9106026, 9107032, 9109020, 9110004, 9110022, 9110062, 9113021, 9114055, 9115016, 9115037, 9129043, 9137019, 9140046, 9140050, 9140070, 9142019, 9143057, 9145042, 9149011, 9151026, 9201027, 9205020, 9206012, 9212010, 9217032, 9218014, 9238011, 9238024, 9240024, 9243044, 9245007, 9247014, 9247015, 9248024, 9249015, 9342029, 9347001, 9401003–9401006, 9401010, 9402028, 9403025, 9405024, 9409040, 9410034, 9411017, 9412027, 9421008, 9421009, 9423038, 9424007, 9425029, 9435031, 9436048, 9436052, 9440012, 9443032, 9443034, 9505015, 9506037, 9507019, 9522043, 9523008, 9524028, 9530017, 9530018, 9533040, 9540007, 9541030, 9544024, 9545015–9545017, 9546012, 9546014, 9549030, 9552045, 9605006, 9609034, 9613007,9622019 (withdrawn by 9631011), 9624013, 9627016, 9630018, 9631008, 9635017, 9637037, 9646018, 9646026, 9627016, 9706006, 9706007, 9722029, 9723042, 9725022, 9731023, 9740005, 9741002, 9742003, 9746035, 9746057, 9809013, 9819023, 9819029, 9823012, 9829024, 9830006, 9831025, 9835045, 9836014, 9844029, 9845018, 9846029, 9848025, 9849003, 9852019, 9852020, 9852043, 9853022, 199905026, 199909048, 199911047, 199913041, 199916045, 199916050, 199924046, 199924063, 199928011, 199928035, 199930028, 199931042, 199942008, 199952049, 199952083, 200003052, 200019023, 200022019, 200031045, 200040016, 200007015, 200008024, 200008039, 200023022, 200109002, 200116069, 200127033, 200151015, 200201001, 200210025, 200214026, 200243023, 200301025, 200318058, 200326012, 200327024, 200334021, 200337006, 200351006, 200403026, 200406024, 200416005, 200418018, 200418044, 200426010, 200426017, 200428015, 200428021, 200430008, 200439033, 200449018,

200453009, 200505013, 200506004, 200510016, 200521005, 200537006, 200538004, 200539006, 200606007, 200610001, 200626027, 200630001, 200637031, 200702022, 200704007, 200727002, 200730019, 200736022, 200738008, 200743011, 200807001, 200808025, 200811010, 200814014, 200817014, 200822019, 200823020, 200827004, 200828026, 200839005, 200839006, 200839009, 200841013, 200841018, 200841019, 200852017, 200908011, 200908013, 200909019, 200915022, 200919022, 200921024, 200924015, 200925032, 200937023, 200942021, 200943025, 200951025, 200953013, 201005024, 201010020, 201036008, 201047011, 201047012, 201047017, 201119008, 201136007, 201136008, 201138014, 201140006, 201142006, 201142016, 201146008, 39761, 201219006, 201219012, 201222018, 201225007, 201230017, 201230019, 201237005, 201245006 (rev'g 200908011), 201303008, 201308010, 201308011, 201314021–201314024, 201318001, 201338029 (mod. by 201509001), 201338034, 201346006, 201425001, 201425010, 201442037, 201515016, 201516031, 201528019, 201537019, 201550026, 201551001, 201551002, 201606004, 201607025, 201634012, 201635004, 39761

448	9439008, 201248011, 200238001
450	200026013, 200303025, 200314024
456	200243040
458	9627016, 9809013, 9822011, 9823029, 9852018, 199906036, 199928011, 199923029, 200116017, 200210024, 200222007, 200243040, 200403026, 200427016, 200827004
459	200551034, 201220005
460	201515016, 201516031, 201528019, 201537019, 39761

Chapter 20

13	200446025
33	200447047, 200508021, 200532051, 200605012, 200606041, 200625043, 200645025, 200708089, 200712045, 200730031, 200733028, 200738032, 200740013, 200740014, 200742029, 200801040, 200801041, 200814028, 200817014, 200817043, 200817055, 200837033, 200840048, 200840049, 200844021, 200844022, 200845053, 200846035, 200850036, 200850038, 200850039, 200850041, 200850042, 200850050, 200850059, 200912038, 200914063, 200914064, 200926036, 200926037, 200926049, 200928045, 200928046, 200943047, 200950049, 200950051, 201002041, 201004045, 201010028, 201014077, 201015045, 201016089, 201017078, 201017079, 201018015, 201021033, 201022029, 201024066, 201028042, 201036030, 201036031, 201037030, 201037039, 201039043, 201039044, 201039050, 201040022, 201040026, 201041047, 201044017, 201044021, 201047033, 201050033, 201050037, 201052022, 201101036, 201108042, 201115025, 201115026, 201120035, 201121032, 201128037, 201130010, 201130011, 201131026, 201143035, 201203022, 201203023, 201203030–201203032, 201204017, 201204019, 201211025, 201211026, 201216040, 201219027–201219029, 201225016, 201227006, 201228041, 201228042, 201229010, 201230025, 201233017, 201233018, 201235023, 201237019, 201237021, 201237022, 201238032, 201241010, 201241011, 201242016, 201242017, 201244021, 201245022, 201245025, 201245026, 201247018, 201250027–201250029, 201251018, 201252021, 201301021, 201302040, 201302041, 201303017, 201305012, 201307014–201307016, 201309015, 201309018,

	201309019, 201309029, 201310046, 201310048, 201311030, 201311033, 201313032, 201313033, 201314046, 201315037, 201321040, 201322042, 201323035, 201325014, 201326019, 201327015, 201327019, 201330037, 201334043, 201337018, 201343028, 201345032, 201346012, 201350047, 201403018, 201411037, 201414021, 201414024, 201415004, 201415006, 201417017, 201417019, 201417024, 201421022, 201424024, 201427018, 201433016, 201433019, 201433020, 201440020, 201440021, 201446029, 201504017, 201507023, 201507025, 201507026, 201538026, 201545028, 201545029, 201548021, 201551010, 201552034, 201615016, 201620011, 201643026, 201647008, 201648020
34	20042703E, 20044004E, 20044032E, 200511016, 200646018, 200649037, 200707161, 200710012, 200725040, 200726032, 200730031, 200732017, 200732019, 200736031, 200736032, 200748019, 200748021, 200752043, 200801040, 200801041, 200809032, 200809033, 200840048, 200844021, 200844022, 200844029, 200846031, 200850038, 200850039, 200850041, 200850042, 200850050, 200850059, 200908051, 200909070, 200930055, 200937039, 201004044, 201004066, 201007072–201007076, 201013062, 201021046, 201035033, 201035038, 201036031, 201037036, 201039034, 201101027, 201113041, 201115025, 201121025, 201122023, 201130018, 201131024, 201142029, 201218018, 201225014, 201252022, 201306028, 201321040, 201322042, 201326019, 201329020, 201331008, 201335023, 201335026, 201337018, 201338049, 201349017, 201350041, 201351026, 201351029, 201402016, 201405017, 201406012, 201418059, 201442057, 201447059, 201450022, 201451032, 201451035, 201451043, 201451045, 201503020, 201503021, 201517010, 201517014, 201518020, 201524026, 201533022, 201534014, 201538026, 201541013, 201543017, 201543019, 201548024, 201603036, 201603042, 201620012, 201627002, 201640025, 201641023, 201647008
64	9525056
84	9112006, 9201035
105	20044013E
115	8731032
119	38394
122	35638
134	9231045, 9621035
136	8838047
140	20044033E
159	8807081, 8808070
162	200511016
164	8807081, 8808070
165	9025089, 37180, 38283, 39670
166	32518, 35865
187	20044004E, 20044032E, 200447050, 200851037, 201505039, 201511026, 201552034, 201637017, 201640019, 201648019
192	201615016
232	201318013

235	201110013
243	200723032
252	9428035
288	39876
299.1	201511024
300	9530024–9530026
309	200852036
346	200635018
358	37789, 39005, 39444, 39546, 39732
361	201634025
362	201432037, 201438030
363	201223020
379	20044004E, 20044032E, 200511017, 200524029, 200606040, 200606041, 200649034, 200711041, 200729042, 200736037, 200737044, 200749026, 200803026, 200806021, 200810025, 200817041, 200817048, 200817049, 200818023, 200818028, 200819021, 200822034, 200822044, 200839040, 200840050, 200841039, 200842057, 200845053, 200936039, 200944053, 201007060, 201017064, 201023058, 201025083, 201029031, 201029032, 201029035, 201030035, 201035034, 201037029, 201049043, 201049048, 201104066, 201109028, 201114036, 201125044, 201125045, 201128030, 201130012, 201147033, 201149045, 201215010, 201217020, 201217021, 201231012, 201234029, 201235021,201249016, 201303018–201303020, 201304011, 201306028, 201309016, 201315028, 201318027, 201322041, 201324020, 201325017, 201327016, 201327017, 201331007, 201338052, 201338053, 201338059, 201343028, 201345030, 201346012, 201404013, 201405024, 201407019, 201407020, 201408029, 201409012, 201414022, 201414023, 201415006, 201422033, 201431032, 201432027, 201434023, 201441017, 201443021, 201451031, 201451036, 201452018, 201514015, 201517019, 201526021, 201529012, 201529013, 201544027–201544029, 201545029, 201548021, 201601014, 201610020, 201610025, 201610026, 201619010, 201626025, 201630017, 201631014, 201632020, 201632023, 201634029, 201636046, 201641026, 20164102, 201643025

Chapter 21

68	200435019–200435022

Chapter 22

15	39694
25	200449035
36	201430014
60	201408030
66	39694
69	9244003
107	9622002
119	9507020
120	9507020

122	9332042
141	9332042, 9347034
212	9510047, 9534021, 9602026, 9636016
215	199919038

Chapter 23

4	9809062
5	20044010E, 2004040E, 200724033, 200748021, 200809038, 200928045, 201416011
33	200830027
42	39694
95	8906062
109	200437040
126	9433001
141	201214035, 201224034
143	9117001
144	200903080
145	200843033, 200903080, 201214035, 201224034
148	200833021, 200843033, 201214035, 201224034, 201424028, 201449002

Chapter 24

30	9120029
35	200027056
56	200704035, 200704036, 200710013–200710016, 200711025–200711039, 200723031, 200732021, 200732022, 200733032, 200733033, 200749023, 200803019, 200803020, 200806019, 200807017, 200810026–200810028, 200810030, 200816034, 200816035, 200817038, 200818025, 200818026, 200821034, 200821035, 200824021, 200824023, 200850048, 200850049, 200904025, 200904037, 200905030, 200905031, 200906053–200906056, 200913063, 200913065, 200919055–200919057, 200922061, 200951037, 200952059, 201003023, 201003024, 201007063, 201011035, 201016082, 201016083, 201016085, 201016086, 201022022, 201105049, 201105050, 201123042–201123044, 201208038, 201209014, 201210014, 201218015, 201223021, 201311032, 201311036, 201408032, 201408034, 201613014, 201613015, 201636043
68	9242035
71	8722082, 9735047, 32896, 36827
72	9217001
76	9325061
92	36827
94	9720035
101	8822057
102	8840020, 8841041
103	8806056, 9318047

110	9042038
115	201306023
128	201113035
129	9438040, 9505020, 9509041, 9510039, 200148085
131	200328045, 200328046, 200328048
145	8829003, 8932004, 9309002
149	8717002, 8717063, 8733037, 8734005, 8901064, 8934050, 8936013, 9003059,
150	9017058, 9018049, 9240937, 9337027, 9340061, 9340062, 9349022, 9425031
167	8922064, 9407005, 9413020
169	9417003
173	9137002, 9417003, 9509002, 9721001
174	199941048
177	8641001
181	9302023
185	9539005
188	8819005, 9723046
199	9535023
204	9750056
205	9641011, 9728034, 9715041
207	8732029, 9041045, 9350045
229	9014069
239	8743081, 8743086, 8743087, 9347036
241	8643091
245	9149002
247	8643049, 9141053, 9150052, 9152039
263	200150033, 200150035
269	200352018, 200352019
274	9107030, 9110012, 9110042, 9137002, 9321072, 9321087, 9323035, 9329041, 9812031, 9814048, 200147059, 200149044, 200203070, 200216036, 200222032, 200230004, 200234071, 200242041, 200243056, 200444030, 200446011, 200528030, 200532058, 200536024, 200804026, 200807016, 201250025, 201406020, 201408031, 201417018, 201424025, 201425016, 201430018
292	201417018, 201424025, 201425016, 201430018
294	9137049, 200752042, 200833022
295	9138003, 9145002, 9147005, 9320050, 9323035, 200501017, 200512025, 39864
301	8025222
324	9137002, 39860
331	8641090
335	9231001
337	8650083

338	9014069
340	39843
341	39762
344	8735004, 8815031, 8817066, 9730941, 9739042
346	8736046
351	8736046, 8817017, 9445024
361	201123045
363	8721103, 8809092, 8921091, 8941082, 9023041
369	9736047
372	9750056, 9803001
373	9110042, 9226055
380	9750056
387	200041030
388	8809092, 8817017
391	201221024
396	199917084
397	8949093
398	8626102, 8640052–8640054, 8640056, 8640057, 8645064, 8833002
400	8814001, 9138003
404	8641060
415	9428035
417	9349024
424	9645027
425	8815002
429	9147054, 9220054, 9550001, 9527001
431	8432003
445	8734004, 39735
449	9029047, 9550001
463	9847001
470	9428035
472	8852002
473	9128003
479	200709073, 200710017, 200710019, 200717029–200717031, 200717033, 200717034, 200725046–200725057
483	9137002, 9147054, 9205037, 9220054, 9306030, 9318005, 9535004 (withdrawn by 9542046), 9612003, 200448048, 39827, 39860
488	9302035
490	9023003, 199914035
491	9325003
492	9128002

497	8726069, 9302023
508	8947002, 9044071, 9234002, 9304001, 9345004, 9724006
513	8932004
519	9023001, 9023002, 9204007, 9402005
525	8403013, 8834006, 8835001, 9023001, 9023002, 9217002, 9247001, 9248001, 9402005, 9419003, 9734002
534	9623035
537	8725058
538	9736046
540	9315001, 9321005
549	9250001
554	200844029
565	9822004
567	9521004
568	8846002
582	201222040
584	9608003, 9711002, 9718029, 9752023, 200108048
586	200910061
591	9814039, 9819049, 9839042, 9853026, 199924065, 199943049, 199949038, 200108045, 200108048, 200108051, 200132139, 200134027, 200215057–200215060, 200233025, 200238051, 200245057, 200108048 200032046, 200036049
592	200108046, 200108047, 200108049
639	200029055
678	200301030
680	200852037
687	201128027, 201221024
688	201221024
693	8708031, 8717066, 200003048
695	8738006, 9144044, 199952089
696	8522040, 8651091, 8906003, 8935058, 9147058, 9204048, 9726005
697	201020022, 201246040
700	200821036, 201206018, 201246040
705	9246032, 9246033
707	201434024, 201434026
708	8950073, 9047040
709	200852037
710	200125096
711	9241052, 200537037
712	9651001

714	8044023, 8104098, 8107114, 8110164, 8338138, 8738006, 8807082, 9031052, 9407023, 9703026, 200041038, 200233032
716	9010025, 9431001, 9533014
717	201407024
719	8818008, 8822057, 8923077, 9012001, 9031052, 9042043, 9047069, 9108021, 9110012, 9218006, 9218007, 9450045, 9508031, 9527033, 9743054, 200150040, 200137061, 200233023, 200318076, 200449033, 200534025, 39826
723	9128020
727	9002030
729	200224014, 200351032
734	8721104, 8721107, 9042038
737	9619077
738	9637053, 9642051
740	9717004

Chapter 25

18	9012058
20	199914042, 199928042, 200518081
21	9042038
22	8708031, 8836037, 9442035, 9826046, 200715015, 201221024
23	200315028, 200315032, 200315034
25	201644019
26	9030048
32	9231045
34	9151001, 9309002, 9306030, 201644019, 39827
40	8839016
43	9346014
44	8827017
45	8222066, 8645050, 8717066, 8717078, 8721102, 8728060, 8808002, 8808003, 8810097, 8824054, 8828011, 8845073, 8846005, 8922084, 8941011, 8941062, 8948023, 9015038, 9023091, 9024026, 9043039, 9108021, 9316045, 9316052, 9319042, 9319043, 9404003, 9404004, 9417036, 9417042, 9417043, 9419033, 9436001, 9440001, 9441001, 9450028, 9503024, 9552019, 9703025, 9705001, 9709029, 9714016, 9723001, 9724006, 9810030, 9816027, 200046039, 200149035, 200149043, 20019037, 200225046, 200601033, 201435017, 39615
46	9139029, 9212030, 9231045, 9234043, 9551019, 200601033, 200621031, 200637041, 35957, 39568
47	9450045, 200041031, 200147058, 200148057, 200148074, 201130005
48	8950072, 9139029, 9141051, 9146047, 9702003
49	8445005, 8720005, 8802009, 8925029, 39825
54	8713072, 8822096, 8932042, 9245036, 9246032, 9246033, 9301024, 9315021, 9703025, 9850020, 200532058
56	201435017

57	200032050
59	201120029–201120032
62	9136037
67	9108034, 9108043, 9127045, 9128030, 9132040, 9132061, 9144032–9144035, 9150047, 9204048, 9247038, 9252028, 9547040, 9551021, 200637041
69	9619068
70	9616039, 9619068, 9619069, 9630031, 9631025, 9631029, 9652028, 9704010, 9745025, 200246032
72	9108034, 9108043, 9128030, 9132040, 9132061, 9144032, 9144035, 9150047, 9252028 (modified by 9428037), 9308040, 9316032, 9319044, 9401029, 9407005, 9411018, 9411019, 9412039, 9414002, 9432019, 9629032, 9651014, 9803024, 9826046, 9844004, 9853034, 199952071, 200151046, 200151062, 200219037, 200237027, 200041038, 200510029, 200530029, 200532057
91	8201024
95	199928042, 199952086, 200315028, 200315032, 200315034
96	9043039
97	8641061, 8831007, 8932004, 8942070, 9033056, 9302023, 9544029, 9605001, 9704012, 199952086, 200251016–200251018
121	200628039
126	39786
128	8832043, 39752
142	8736046, 9241055
146	201434024, 201434026
149	200628039
151	8915005, 9217001
160	8728080
164	200531020
169	39734
176	9302035, 9303030
182	9232003
183	8920084
190	9726030
195	9652004
215	9319044, 9750056
217	201434025
220	9847002
223	9145003, 9328003
232	9141003, 9141004, 9145031, 9145032, 9147059, 9216033, 9242014, 9247039
234	9247039, 9517035, 9841003
235	8905002, 8943009, 9721034, 9310034, 9344028, 9628022, 199932050, 39773, 200003036

238	8728008, 8728009, 8925091, 9016039, 9310034, 9351042, 9410048, 9413042, 9818001

Chapter 26

26	200846040
40	200540016
45	20044034E, 200536021, 200845053
52	200930049
53	201023058, 201215013, 201219025, 201229010, 201242015, 201244021, 201310045, 201322041, 201325017, 201332013, 201334044, 201340021, 201404012, 201408030, 201427018, 201433017, 201433019, 201503016, 201552032, 201603035, 201649016
158	9145001
226	9145039
227	201330043
237	39833
287	39830
288	39830

Chapter 27

27	9408066
55	201409010, 201413013, 201419018
243	201150031, 201150033, 201209007, 201209008, 201218022, 201225015, 201231017, 201237022, 201240028, 201240029, 201241010, 201245023, 201247025, 201252020, 201252028, 201317012, 201317020, 201321038, 201323027, 201327011, 201329019, 201330042, 201333016, 201338054, 201340021, 201404012
249	200634047, 200636102, 200636104, 200646018, 200649037, 2006650027, 200651035, 200714028, 200720028, 200723028, 200743039, 200749027, 200751036, 200752039–200752041, 200802034, 200802037, 200802038, 200803023–200803025, 200803027, 200803028, 200805024, 200808033, 200808035, 200808037, 200808040, 200808041, 200809036, 200817047, 200817052–200817054, 200817063, 200822030–200822033, 200822035–200822039, 200822043, 200829036, 200829039, 200829040, 200829042, 200829047, 200829052, 200829055, 200833019, 200833020, 200833023, 200833025, 200833026, 200834023, 200837034, 200837037–200837039, 200837048, 200837049, 200837051, 200837053, 200842054, 200852056, 200844018, 200844019, 200844023–200844026, 200844031, 200846027, 200846030, 200846032, 200846035, 200850040, 200850044, 200850047, 200903083–200903088, 200903091, 200903092, 200903095, 200909063, 200909067, 200909068, 200910062–200910065, 200915056, 200919054, 201007068, 201007070, 201007003–201007075, 201013057–201013059, 201013063, 201013064, 201021031, 201021032, 201023061, 201029030, 201029033, 201029034, 201029041, 201035024, 201035025, 201035027, 201035028, 201035031, 201037031, 201037033, 201039045, 201040023, 201040029, 201040031, 201040032, 201040035, 201040038, 201042038, 201042039, 201045025, 201045026, 201045028–201045030, 201049044, 201049045, 201050035, 201050038, 201050041, 201101025, 201101026,

201102065, 201102066, 201103056, 201103061, 201105042, 201105044, 201106016, 201006017, 201108048, 201111014, 201113049, 201116031–201116033, 201118022, 201119035, 201120037, 201121023, 201121026, 201122024, 201122026, 201123039, 201124027, 201124028, 201127015–201127017, 201129041–201129043, 201146021, 201149034, 201330042, 201333016, 201338054, 201340021, 201340022, 201404012, 201414022, 201414026, 201418054, 201418057, 201428024, 201445011, 201445012, 201451046, 201502016, 201505043, 201514010, 201519032, 201520013, 201526018, 201526019, 201526022, 201527044, 201527045, 201539033, 201552032, 201603035, 201603041, 201618013, 201630017, 201631012, 201641024, 201645014–201645016, 201646006, 201649014

Chapter 28

2	9141050
4	9446033, 9446034
9	201203019
22	8906008
87	8728057, 8728058, 8728073
88	200606039, 200649037, 200709071, 200720027, 200720029, 200720030, 200725041, 200725042, 200732018, 200735031, 200738031, 200740015, 200746020, 200746021, 200748 020, 200749027, 200751306, 200802034, 200802037, 200802038, 200803023, 200803028, 200805024, 200817047, 200817050, 200817052–200817054, 200817056, 200817057, 200817061–200817063, 200840051, 200844017, 200844028, 200844029, 200846027, 200846030–200846032, 200846035, 201017059, 201017061–201017063, 201017065, 201021031, 201021032, 201023061, 201035028, 201040023, 201040029, 201040031, 201040032, 201040035, 201040038, 201042038, 201042039, 201045025, 201045026, 201045028–201045030, 201103056, 201103061, 201105042, 201105044, 201106016, 201006017, 201113049, 201115025, 201118022, 201119035, 201121023, 201121026, 201144031, 201231017, 201247025, 201317020, 201318011, 201318025, 201218028, 201317020, 201323026, 201323030, 201330040, 201335015, 201335016, 201335025, 201338049, 201406014, 201406015, 201406017, 201407025, 201418058, 201445011, 201445012, 201449001, 201517013
99	8642083, 8709049, 8724057, 8738039, 8747032, 8818046, 8819037, 8819057, 8819071, 8825044, 8834010, 9040038, 9103047, 9253044, 9310045, 9310068, 9518021, 9619024, 200545047, 200615027
104	9803015
119	8710016, 8715013, 8725010, 8725024, 8738077, 8823091, 8926078, 8932031, 8944068, 9029043, 9150055, 9348021, 9401010, 9409040, 9421009, 9436052, 9540007, 200049035, 200049036
122	9411011
123	9825030, 200436019, 2005198083, 200527019, 200549009, 200601036–200601039, 200607022, 200607024, 200607025, 200612016, 200612017, 200616034, 200616036, 20061307, 200622054, 201217025, 201551001
328	9042043, 39826
349	8725056, 9201039, 200449033, 39718, 39737, 39799, 39828, 39829, 39866
350	201218016, 201445012, 201517013

352	39761
354	9752023
356	9645007
357	39829
361	39655, 39764
363	9108021, 9110012, 9743054, 200449033
384	39778
399	39684, 39874
402	9527035
420	9033056
441	9010011
473	201150027, 201202017, 201230002, 201234004, 201303001, 201316007, 201320013, 201332008, 201425002, 201447018, 201505029–201505033, 201506007, 201507014, 201507015, 201508004–201508007, 201516021, 201516052, 201536003, 201538003, 201543005, 201548010, 201606005, 201609002, 201642010
546	201322041
558	200441012, 200441016
559	200931059
560	200931059, 201144031, 201149033, 201149034, 201150031, 201150033, 201222047, 201240030, 201252021, 201252028, 201318015, 201321040, 2011329019, 201338038, 201338049, 201350046, 201349017, 201402015, 201418056, 201449001

Chapter 29

16	9740001–9740004
27	200714026
38	9002036, 9014061
47	9119069, 9547013
48	9828032, 199943035, 200004041, 200622049–200622051, 200622059, 200634039
50	9629020
54	9135003
55	8714050
59	9031051
70	201222069
72	201113036
79	9119069, 9242002
80	9246033
98	199924065, 199949038
99	9839038, 9839042
108	8810048

109	8417019, 9335022
117	7903079, 9042004

Chapter 30

7	9308047
18	8606056, 8705087, 8706012, 8709071, 8720048, 8749058, 8749059, 8805059, 8810082, 8811003, 8819034, 8821044, 8833002, 8840056, 8846053, 8901012, 8901050, 8903083, 8909029, 8925051, 8934064, 8952076, 9005068, 9024068, 9024026, 9024086, 9030063, 9033069, 9108016, 9119060, 9131058, 9245031, 9308047, 9311031, 9316052, 9341024, 9346013, 9402031–9402933, 9408026, 9417036, 9417042, 9417043, 9421006, 9438041, 9447043, 9523027, 9528020, 9530009, 9535022, 9539014, 9542045 (amended by 9720036), 9547039, 9626021, 9630014, 9637051, 9705028, 9721038, 9726010, 9720031, 9722032, 199941048, 200425050 (reissued as 200444044), 201406019, 201644019
28	8934064, 9242038, 9408026, 9421006, 199941051, 201503018
31	199929006
36	39598, 39646, 39866
37	39776
41	8625078, 8720048, 8732040, 8743070, 8840056, 8934064, 9027050, 9305026, 9734026, 9734027, 9734036, 9734037, 9734039, 9734040, 199938041, 200037050, 200130048, 200130049, 200130055, 200132040, 200149043, 200405016
49	201644019
51	200602040, 200602041
55	201328035
63	8839002
65	8709051, 9305026
84	9105029, 9303030, 9305026, 39866
108	8729005, 8832084, 8833002, 8903083, 8922047, 9010073, 9027051, 9045003, 9108016, 9308047, 9404004, 9438029, 9535022, 9547039, 9705028, 200132040
126	200602040, 200602041
132	200139006
134	8849072, 9136032, 9148051

Chapter 31

28	8925052, 8945063
31	9105029, 9105031, 9215046, 9308034, 9323030, 9352030, 9407022, 9518014, 8621060, 8903060, 8912003, 8925052, 8936073, 8945063, 9029034, 9035072, 9517029, 200206058
34	200304042, 200448048
39	20044018E, 20044020E, 20044030E
40	8925051, 9547039
46	20044020E–20044030E
49	9230001, 9350044

65	8628049, 8705089, 8715039, 9715040, 8717057, 8723065, 8724060, 8727080, 8806057, 8807012, 8814047, 8817039, 8818008, 8820093, 8833009, 8901054, 8909036, 8912003, 8912041, 8915065, 8917055, 8931083, 8936047, 8936077, 8938002, 8939024, 8940039, 8941006, 8942099, 8943050, 8943064, 9021050, 9029034, 9109066, 9122061, 9122062, 9122070, 9147058, 9318033, 9319044, 9323030, 9345057, 9349032, 9352030, 9438030, 9502035 (updating 8528080), 9603839, 9642051, 9736039, 9736043, 9739001, 9709014, 9718036, 9722032, 39732
66	200211052

Chapter 32

18	9451001
29	199913044–199913046
33	8944017
41	8640054, 8640056, 8640057
53	200236049
55	9435029, 9752062, 9752063, 9752065, 9752067, 9839032, 200027057, 200108048
56	9425009, 200704032, 200813037–200843039
58	200702035
60	9623057, 9623059, 9623060, 9738055, 9738056, 9620027, 200150026
61	20003029, 200124021
64	200541043, 200541044
65	200714020–200714024
66	200843041
73	201446026
74	200149035, 200418047, 200446011, 200831032, 200831033
98	200044040, 200218037
102	200325003, 200325004, 200327065, 200327067
103	200102053
110	200325004
112	200333032, 200333033, 200510030
114	200333032, 200333033
121	8921203, 8932085, 8941006, 8949034, 9001030, 9521013
125	200606047
183	8219066, 9538026–9538031

Cumulative Table of Cases
Discussed in *Bruce R. Hopkins'*
Nonprofit Counsel

The following cases, referenced in the text, are discussed in greater detail in one or more issues of the author's monthly newsletter, as indicated.

Case	Book Sections	Newsletter Issue
ABA Retirement Funds v. United States	14.1(c), 14.2(a), 14.2(b)	July 2013, Oct. 2014
Airlie Found., Inc. v. United States	20.3, 26.5(b)(iv)	July 1993, Nov. 2003
Alpha Medical, Inc. v. Comm'r	20.4	July 1999
Alabama Cent. Credit Union v. United States	24.12(c)	June 1987
Alive Fellowship of Harmonious Living v. Comm'r	10.9, 26.5(b)(iv)	May 1984
Allen v. Wright	6.2(b)(iii)	Aug. 1984, July 1985
Alumni Ass'n of the Univ. of Oregon, Inc. v. Comm'r	24.5(i)(ii)	Dec. 1999
Amend16Robert Wirengard v. Comm'r American Academy of Family Physicians v. United States	4.5(a) 24.2(b), 24.2(g)	May 2005 June 1995, Oct. 1996
American Ass'n of Christian Schools Voluntary Employees Beneficiary Ass'n Welfare Plan Trust v. United States	13.1(b), 18.3, 27.13(a)	Oct. 1996
American Campaign Academy v. Comm'r	4.5(a), 4.5(b), 8.3(a) (i), 8.4, 20.3, 20.11(a), 20.11(c)	July 1989, June 2001, Feb. 2005
American Civil Liberties Union Found. of Louisiana v. Crawford	1.4, 10.1(b)	June 2002
American College of Physicians v. United States	4.9, 24.5(h)(iii)	Oct. 1984, June 1986
American Hosp. Ass'n v. United States	24.5(h)(ii)	May 1987
American Medical Ass'n v. United States	24.1, 24.5(h)	Oct. 1987, Nov. 1987, Jan. 1990
American Plywood Ass'n v. United States	14.1(c)(ii), 14.2(c)	Apr. 2008
American Postal Workers Union, AFL-CIO v. United States	16.1, 24.5(f)	Feb. 1990, Apr. 1991
American Society of Ass'n Executives v. United States	22.9	Jan. 1999, Jan. 2000, July 2000

Case	Book Sections	Newsletter Issue
American Tradition Partnership, Inc., fka Western Tradition Partnership, Inc. v. Bullock	23.2(b)(ii)	Aug. 2012
Americans for Prosperity Foundation v. Harris	28.3(i)	Mar. 2016, July 2016, Aug. 2016
AmeriDream, Inc. et al. v. Jackson	7.5	Jan. 2008
Anclote Psychiatric Center, Inc. v. Comm'r	20.5(c), 21.4(a), 26.5(b)(i), 31.9(b)	June 1992, Sep. 1998
Anonymous v. Comm'r	28.11(a)(ii)	Jan. 2016
Aries Communications, Inc. v. Comm'r	20.4(b)	June 2013
Asmark Institute, Inc. v. Comm'r	4.11	Mar. 2011, Sep. 2012
Ass'n of the Bar of the City of New York v. Comm'r	23.2(c)	Nov. 1987, Nov. 1998
At Cost Services, Inc. v. Comm'r	4.10(b), 24.1	Jan. 2001
Atlanta Athletic Club v. Comm'r	15.5, 15.6	Mar. 1993
Beiner, Inc. v. Comm'r	20.4(b)	Dec. 2004
Bellco Credit Union v. United States	19.7, 24.4(a), 24.5(g)	Apr. 2009, June 2010, June 2014
Bethel Conservative Mennonite Church v. Comm'r	4.3(b), 4.4, 27.13(a)	Dec. 1984
Bluetooth SIG, Inc. v. United States	14.1(c)(iii), 14.2(b)(i), 14.2(c)(ii)	Apr. 2008, Sep. 2010
Bluman v. Federal Election Commission	____	Mar. 2012
Bob Jones Univ. Museum and Gallery, Inc. v. Comm'r.	28.1	Aug. 1996, Oct. 2013
Bobo v. Christus Health	6.3(j)-(m)	Aug. 2005
Boy Scouts of America v. Dale	1.7, 6.2(d)	Nov. 1999, Aug. 2000
Branch Ministries v. Richardson	23.2(v)	Sep. 1997
Branch Ministries v. Rossotti	23.2(v), 23.3	June 1999, July 2000
Brentwood Academy v. Tennessee Secondary Schools Athletic Ass'n	4.8(a)	Apr. 2001
Brown v. Buhman	10.1(a)(i)	Feb. 2014
Brook, Inc. v. Comm'r	15.3,15.5	Oct. 1986
Brown Shoe Co. v. Comm'r	15.3	Oct. 2001
Buckley v. Valeo	23.2(b)(ii)	Oct. 2012
Budlong v. Graham	10.1(b)	June 2006
Buder v. United States	7.15(b)	Dec. 1993
Burton v. William Beaumont Hosp.	6.3(j)-(m)	Feb. 2005
Burwell v. Hobby Lobby Stores, Inc.	____	Sep. 2014
Calhoun Academy v. Comm'r	6.2(b)(iii)	Apr. 1990

Case	Book Sections	Newsletter Issue
Camps Newfound/Owatonna, Inc. v. Town of Harrison	1.1, 1.l(a), 12.3(b)(iv)	July 1997
Capital Gymnastics Booster Club, Inc. v. Comm'r	7.16(c), 20.11	Nov. 2013
Caracci v. Comm'r	20.5(c), 21.1, 21.4(a), 21.11, 31.9(b)	Feb. 2000, July 2002, Sep. 2006
Catholic Answers, Inc. v. United States	23.3	June 2009, Dec. 2009, Jan. 2012
Center for Competitive Politics v. Harris	28.3(i)	July 2015, Mar. 2016
Chicago Metropolitan Ski Council v. Comm'r	24.5(h)	May 1995
Chief Steward of the Ecumenical Temples & Worldwide Peace Movement v. Comm'r	4.3(b), 4.5(a), 25.1(a)(i)	May 1985
Child Adult Intervention Servs., Inc. v. Comm'r	27.2(a)(v)	May 2012
Christian Coalition of Florida, Inc. v. United States	23.5, 26.5(a)	June 2009, Oct. 2010, Jan. 2012
Christian Coalition Int'l v. United States	27.9(a)(ii)	Nov. 2002
Church by Mail, Inc. v. Comm'r	4.5(a), 20.5, 20.11(b)	Oct. 1984
Church of Ethereal Joy v. Comm'r	20.11	Sep. 1984
Church of Spiritual Technology v. United States	4.6, 25.1(a)(i), 26.5(b)(iv)	Dec. 1989
Citizens United v. Federal Election Comm'n	17.1(a), 23.2(g)(ii)	June 2009, Aug. 2009, Nov. 2009, March 2010, Apr. 2010, Aug. 2012, Oct. 2012
Citizens United v. Schneiderman	28.3(i)	Oct. 2015
City of Arlington v. FCC	App. A	Apr. 2014
Cleveland Athletic Club, Inc. v. United States	15.3, 15.5	Feb. 1986
CNG Transmission Management VEBA v. United States	18.3, 24.10	Jan. 2009
Colony, Inc. v. Comm'r	App. A	June 2012
Colorado State Chiropractic Soc'y v. Comm'r	4.3(a), 26.5(b)(iv)	Dec. 1989
Columbia Park & Recreation Assn, Inc. v. Comm'r	13.2(a), 20.3	Feb. 1987
Common Cause v. Schultz	26.5(a)	Aug. 1999
Community Education Found. v. Comm'r	4.9(a)	Mar. 2017
Community First Credit Union v. United States	19.7, 24.5(g)	Mar. 2008, July 2009, June 2014

Case	Book Sections	Newsletter Issue
Community Humanitarian Assoc., Inc. v. Town of Ramapo	6.3(i)	May 2016
CORE Special Purpose Fund v. Comm'r	24.5(h), 24.14	May 1985
Council for Education, The v. Comm'r	5.2	Feb. 2014
CRSO v. Comm'r	12.3(c), 27.13	July 2007
Credit Union Ins. Corp. v. United States	14.1(a)(i), 19.8	July 1995, Sep. 1996
Cutter v. Wilkinson	10.1(a)(i)	May 2005, Sep. 2005
Davenport v. Washington Education Ass'n	15.1	Mar. 2007
Delaware County, PA v. Federal Housing Finance Agency	____	June 2013
Democratic Leadership Council, Inc. v. United States	26.3	June 2008, Aug. 2008, Mar. 2009
Devine Brothers, Inc. v. Comm'r	20.4(b)	Mar. 2003
Dexsil v. Comm'r	20.4(b)	Aug. 1998, Jan. 2000
Disabled Am. Veterans v. Comm'r	24.1(a)	Apr. 1990
Doe v. Kamehameha Schools/Bernice Pauahi Bishop Estate	6.2(e)	Oct. 2005, Feb. 2007, July 2007
Dzina v. United States	21.1	Jan. 2005
Easter House v. United States	4.4, 4.9, 4.10(b)	Aug. 1987
Ecclesiastical Order of the Ism of Am. v. Comm'r	4.10(a), 10.2(c), 24.5(i) (v)	Dec. 1985
Educational Assistance Found. for the Descendants of Hungarian Immigrants in the Performing Arts, Inc. v. United States	20, 27.3	Sep. 2015
E.J. Harrison & Sons, Inc. v. Comm'r	20.4(b), 20.4(g)	Sep. 2005, Sep. 2006
Elk Grove Unified School District v. Newdow est of Hawaii v. Comm'r	10.1(a)(ii) 4.5(a), 8.6,20.11(b)	Mar. 2004, May 2004 June 2001
Exacto Spring Corp. v. Comm'r	20.4(b)	Jan. 2000
Executive Network Club, Inc. v. Comm'r	24.7(a)	Mar. 1995
Exploratory Research, Inc. v. Comm'r	5.6(n), 25.1(b)	July 2008
FEC v. Wisconsin Right to Life, Inc.	17.1(a)	July 2007, Sep. 2007
Families Against Government Slavery v. Commissioner	8.2, 25.1(a)(i)	May 2007
Family Trust of Massachusetts, Inc. v. United States	20.4(b)	Nov. 2012, Sep. 2013
Federal Election Comm'n v. Beaumont	23.2(b)(ii)	Oct. 2012
First National Bank of Boston v. Bellotti	23.2(b)(ii)	Oct. 2012
Fisher v. Univ. of Texas at Austin	6.2(e)	Apr. 2012, Dec. 2012, Sep. 2013, Oct. 2014, Feb. 2016, Sep. 2016

Case	Book Sections	Newsletter Issue
Florida v. Department of Health and Human Services	____	Apr. 2011, Oct. 2011
Florida Hosp. Trust Fund v. Comm'r	27.13(b)	Sep. 1994, Mar. 1996
Florida Independent Colleges and Universities Risk Management Ass'n, Inc. v. United States	11.6, 27.13(b)	May 2012
Fondel v. United States	26.5(b)(i)	Oct. 1996, Mar. 1999
Found. of Human Understanding v. United States	10.3(a), 10.3(b), 10.3(c)	Oct. 2009, Oct. 2010
Founding Church of Scientology v. United States	5.2, 10.2(a), 20.3, 20.4(b), 20.5(a), 25.1(a)(i)	July 1992
Fraternal Order of Police, Ill. State Troopers Lodge No. 41 v. Comm'r	24.5(h)(i), 24.6(g)	Nov. 1986
Free Fertility Found. v. Comm'r	5.2, 7.6	Sep. 2010
Freedom From Religion Found. v. Koskinen	27.7(c)	June 2016
Freedom From Religion Found., Inc. v. Lew	10.1(a)(ii)	Jan. 2014, June 2016
Freedom From Religion Found., Inc. v. Shulman	10.1(a), 23, 26.6(c)	Oct. 2013
Freedom From Religion Found., Inc. v. Werfel	10.1(a), 25.2(b), 27.2(b)(i)	Oct. 2013
Freedom Path, Inc. v. Lerner	26.15	Aug. 2016
Fund for Anonymous Gifts v. Internal Revenue Serv.	11.8(c)	July 1997, June 1999
Fund for the Study of Economic Growth Tax Reform v. Internal Revenue Serv.	22.3(c)(i), 22.3(c)(iii)	Feb. 1999
GameHearts v. Comm'r	4.11(d)	Jan. 2015, Jan. 2016
Gardner v. Comm'r	28.18(c), (e), (f)	Nov. 2015
Gardner v. North Mississippi Health Services, Inc.	6.3(j)-(m)	Aug. 2005
Gaylor and Freedom From Religion Found. v. U.S.	10.1(c)	Jan. 2017
Geisinger Health Plan v. Comm'r	7.6(e), 25.10(a)	Mar. 1993, Sep. 1994, Jan. 2016
George v. Comm'r	4.1(a)	Oct. 2015
Gonzales v. O Centro Espirita Beneficente Uniao Do Vegetal	10.1	Apr. 2006
Good News Club v. Milford Central School	3.3(h), 10.1(a)(iii)	Aug. 2001
Good Samaritan Hosp. v. Shalala	____	Oct. 2012
Green v. Connally	6.3(i)	Oct. 2013

Case	Book Sections	Newsletter Issue
Gwaltney of Smithfield, Ltd. v. Chesapeake Bay Found., Inc.	———	Oct. 2012
H.W. Johnson v. Comm'r	20.4(b)	July 2016
Haffner's Service Stations, Inc. v. Comm'r	20.4(b)	June 2003
Hager v. Federal Nat'l Mortgage Ass'n	———	Oct. 2012
Harlan E. Moore Charitable Trust v. United States	24.5(m), 30.1(a)	Apr. 1993
Hattem v. Schwarzenegger	24.1	Sep. 2005, Sep. 2006
Hein v. Freedom From Religion Found., Inc.	26.5(b)	Sep. 2007
Henry E. & Nancy Horton Bartels Trust for the Benefit of Cornell Univ. v. United States	24.12(c)	Sep. 2009
Henry E. & Nancy Horton Bartels Trust for the Benefit of the Univ. of New Haven v. United States	24.12(c)	July 2000
Higgins v. Comm'r	24.2(a)	Oct. 2013
High Adventure Ministries, Inc. v. Comm'r	26.5(b)(i)	Apr. 1984
Hosanna-Tabor Evangelical Lutheran Church and School v. Equal Employment Opportunity Comm'n	———	Mar. 2012
Housing Pioneers, Inc. v. Comm'r	4.1(a), 20.11(b), 30.2	Apr. 1995, Sep. 1995
IHC Health Plans, Inc. v. Comm'r	7.6(e), 25.10(a)	Dec. 2001
IIT Research Inst. v. United States	9.1, 9.2, 24.6(1)	Dec. 1985
Illinois Ass'n of Professional Ins. Agents, Inc. v. Comm'r	8.6, 24.5(e)(ii)	Nov. 1986
Jellison v. Florida Hosp. Healthcare System, Inc.	6.3(j)-(m)	Aug. 2005
Judicial Watch, Inc. v. Rossotti	26.5(a)	Nov. 2002
Julius M. Israel Lodge of B'nai Brith v. Comm'r	24.7(h)	Dec. 1995
Junaluska Assembly Hous., Inc. v. Comm'r	4.4, 4.9, 10.8, 26.5(b)(iv)	Aug. 1986
King v. Burwell	5.7	Sep. 2015
Kizzire v. Baptist Health System, Inc.	6.3(j)-(m)	May 2006
Knights of Columbus Bldg. Ass'n v. United States	3.1, 7.13, 19.2(a)	Sep. 1988
Laborer's Int'l Union of North Am. v. Comm'r	24.2(b), 24.2(c), 30.1(c)	Oct. 2001
Lapham Found., Inc. v. Comm'r	12.3(c)	Feb. 2005

Case	Book Sections	Newsletter Issue
Lehrfeld v. Richardson	27.9(a)(iii)	Mar. 1998
Liberty University, Inc. v. Geithner	——	Jan. 2013
Lima Surgical Assocs., Inc., Voluntary Employees' Beneficiary Ass'n Plan Trust v. United States	18.3	Sep. 1990, Dec. 1991
Linchpins of Liberty v. U.S.	26.1(j), 26.15	Oct. 2016
Lintzenich v. United States	21.15	Dec. 2005
Littriello v. United States	4.1(b)(i)	Sep. 2005, July 2007
Living Faith, Inc. v. Comm'r	4.5(a), 4.10(b), 23.2(a), 24.4(b)	Nov. 1990, Feb. 1992
Locke v. Davey	10.1	Apr. 2004
Loving v. IRS	5.7(b)	Apr. 2014, Oct. 2014
Louisiana Credit Union League v. United States	4.9, 8.6,14.2(c)(ii), 24.1, 24.2(b), 24.4(a), 24.5(c)(ii)	Apr. 2005
Lutheran Social Servs. v. United States	10.3,10.4, 10.5	May 1984, June 1985
Maimonides Medical Center v. United States	1.1(a)	Mar. 2016, Oct. 2016
Manning Ass'n v. Comm'r	4.5(a), 8.4, 20.5(h), 24.1	Jan. 1990
Marek v. Lane	6.3(g)	Jan. 2014
Mayo Found. for Medical Education and Research	App. A	Mar. 2011, May 2016
McConnell v. Federal Election Comm'r	23.2(b)(ii)	Feb. 2004, Sep. 2007,
McCreary County v. American Civil Liberties Union	10.1(a)(ii)	Sep. 2005
McCutcheon v. Federal Election Comm'n	23.2(b)	Dec. 2013, June 2014
Mead v. Holder	——	May 2011
Mellon Bank v. United States	7.15(f), 19.6	Aug. 1984, July 1985
Menard, Inc. v. Comm'r	20.4(b)	Nov. 2004
Meredith v. Jefferson County Board of Education	6.2(b)	Feb. 2007, Sep. 2007
Michigan v. United States	19.21(c)	Dec. 1994
Miller & Son Drywall, Inc. v. Comm'r	20.4(b)	Aug. 2005
Minority Television Project, Inc. v. Federal Communications Comm'n	——	June 2012
Missall v. Comm'r	4.1(a)	Jan. 2009
Mobile Republican Assembly v. United States	27.6(a)	Mar. 2004
Montgomery County, MD v. Federal Nat'l Mortgage Ass'n	——	Apr. 2014

Case	Book Sections	Newsletter Issue
Morganbesser v. United States	16.1	Mar. 1992
Multi-Pak Corp. v. Comm'r	20.4(b), 20.11(a), 21.9(b)	Aug. 2010
Music Square Church v. United States	26.5	Sep. 2000
Mutual Aid Ass'n of the Church of The Brethren v. United States	13.1(b), 27.13(a)	June 2005
Myers v. Loudoun County Public Schools	10.1(a)(ii)	Oct. 2005
National Ass'n of Am. Churches v. Comm'r	24.5(i)(v), 25.1(a)(i), 25.7	Feb. 1984
National Ass'n of Postal Supervisors v. United States	16.1, 24.5(f)	Oct. 1990, Apr. 1991, Dec. 1991
National Collegiate Athletic Ass'n v. Comm'r	24.3(b), 24.3(d)	Apr. 1989, Sep. 1990, Oct. 1990, Nov. 1990
National Education Ass'n of the United States v. Comm'r	24.5(h)(ii)	Dec. 2011
National Federation of Independent Business v. Sebelius	——	Sep. 2012, Jan. 2013
National Federation of Republican Assemblies v. United States	25.9, 27.6(a)	Nov. 2002
National Foundation, Inc. v. United States	4.5(a), 20.4(c)	Jan. 1998
National League of Postmasters v. United States	24.5(e)(iii)	Sep. 1996
National Prime Users Group, Inc. v. United States	14.1(c)(iii)	Oct. 1987
National Water Well Ass'n, Inc. v. Comm'r	24.5(e)(ii)	Mar. 1989
Nehemiah Corporation of America v. HUD	7.5	Nov. 2007
Neonatology Associates, P.A. v. Comm'r	18.3, 27.16(e)	Sep. 2002
New Concordia Bible Church v. Comm'r	25.1(a)(i)	Mar. 1985
New Dynamics Found. v. United States	1.2, 4.4,11.8(a)	June 2006
New York State Club Ass'n v. New York City	6.2(c)	Aug. 1988
Newdow v. U.S. Congress et al.	10.1(a)(ii)	Aug. 2002
Nonprofits' Ins. Alliance of Calif. v. United States	4.10(b), 7.13, 27.13(b)	Dec. 1994
NorCal Tea Party Patriots v. Internal Revenue Service	26.1(j), 28.11(a)	Mar. 2016, Oct. 2016
North Carolina Citizens for Business & Indus. v. United States	24.5(h)(ii)	Oct. 1989
North Ridge Country Club v. Comm'r	15.3,15.5	Nov. 1987, Aug. 1989

CUMULATIVE TABLE OF CASES DISCUSSED IN *NONPROFIT COUNSEL*

Case	Book Sections	Newsletter Issue
Obergefell v. Hodges	6.2(d)	Sep. 2015
Ocean Pines Ass'n, Inc. v. Comm'r	13.2, 24.6(h)(i)	Nov. 2010, May 2012
Ohio Disability Ass'n v. Comm'r	5.2	Jan. 2010
Ohio Farm Bureau Fed'n, Inc. v. Comm'r	24.3(b)	June 1996
Oregon State Univ. Alumni Ass'n v. Comm'r	24.5(i)(ii)	Apr. 1996, Dec. 1999
PNC Bank, N.A. v. PPL Electric Utilities Corp.	18.5	Sep. 2006
Paratransit Ins. Corp. v. Comm'r	4.10(b), 27.13(b)	Aug. 1994
Parents Involved in Community Schools v. Seattle School District No. 1	6.2(b)	Feb. 2007, Sep. 2007
Parks v. Comm'r	8.2, 22.3(d)	Jan. 2016
Partners in Charity, Inc. v. Comm'r	7.5, 26.3	Nov. 2013
People of God Community v. Comm'r	20.2, 20.4(c)	Feb. 1984
Peters v. Comm'r	6.3(a), 6.3(i), 20.4(b), 21.4(c), 26.4(a)	Dec. 2000
Peterson v. Fairview Health Servs.	6.3(j)-(m)	Aug. 2005
Phi Delta Theta Fraternity v. Comm'r	8.5, 15.5	June 1988
Planned Parenthood Federation of America, Inc. v. Comm'r	24.6(g)	Aug. 1999
Pleasant Grove City, Utah v. Summum	10.1(a)(iii)	May 2009
Polm Family Found. v. United States	12.3(c)	Nov. 2009
Portland Golf Club v. Comm'r	1.4, 15.1(a), 15.5	Jan. 1991
Presbyterian & Reformed Publishing Co. v. Comm'r	4.9, 4.10(a)(v), 26.3	Oct. 1984
Professional Ins. Agents of Wash. v. Comm'r	8.6, 24.5(e)(ii)	Mar. 1987
Quality Auditing Co. v. Comm'r	20.11(c), 31.1(d)	Sep. 2000
Rameses School of San Antonio Texas v. Commissioner	20.3, 21.1	July 2007
Rapco, Inc. v. Comm'r	20.4(b)	Aug. 1996, Jan. 2000
Reed v. Town of Gilbert, Arizona	10.1(a)(iii)	Oct. 2015
Redlands Surgical Servs. v. Comm'r	20.11, 20.11(a), 20.11(b), 30.3(b)(iv)	Sep. 1999, June 2001
Research Corp. v. Comm'r	____	May 2012
Ridgely v. Lew	5.7(b)	Oct. 2014
Roberts, Acting Comm'r, Minn. Dep't of Human Rights v. United States Jaycees	6.2(c)	Aug. 1984
Rodriguez v. Comm'r	24.6(n)	Sep. 2013
St. David's Health Care System, Inc. v. United States	20.11(b), 30.3(b)(iv), 31.1(b)	Aug. 2002, Jan. 2004, July 2004, Aug. 2004

Case	Book Sections	Newsletter Issue
St. Louis Science Fiction, Ltd. v. Comm'r	7.12, 8.4, 20.11(c)	July 1985
Salus Mundi Found., Transferee v. Comm'r	____	May 2012, Oct. 2016
Salvation Navy, Inc. v. Comm'r	4.5(a)	Jan. 2003
Schuette v. Coalition to Defend Affirmative Action	6.2(e)	Dec. 2013
Self-Realization Brotherhood, Inc. v. Comm'r 10.2(c)	Sep. 1984	
Senior Citizens of Missouri, Inc. v. Comm'r	20.4(h)	Mar. 1989
Service Bolt & Nut Co. Profit Sharing et al. Trust v. Comm'r	24.9	Apr. 1984
Seven-Sky v. Holder	____	Jan. 2012
Shays & Meehan v. Federal Election Comm'n	17	Nov. 2004, Nov. 2005, Feb. 2006, Oct. 2007
Sherwin-Williams Co. Employee Health Plan Trust v. Comm'r	18.3, 24.10	Jan. 2001, Aug. 2003, Jan. 2009
Sierra Club, Inc. v. Comm'r	24.5(i)(ii), 24.6(g), 24.7(k)	July 1993, Oct. 1994, Aug. 1996, May 1999
Skillman Family Reunion Fund, Inc., The v. United States	15.4	June 2002
Sklar v. Comm'r	10.2(a)	Apr. 2002
Smith v. United States	4.4, 19.6	May 1985
Snyder v. Phelps	____	May 2011
Solution Plus, Inc. v. Comm'r	7.3(d)	Apr. 2008
Sound Health Assoc. v. Comm'r	7.6(f), 13.1(b), 13.2	Jan. 2016
South Community Ass'n v. Comm'r	24.7(a)	Feb. 2006
Southern Faith Ministries, Inc. v. Geithner	26.6(c)	Dec. 2009
Spiritual Outreach Soc'y v. Comm'r	10.3(c)	Apr. 1991
Stahl v. United States	10.7	Feb. 2010, Jan. 2011, May 2012
State Police Ass'n of Massachusetts v. Comm'r	24.5(h)(ii)	Nov. 1997
Stichting Pensioenfonds Voor de Gezondheid v. United States	16.1	Jan. 1998
Sun Capital Partners III, LP v. New England Teamsters & Trucking Industry Pension Fund	24.2(a)	Oct. 2013, May 2014, , June 2016
Sunrise Constr. Co. v. Comm'r	18.3	May 1987
Tamarisk Country Club v. Comm'r	15.6	June 2012

Case	Book Sections	Newsletter Issue
Tax Analysts v. Internal Revenue Serv.	27.9(a)(i), 27.9(a)(ii), 27.9(b)	Nov. 2002, Feb. 2004, Mar. 2005, May 2006, May 2012
Tax Analysts v. IRS and Christian Broadcasting Network, Inc.	27.9(b)	Sep. 2005
Tennessee Baptist Children's Homes, Inc. v. United States	10.5	July 1985
Texas Apartment Ass'n v. United States	24.5(d)(i)	Apr. 2005
Texas Farm Bureau v. United States	24.5(e)(ii)	Aug. 1995
Texas Learning Technology Group v. Comm'r	23.8(a), 25.10(a)	May 1992
Texas Medical Ass'n Ins. Trust v. United States	19.24	Mar. 2006
Texas Monthly, Inc. v. Bullock	10.1(a)(ii)	Jan. 2014
Thomas More Law Center v. Harris	28.3(i)	Feb. 2017
Thomas More Law Center v. Obama	____	Sep. 2011
Triune of Life Church, Inc. v. Comm'r	4.9	Sep. 1985
True the Vote, Inc. v. IRS	26.1(j), 26.15	Oct. 2016
Trust U/W Emily Oblinger v. Comm'r	24.5(m), 30.1(a)	May 1993
Tupper v. United States	16.1	Mar. 1998
Twin Oaks Community, Inc. v. Comm'r	10.7	Jan. 1987
United Cancer Council, Inc. v. Comm'r	4.7(a), 4.11 (b), 20.3, 20.11(c), 21.8, 26.5, 29.2	Jan. 1998, Apr. 1999
United States v. American Bar Endowment	8.6, 24.2(b), 24.5(i)(ii), 26.4(a)	Apr. 1984, Aug. 1986
United States v. Chicago, Burlington & Quincy Railroad Co.	15.3, 26.4(a)	Oct. 2001
United States v. Church of Scientology	26.6(a)	Sep. 1990
United States v. Danielczwk, Jr.	23.2(b)(ii)	Aug. 2011, Oct. 2012
United States v. Detroit Medical Center	1.1(a)	Oct. 2016
United States v. Hartshorn	____	May 2012
United States v. Home Concrete and Supply, LLC	App. A	Mar. 2012, June 2012
United States v. Hovind	4.1(a)	Oct. 2009
United States v. Living Word Christian Center	26.6(c)	Jan. 2009, Feb. 2009, Apr. 2009, June 2009
United States v. Missouri Pacific R. R. Co.	____	May 2012
United States v. Mubayyid	27.2(a)(vii)	Nov. 2011
United States v. NorCal Tea Party Patriots	28.11(a)(ii)	May 2016
United States v. Wells Fargo Bank		Oct. 2012

CUMULATIVE TABLE OF CASES DISCUSSED IN *NONPROFIT COUNSEL*

Case	Book Sections	Newsletter Issue
United States Catholic Conference & Nat'l Conference of Catholic Bishops, In Re	26.5(b)	Oct. 1989, Nov. 1989
United States Nat'l Bank of Oregon v. Independent Ins. Agents of America, Inc.	____	May 2012
University Med. Resident Servs., P.C. v. Comm'r	7.7, 7.8	Oct. 1996
U.S. House of Representatives v. Burwell	____	July 2016
Van Orden v. Perry	10.1(a)(ii)	Sep. 2005
Variety Club Tent No. 6 Charities, Inc. v. Comm'r	20.1, 20.3, 20.5(k), 21.8, 24.7(h)	Mar. 1998
Veterans of Foreign Wars, Dep't of Mich. v. Comm'r	24.5(i)(i), 26.4(a)	Aug. 1987
Veterans of Foreign Wars, Dep't of Mo., Inc. v. United States	24.5(i)(i)	Dec. 1984
Vigilant Hose Co. of Emmitsburg v. United States	24.2(a), 24.4(g), 30.1(c)	Aug. 2001
Virginia v. Sebelius	____	Feb. 2011
Vision Serv. Plan v. United States	13.2(a)	Feb. 2006, Apr. 2008, Apr. 2009, Jan. 2016
Vision Serv. Plan Tax Litigation, In re	7.11, 13.1(b), 13.2	Aug. 2010
Walz v. Tax Comm'n of City of New York	10.1(a)(ii)	Jan. 2014
Washington v. Washington Education Ass'n	15.1	Mar. 2007
Wayne Baseball, Inc. v. Comm'r	4.4, 7.15(c), 8.4	Dec. 1999
Wendy L. Parker Rehabilitation Found., Inc. v. Comm'r	6.3(a), 20.5(h)	Nov. 1986
West Va. State Med. Ass'n v. Comm'r	15.5, 24.2(b), 24.14	Nov. 1988
Whipple v. Comm'r	24.2(a)	Oct. 2013
Westward Ho v. Comm'r	4.6	June 1992
Wiccan Religious Cooperative of Florida, Inc., The v. Zingale	8.1(b)	June 2005
Woodrum v. Integris Health, Inc.	6.3(j)-(m)	Mar. 2005
Z Street, Inc. v. Koskinen	26.15	Aug. 2014, Aug. 2015
Zagfly, Inc. v. Comm'r	4.10(b)	Apr. 2013

Cumulative Table of IRS Private Determinations Discussed in *Bruce R. Hopkins' Nonprofit Counsel*

The following IRS private letter rulings and technical advice memoranda, referenced in the text, are discussed in greater detail in one or more issues of the author's monthly newsletter, as indicated.

Private Determination	Book Sections	Newsletter Issue
8306006	9.5	Dec. 1993
8505044	29.3(a)	May 1985
8512084	9.5	Dec. 1993
8606056	9.5, 29.2	Apr. 1986
8621059	30.1(b)	Aug. 1986
8706012	29.1(a)	Apr. 1987
9017003	28.2(a)	July 1990
9029047	26.5(e)(ii)	Sept. 1990
9042038	24.6(i)	Jan. 1991
9130002	20.1, 20.5(c), 20.5(d), 30.2, 31.9(b)	Nov. 1991
9242002	19.2(a), 28.2(d)	Dec. 1992
9243008	9.5	Dec. 1992
9305026	29.3(a), 29.6(b)	Apr. 1993, Apr. 1997
9316052	9.5, 20.4(i)	Dec. 1993
9345004	24.5(e)(iii)	June 1994
9416002	24.5(e)(iii)	June 1994
9425032	17.5	Aug. 1994
9434041	7.6(b)	Oct. 1994
9438029	29.8	Nov. 1994
9438030	30.2(b)(i), 31.1(b)	Nov. 1994
9448036	20.9	Jan. 1995
9506046	31.3	Mar. 1995
9530024	7.7	Nov. 1995
9542002	11.4	Dec. 1995
9550001	14.1(d), 14.2(c)(i), 24.4(g), 24.5(e)(i), 24.5(k)	Feb. 1996
9603019	24.12(g)	Mar. 1996

IRS PRIVATE DETERMINATIONS DISCUSSED IN *NONPROFIT COUNSEL*

Private Determination	Book Sections	Newsletter Issue
9608003	24.5(k)	Apr. 1996
9615030	6.3(b), 20.11(a)	June 1996
9615045	24.6(h)(iii)	July 1996
9619069	25.6(j)	Aug. 1996
9635001	24.7(k)	Nov. 1996
9635003	23.2(c), 23.3	Nov. 1996
9637050	29.1(b)	Nov. 1996
9637051	29.6	Apr. 1997
9641011	24.5(k)	Dec. 1996
9645004	24.2(f), 24.4(d), 24.7(b)	Jan. 1997
9645017	29.6, 29.8	Feb. 1997, Apr. 1997
9651047	7.6(f), 24.5(k)	Jan. 1997
9652026	17.1(a), 17.4, 22.3	Jan. 1998
9702004	8.4, 24.2(f), 24.5(j), 28.2(e), 31.8(g)	Mar. 1997
9711002	24.5(k)	May 1997
9711003	4.7, 24.1	June 1997
9711004	25.7	June 1997
9712001	24.3(d)	June 1997
9720002	24.5(c)	Sept. 1997
9722006	19.5(b), 29.2	Feb. 1999, Nov. 2002
9732022	16.2	Oct. 1997
9732032	7.6(h), 8.5, 24.5(a), 24.5(b)(iv)	Oct. 1997
9739043	24.5(b)(iii)	Dec. 1997
9740032	24.1(h)(i)	Dec. 1997
9747003	19.11(a)	Jan. 1998
9750056	31.3	Feb. 1998
9803001	4.11(b), 7.6(a), 24.5(b)	Apr. 1998
9805001	13, 24.8	Mar. 1998
9811001	24.5(k)	May 1998
9812001	23.2(b)(iv)	May 1998
9815061	13, 15, 19.4, 19.11(a), 27.17	July 1998
9816027	24.6(g)	June 1998
9821049	24.4(f)	Aug. 1998
9821063	24.5(b)(vi)	Aug. 1998
9821067	24.4(g)	Aug. 1998
9822004	24.5(k)	Oct. 1998
9822006	24.4(g)	Oct. 1998

Private Determination	Book Sections	Newsletter Issue
9822039	24.5(b)(vi)	Oct. 1998
9825030	24.4(f)	Aug. 1998, Nov. 1998
9835003	20.7, 25.1(f), 27.1(a)	Nov. 1998
9839039	24.5(k), 24.9, 30.7, 31.5	Dec. 1998
9841003	18.3	Jan. 1999
9847002	24.5(k)	Mar. 1999
9847006	17.5	Jan. 1999
9849027	24.5(k), 27.14	Mar. 1999
9853001	24.4(g)	Mar. 1999
199901002	24.4(g)	Mar. 1999
199932052	7.7	Oct. 1999
199938041	28.1(a)	May 2000
200020056	14.1(a)(iii)	July 2000
200020060	20.4(b)	Aug. 2000
200021056	4.4, 4.10(a)(ii), 4.10(b), 8.6, 24.1, 24.2(d), 24.2(f), 24.4(a)	Aug. 2000
200022056	24.5(k)	July 2000, May 2001
200026013	19.19(d)	Aug. 2000
200027056	14.1, 24.6(j), 29	Sept. 2000
200037053	11.8(d)	Dec. 2000
200044038	23.2(b)(iv)	Jan. 2001
200044039	27.12(b)	Jan. 2001
200051046	15.6	Feb. 2001
200051049	7.6(h), 24.1	Feb. 2001
200108045	24.5(k)	May 2001
200114040	20.11(a)	June 2001
200117043	31.5	July 2001
200118054	30.1(b), 30.4, 31.5	July 2001
200119061	24.2(h), 24.6(j)	Aug. 2001
200128059	24.5(i)(iv)	Sep. 2001
200133036	15.3	Oct. 2001
200133037	15.3	Oct. 2001
200132040	29.2, 31.1(d)	Nov. 2001
200134025	4.1(b)(i), 25.2(c), 27.2(c)	Nov. 2001
200147058	24.9	Jan. 2002
200151060	23.2(b)(iv), 28.3	Mar. 2002
200152048	19.6, 29	Mar. 2002
200203069	29	May 2002

Private Determination	Book Sections	Newsletter Issue
200204051	24.4(f)	Apr. 2002
200217044	31.8(c)	July 2002
200222030	8.3(b), 8.6, 24.5(c)	Sept. 2002
200225044	24.4(f)	Sept. 2002
200225046	29	Oct. 2002
200230005	24.7(c), 28.5	Oct. 2002
200243057	27.16(e)	Dec. 2002
200244028	21.4(a), 21.9(b)	Jan. 2003
200247055	21.4(a)	Feb. 2003
200303051	31.10(c)	Mar. 2003
200303062	24.5(h)(i), 24.5(o), 24.8	Mar. 2003
200304041	30.1(b), 31.5	Apr. 2003
200305032	31.3	Apr. 2003
200311034	19.19(c), 31.5	May 2003
200313024	19.19(c), 24.5(a)	June 2003
200314030	15.6	June 2012
200314031	24.5(k), 24.6(h)(iii)	June 2003, Aug. 2003
200325003	31.5	Sept. 2003
200326035	9.2, 9.5, 20.11(b), 24.4, 24.6(g), 29.7	Sept. 2003
200333031	31.5	Oct. 2003
200333034	8.5	Nov. 2003
200335037	21.4(a), 21.7	Nov. 2003
200341023	31.6	Dec. 2003
200343027	4.5(a)	Dec. 2003
200345041	24.4(f)	Jan. 2004
200347009	9.5	Jan. 2004
200347023	12.4	Jan. 2004
200348029	31.3	Feb. 2004
200350022	12.4(a)	Feb. 2004
200352021	12.4(a)	Mar. 2004
200402003	31.10(c)	Mar. 2004
200405016	29.2	Apr. 2004
200411044	31.5	May 2004
200413014	21.9(b)	June 2004
200421010	21.4(a)	July 2004
200427016	19.21(c)	Nov. 2004
200428021	19.21(d)	Nov. 2004

Private Determination	Book Sections	Newsletter Issue
200431018	31.6	Oct. 2004
200432026	24.12(b)	Oct. 2004
200435018	21.4(c)	Nov. 2004
200435019	21.4(c)	Nov. 2004
200435020	21.4(c)	Nov. 2004
200435021	21.4(c)	Nov. 2004
200435022	21.4(c)	Nov. 2004
200436019	27.2(b)	Nov. 2004
200436022	4.1(b), 7.6, 30.4, 31.6	Nov. 2004
200437040	5.2, 10.3(a), 21.4(c), 21.16, 23.2(b), 29.4	Nov. 2004
200439043	7.6(g), 8.7, 24.5(g)	Dec. 2004
20044008E	4.5, 13, 20.11(c)	Feb. 2005
200446033	23.2(b)(iv), 23.3, 28.3	Jan. 2005
200450037	7.3(c)	Feb. 2005, Mar. 2005
200450038	7.4	Feb. 2005
200450041	4.1(a), 4.3, 4.3(d), 4.4, 15.1(b)	Mar. 2005
200451031	15.6	June 2012
200501017	24.4(g), 29	Mar. 2005
200501021	12.4(a), 24.6(d)	Mar. 2005
200501022	12.4(a), 24.6(d)	Mar. 2005
200504035	19.5(b)	Apr. 2005
200505024	14.1(c)(iii)	Apr. 2005
200505032	7.15(d)	Apr. 2005
200506024	4.5(a)	Apr. 2005
200506025	24.4(f)	Apr. 2005
200510029	24.2(h), 24.6(j)	May 2005
200510030	31.6	May 2005
200511003	18.3	May 2005
200511023	4.10(b), 13.4	June 2005
200511024	13, 27.17	May 2005
200512023	4.10(b), 13.4	June 2005
200512025	24.2(f)	June 2005
200512027	4.10(g)	June 2005
200513030	12.3(b)	July 2005
200520035	19.9	Aug. 2005
200522022	14.2(c)(ii), 14.2(c)(iii)	Sept. 2005
200525020	4.10(b)	Sept. 2005

Private Determination	Book Sections	Newsletter Issue
200528008	19.24	Sept. 2005
200528029	4.5(c), 30.1(b)	Sept. 2005
200530028	10.3(a), 10.3(b)	Oct. 2005
200530029	24.2(h), 24.6(j)	Oct. 2005
200531020	14.1, 24.7(f)	Dec. 2005
200531024	27.2(a)(vi)	Oct. 2005
200532052	28.2(c)	Dec. 2005
200532056	15.6	Oct. 2005
200532058	7.7	Dec. 2005
200534022	7.5	Nov. 2005
200535029	5.2, 20.1, 25.1(a)(i)	Dec. 2005
200536023	14.2(c)(ii)	Dec. 2005
200536024	7.15(c)	Dec. 2005
200536025	19.16(a)	Dec. 2005
200536026	14.1(c)(iii)	Dec. 2005
200536027	12.4(a), 12.4(e)	Dec. 2005
200537037	24.12	Feb. 2006
200537038	7.15(e), 24.12(b)	Dec. 2005
200538026	8.3(a)(i)	Feb. 2006
200538027	24.6(h)(iii), 24.12(b)	Dec. 2005
200539027	4.10(b)	Feb. 2006
200541042	31.13	Dec. 2005
200542037	12.4(a)	Feb. 2006
200544020	4.11(b), 13, 20.11(a)	Feb. 2006
200549009	12.3(c), 27.2(b)	Feb. 2006
200552013	26.3	Mar. 2006
200601030	20.4(c)	Mar. 2006
200601033	24.6(g)	Mar. 2006
200601035	14.1(b), 14.1(c)	Apr. 2006
200602039	29.2, 29.7(c)	Apr. 2006
200606042	7.6, 20.1, 20.11, 24.4	May 2006
200607027	4.1(a), 27.2, 27.9	Apr. 2006
200611033	7.7, 24.4	May 2006
200614030	8.3(a), 12.3(c), 20.11(b)	July 2006
200619024	24.2(h)	Sept. 2006
200621023	4.4, 13	Aug. 2006
200621025	6.3(a)	Aug. 2006
200622055	5.6(f), 6.3(h), 8.3, 30.1(c)	Aug. 2006

Private Determination	Book Sections	Newsletter Issue
200623069	24.6(n)	Aug. 2006
200623072	4.4, 15.2	Aug. 2006
200623075	7.5	Aug. 2006
200624068	7.7, 13.1(a)	Nov. 2006
200625033	19.5(b)	Nov. 2006
200625035	24.5(a), 24.7(b)	Sept. 2006, April 2011
200634036	7.7	Feb. 2007
200635018	20.11(a), 20.11(b)	Nov. 2006
200638027	18.3, 20.1	Nov. 2006
200642009	7.4, 31.6	Dec. 2006
200648031	24.2, 24.6(h)	Feb. 2007
200649034	20.11(b)	Apr. 2007
200702042	20.11(b)	Apr. 2007
200703037	24.2(b), 24.5(j)	Mar. 2007
200708087	20.11	June 2007
200709064	4.11(a), 20.5	June 2007
200709065	7.13, 12.4(c)	June 2007
200709070	12.4(c)(iii)	June 2007
200709072	24.4(a), 24.5(g)	June 2007
200713024	24.6(g), 24.7(f)	June 2007
200716026	14	July 2007
200716034	24.4(b), 29.7	July 2007
200717019	27.7	July 2007
200717020	19.5(b)	July 2007
200721025	7.5	Aug. 2007
200722028	24.5(1)	Aug. 2007, Oct. 2016
200727021	10.3(a), 10.3(b)	Oct. 2007
200731034	12.3(c)	Oct. 2007
200736037	5.1b, 20.11(d)	Nov. 2007
200750020	12.2(e), 12.4(a)	Feb. 2008
200752043	12.3(c), 20.11, 26.3	Feb. 2009
200810025	12.3(c), 20.11, 26.3	Feb. 2009
200815035	4.10(b), 25.1(a)(i)	June 2008
200819017	21.14	July 2008
200825046	4.7	Aug. 2008
200826038	15.6	Aug. 2008
200816043	6.2(a)	Aug. 2008
200829029	13.2(b)	Sep. 2008

Private Determination	Book Sections	Newsletter Issue
200830028	5.7(b), 20.11(d)	Oct. 2008
200832027	4.10(c), 24.2(g), 24.4(h), 24.5(h)	Mar. 2009
200833021	23.5, 23.5(a)	Dec. 2008
200837035	14.1(c)(iii), 14.2(a)	Dec. 2008
200841038	19.12	Jan. 2009
200843032	5.7(b), 20.11	Jan. 2009
200843036	24.12(b)	Jan. 2009
200844021	20	Feb. 2009
200844022	12.3(c), 20.11, 26.3	Feb. 2009
200845053	5.7(b), 20.11(d)	Feb. 2009, Sep. 2012
200846040	5.7(b)	Feb. 2009
200849016	19.5(b)	Feb. 2009
200849017	4.11, 9.2, 12.3(c)	Feb. 2009
200849018	11.2	Feb. 2009
200851031	4.3, 4.5(a), 20	Feb. 2009
200851037	6.3(a), 20	Feb. 2009
200851040	6.3(a), 10.2, 20.11, 24.2(e)	Feb. 2009
200902013	30.1(b)	Apr. 2009
200903081	4.5, 12.3(c), 20	Mar. 2008
200904026	25.1(a)(i)	May 2009
200905028	4.3(b), 4.5(a), 10.2, 20	May 2009
200905029	8.1, 15.1, 19.4(a)	May 2009
200905033	9.2, 20	Apr. 2009
200906057	15.1(a), 15.2	Apr. 2009
200908050	23.10	May 2009
200909064	6.2(a), 6.2(b)(iii)	May 2009
200909072	13, 15	May 2009
200910060	11.3	May 2009
200912039	10.3(b)	Aug. 2009
200913067	20	July 2009
200916035	5.7(b), 20.11(d)	July 2009
200917042	14, 20.9	July 2009
200926033	7.2(b)	Sep. 2009
200926036	10.3(b), 20	Sep. 2009
200926037	5.7(b)	Sep. 2009
200926049	10.3(b)	Sep. 2009
200928045	23.2(b), 23.10, 26.6(a)	Oct. 2009

Private Determination	Book Sections	Newsletter Issue
200930049	4.3(a), 4.39(b), 25.1(b)	Nov. 2009
200931059	4.5(a), 18.3, 27.17	Oct. 2009
200931064	19.7, 24.4(a), 24.5(g)	Oct. 2009
200941038	4.11, 7.7, 11.6, 27.12(b)	Dec. 2009
200943042	22.3(d)(iv)	Dec. 2009
200944053	4.11, 7.6, 8.4, 8.5, 9.2, 20.11(b), 24.2(e)	Jan. 2010
200944055	20.4(b)	Jan. 2010
200947064	7.6(a)(i)	Jan. 2010
200947065	12.4, 24.2	Jan. 2010
200950047	4.11(b)	Apr. 2010
200950049	18.3, 20	Feb. 2010
201002040	19.4(b)	Apr. 2010
201002042	19.5	Apr. 2010
201002043	15.6	Apr. 2010
201003022	15.6	Apr. 2010
201005061	14.2(c)(iii), 14.2(c)(iv)	Apr. 2010
201007060	24.2(e)	May 2010
201007076	—	May 2010
201008050	—	May 2010
201012051	14.2(c)(ii)	July 2010
201002052	24.4(f)	July 2010
201014068	7.4, 13.2	July 2010
201016088	4.10(b)	Aug. 2010
201017064	4.5, 20.11(a)	Aug. 2010
201017067	6.3(a), 7.8	Aug. 2010
201019033	4.10(c), 24.2(e)	Aug. 2010
201020021	4.5	Aug. 2010
201023058	4.3, 20.11	Aug. 2010
201024066	14.1(a)(ii), 14.1(c), 20	Aug. 2010
201025078	15.1, 20	Sep. 2010
201028042	20.3, 20.10	Sep. 2010
201029031	4.11, 20.11(a)	Sep. 2010
201031033	4.4, 4.6	Oct. 2010
201033039	6.2(b)	Oct. 2010
201035034	11.2, 20	Nov. 2010
201035035	19.11(a)	Nov. 2010
201036031	12.3(c), 20, 27.2, 27.15	Nov. 2010

Private Determination	Book Sections	Newsletter Issue
201037029	8.4, 20.11(a)	Nov. 2010
201038015	14.1(c), 14.2(a)	Nov. 2010
201038020	25.6	Nov. 2010
201039034	20, 21.4(a)	Dec. 2010
201039045	4.10(b), 6.3(a)	Dec. 2010
201039046	20	Dec. 2010
210139048	4.10(b), 20.11(a)	Dec. 2010
201040020	14.2(c)	Jan. 2011
201040036	4.5(a), 15.1	Jan. 2011
201041045	4.10(b), 6.3(a), 24.2(e)	Dec. 2010
201042040	20.11(a)	Dec. 2010
201043041	24.6(b), 29.2	Jan. 2011
201044015	12.3(c), 28.3	Jan. 2011
201044016	29.2	Jan. 2011
201044025	20	Jan. 2011
201045034	14.1(a)(i), 14.2(a), 14.2(c)	Jan. 2011
201046016	4.10(b)	Jan. 2011
201047024	11.6	Jan. 2011
201048045	9.7	Feb. 2011
201049046	31.6	Feb. 2011
201049047	24.6(j)	Feb. 2011
201051024	4.10	Mar. 2011
201052022	12.3(c)	Mar. 2011
201103057	4.7	Mar. 2011
201104066	16.2, 20.11	April 2011
201105043	14.1(c)	April 2011
201105048	14.29(c)	April 2011
201106019	24.5(a)	April 2011
201107028	14.2(c)	June 2011
201108041	4.10, 20.11	June 2011
201109028	6.3(a), 20.11	June 2011
201109029	4.3(b), 4.10	June 2011
201110012	7.8, 7.16(c)	June 2011
201110013	20.9	June 2011
201113036	29.2, 20.11	June 2011
201113041	5.7(b), 20	June 2011
201114035	9.1–9.3	June 2011
201114036	4.10, 20.11	June 2011

IRS PRIVATE DETERMINATIONS DISCUSSED IN *NONPROFIT COUNSEL*

Private Determination	Book Sections	Newsletter Issue
201115026	5.7(b), 20, 29.2	June 2011
201115030	12.3(c)	June 2011
201116028	4.10, 20.11	June 2011
201116046	4.5	June 2011
201117035	8.4, 8.7, 20.11	July 2011
201119036	7.4	July 2011
201120035	12.3(c), 20.5(b)	July 2011
201120036	7.8, 20.11	July 2011
201121021	4.3, 4.5, 4.10, 7.3(d), 20	July 2011
201121027	16.1	July 2011
201122022	4.10(b)	Aug. 2011
201122028	4.10(b)	Aug. 2011
201123035	3.2, 19.5(b), 25.11	Aug. 2011
201123041	4.3, 4.5, 25.7	Aug. 2011
201123045	24.5(b)(iv)	Aug. 2011
2–1123046	27.10(f)	Aug. 2011
201124024	12.3(c)	Aug. 2011
201124025	4.10(b)	Aug. 2011
201125043	29.3	Aug. 2011
201125045	8.1, 20.11	Aug. 2011
201126039	4.10, 20.11	Sep. 2011
201126040	13, 15, 19.4, 27.18	Oct. 2011
201127013	23.1, 23.2, 29.2	Sep. 2011
201128027	7.11, 24.5(1)	Sep. 2011
201128028	4.10	Sep. 2011
201128030	20.11	Oct. 2011
201128032	20.11(d)	Sep. 2011
201129050	12.4(e)	Sep. 2011, Mar. 2014
201133011	19.2(b)	Oct. 2011
201133012	12.3(c)	Oct. 2011
201133013	12.4	Oct. 2011
201134023	31.6	Nov. 2011
201135032	7.16(e)	Nov. 2011
201135036	14, 20.11	Nov. 2011
201136027	4.3(b), 16.1	Nov. 2011
201137012	12.4(e)	Nov. 2011
201138031	27.15(g)	Nov. 2011
201140013	27.15(g)	Dec. 2011

Private Determination	Book Sections	Newsletter Issue
201140028	7.7, 7.8	Dec. 2011
201141021	20.4(b)	Dec. 2011
201142026	24.6(g), 24.12(c)	Dec. 2011
201142027	20.11(d)	Dec. 2011
201143020	20.11(d)	Jan. 2012
201144030	4.5(a), 20.11	Jan. 2012
201144032	9.2	Jan. 2012
201145025	4.5(a), 20.11	Jan. 2012
201146022	15, 20, 28.2	Jan. 2012
201147033	20.11(d)	Feb. 2012
201147034	14.2(a), 14.2(c)	Feb. 2012
201147035	28.2(c)	Feb. 2012
201148008	20.5(h)	Feb. 2012
201149032	4.3(b), 18.3, 18.7	Feb. 2012
201149035	4.10	Feb. 2012
201149036	12.3(c)	Feb. 2012
201149043	7.7, 13	Feb. 2012
201149044	4.5(a), 12.3(c)	Feb. 2012
201149045	4.10, 20.11	Feb. 2012
201150027	27.15(g)	Feb. 2012
201150032	14.2(a), 14.2(c)	Feb. 2012
201150034	20.11	Feb. 2012
201150035	20.11	Feb. 2012
201150036	14.2(a), 14.2(c)	Feb. 2012
201151028	7.11, 20.11	Feb. 2012
201152019	6.3(a), 7.3(d), 8.4, 20.11	Mar. 2012
201152020	4.10	Mar. 2012
201152021	12.4(b)	Mar. 2012
201202038	4.10, 20, 29.2	Mar. 2012
201202039	4.10, 7.3(d)	Mar. 2012
201203018	14.2(a), (c)	April 2012
201203025	5.7(b)	April 2012
201204016	27.2(b)(i)	April 2012
201204018	5.7(b), 15.1, 15.2	April 2012
201204020	4.3. 4.5	April 2012
201204021	4.10, 20	April 2012
201205010	20	April 2012
201205011	20	April 2012

Private Determination	Book Sections	Newsletter Issue
201205013	4.10, 20	April 2012
201209009	4.10	May 2012
201209010	7.7	May 2012
201209011	20	May 2012
201210041	20	May 2012
201210042	20	May 2012
201210043	20	May 2012
201211025	20, 21.16	May 2012
201211026	20	May 2012
201213032	13.2, 14.2(a)	June 2012
201213033	15.1(b), 20.10	June 2012
201213034	15.6	June 2012
201213035	15.6	June 2012
201213036	15.1(b)	June 2012
201214035	13.3(b), 23.5	June 2012
201215011	28.2(e)	June 2012
201215013	23.5, 25.1(a), (b)	June 2012
201216040	20.11	June 2012
201217020	4.10, 20.11	June 2012
201217022	4.3(b), 31.2(a)	July 2012
201217026	7.15(d), 1.16(d), 20.11	July 2012
201218016	4.10, 11.4, 27.13(b)	July 2012
201218018	14, 20	July 2012
201218023	4.10	July 2012
201218041	5.7(b), 20.4(a), 20.11	July 2012
201219024	31.2(a)	July 2012
201219026	15.1	July 2012
201219030	4.10, 15	Aug. 2012
201219032	15.1, 15.2, 20.3, 20.11	Aug. 2012
201221022	5.7(b), 20.11	July 2012
201220034	14.2(c)	Aug. 2012
201220035	6.3(a)	Aug. 2012
201220037	12.4(c)	Aug. 2012
201221022	10.3	Aug. 2013
201221023	4.10, 7.15(a), 20.11	Sep. 2012
201221024	6.3(a), 24.6(g), 24.6(h)(iii), 24.12(b)	Aug. 2012
201221025	12, 20.11	Aug. 2012

Private Determination	Book Sections	Newsletter Issue
201221030	18.3	Aug. 2012
201221031	12.4(a)	Aug. 2012
201222040	12.3(c), 24.2(g), 24.5(k)	Sep. 2012
201222042	12.3(c), 24.2(g), 24.5(k)	Sep. 2012
201222043	24.4(f)	Sep. 2012
201222050	14.1(a)(ii), 14.1(d), 14.2(c)(iii)	Aug. 2012
201222069	5.7(b), 28.2(e)	Sep. 2012
201223020	13.1(a), 20.11	Sep. 2012
201224034	5.7(b), 23.5	Aug. 2012
201234036	6.3(i), 20.11	Aug. 2012
201224037	18.3	Aug. 2012
201225019	24.10	Oct. 2012
201227006	4.4, 20	Sep. 2012
201228026	19.1	Oct. 2012
201231012	4.10(b), 20.11	Oct. 2012
201232034	5.7(b), 10.3(b)	Oct. 2012
201232036	4.10, 7.7	Nov. 2012
201233017	5.7(b)	Oct. 2012
201234004	27.15(g)	Nov. 2012
201234028	13.1, 13.2	Nov. 2012
201234029	20	Nov. 2012
201235021	20.11	Nov. 2012
201235024	15.6	Jan. 2013
201236033	5.7(b)	Nov. 2012
201240026	19.4(b)	Jan. 2013
201242014	5.7(b)	Dec. 2012
201242016	5.7(b), 14.1(a)(ii), 14.12(c)(iii), 20.9	Dec. 2012
201243015	12.4(a), (e)	Jan. 2013
201244020	5.7(b), 12.4(f)	Jan. 2013
201244021	4.10, 27.1(a)(1), 29.2	Jan. 2013
201245025	20	Jan. 2013
201246037	10.5	Jan. 2013
201246039	14.1(c), 14.2(d)	Jan. 2013
201247016	4.10, 6.3(a), 7.8, 7.9, 20.11	Jan. 2013
201247019	19.5(a)	Jan. 2013
201249016	4.3(a), 4.5(a), 7.3(d), 8.1, 20.11	Mar. 2013
201250075	4.10(c), 7.6(k), 20.3, 20.11(b)	Feb. 2013

IRS PRIVATE DETERMINATIONS DISCUSSED IN *NONPROFIT COUNSEL*

Private Determination	Book Sections	Newsletter Issue
201251018	10.3	Mar. 2013
201251019	24.3(d)	Mar. 2013
201301014	7.3(d), 8.4, 8.5, 20.11(b)	Mar. 2013
201301015	21.7	Mar. 2013
201303018	4.10, 8.4, 20.11	Mar. 2013
201303019	4.10, 7.3(d), 20.11	Mar. 2013
201303020	4.10, 7.3(d), 20.11	Mar. 2013
201305012	4.10, 20.5(a)	Apr. 2013
201306023	24.2(h), 24.6(j)	Apr. 2013
201307008	12.3(b)(iii)	Apr. 2013
201309014	19.2(a)	May 2013
201309016	4.10, 20.4, 20.11(a)	May 2013
201309017	19.5(b)	May 2013
201310047	6.2(a), 10.7	May 2013
201311028	4.10, 7.16(a), 8.5, 9.1	May 2013
201311035	12.4(c)	May 2013
201313034	11.8, 20.11	June 2013
201314044	3.2A, 7.6(a)	June 2013
201314046	20.5(h)	June 2013
201315027	4.10(b)	June 2013
201315028	4.10(b)	June 2013
201317011	7.13	July 2013
201317013	20.2, 20.3	July 2013
201318013	20.8	July 2013
201318034	26.3	July 2013
201319031	4.10, 13.2	July 2013
201320023	19.4(a), 24.4(a)	Aug. 2013
201321026	4.10, 14.2(a), (c)	Aug. 2013
201321036	19.3, 27.13(b)	Aug. 2013
201322041	4.5(a), 20.11, 25.1(a)(i), 27.17(a)	Aug. 2013
201323029	12.4(b), 12.4(c), 24	Aug. 2013
201323037	4.10	Aug. 2013
201323038	20	Aug. 2013
201324020	4.10, 20.11	Aug. 2013
201325016	4.10, 7.3(d), 13	Sep. 2013
201325017	5.7(b), 10.3, 20.11(a), 25.1(a)(iii)	Sep. 2013

Private Determination	Book Sections	Newsletter Issue
201327014	13.1, 20.11(a), 24.5(q)	Sep. 2013
201328035	12.3(c), 24.7(m)	Sep. 2013
201329021	6.3(a), 8.6, 9.2, 20.11(a)	Sep. 2013
201330043	4.5(a), 4.10, 25.7	Sep. 2013
201332013	5.7(b), 25.1	Oct. 2013
201332015	4.7(a), 19.4(a)	Oct. 2013
201333014	6.3(i), 19.10	Oct. 2013
201333015	4.5(a), 27.2, 27.5, 27.18	Oct. 2013
201336020	21.3	Nov. 2013
201338029	19.5(b), 19.21(b)	Dec. 2013
201338034	7.8, 19.21(b)	Dec, 2013
201338052	6.3(a), 20.11	Nov. 2013
201338053	13, 20.11	Dec. 2013
201338059	12.3(c), 26.3	Dec. 2013
201340020	4.4, 4.10, 6.3(a), 8.5	Dec. 2013
201342011	12.3(b)(i)	Jan. 2014
201343028	20.11(a)	Jan. 2014
201344009	7.6(i), 7.11	Jan. 2014
201344011	24.7(h)	Jan. 2014
201345031	28.2(e)	Jan. 2014
201347022	14.1(c), 14.2(c)	Feb. 2014
201347023	20.3, 20.5(b), 14.1(c), 14.2(a)	Jan. 2014
201347024	22.3(d)(v)	Jan. 2014
201349019	14.1(c)	Feb. 2014
201349021	14.1(a)(ii)	Feb. 2014
201350042	4.10, 20.11	Feb. 2014
201351024	4.10, 13.2(b), 20.11, 25.1(a)(i)	Mar. 2014
201351027	12.4(e)	Mar. 2014
201403017	4.10	Mar. 2014
201403020	23.5	Mar. 2014
201405018	7.15, 20.11, 12.3(b)	Apr. 2014
201405029	24.5(h)(ii), 24.8	Apr. 2014
201406019	29.2	Apr. 2014
201406020	14.1(f)	Apr. 2014
201407014	4.10, 20.11, 24.8	May 2014
201409009	29.2	May 2014
201409010	26.3	May 2014
201409012	4.10, 20.11	May 2014

IRS PRIVATE DETERMINATIONS DISCUSSED IN *NONPROFIT COUNSEL*

Private Determination	Book Sections	Newsletter Issue
201409013	13.2	May 2014
201410035	4.10, 7.14	May 2014
201411037	20.5(a)	May 2014
201411038	4.10	May 2014
201411039	13, 20.8	May 2014
201413012	7.7	June 2014
201413013	27.3	June 2014
201414029	15.4	June 2014
201415003	4.7(a), 7.14, 25.2(h)	June 2014
201415009	26.13(b)	June 2014
201416011	23.2(b)	July 2014
201417017	26.1(a)(i)	July 2014
201418061	24.9(c)	July 2014
201419015	20.12	July 2014
201420020	10.3	July 2014
201421022	5.7(b)	July 2014
201422025	18.3	Aug. 2014
201422027	12.4(c), 25.1(h)	Aug. 2014
201424023	14.2(a), (c)	Aug. 2014
201424028	23.5	Aug. 2014
201425025	7.6, 12.3(c)	Aug. 2014
201426028	28.1(b)	Sep. 2014
201426029	16.1(g)	Sep. 2014
201428009	15.2, 15.3	Oct. 2014
201428011	19.6, 20.5	Sep. 2014
201428030	24.5(b)(iii)	Sep. 2014
201428022	4.11	Nov. 2014
201429027	7.14	Oct. 2014
201429029	24.5(c)	Oct. 2014
201430014	22.3(c)(iii)	Oct. 2014
201430019	15.2–15.4	Oct. 2014
201431031	19.5(b)	Oct. 2014
201431032	13.2(b), 14.2(c)(iii), 16.1, 20.12(a)	Oct. 2014
201432037	20.12(a)	Oct. 2014
201433016	7.6(c)	Nov. 2014
201434022	15.1(b)	Oct. 2014
201434023	7.1, 7.2, 7.7, 7.8, 7.11, 20.12	Nov. 2014

Private Determination	Book Sections	Newsletter Issue
201434025	25.3	Oct. 2014
201436050	7.6(a), (m), 20	Nov. 2014
201436051	6.3(a), 20.12(b)	Nov. 2014
201438034	4.4, 27.3	Nov. 2014
201440020	4.3(a), (b), 5.7(b)	Dec. 2014
201440023	20.12(b)	Dec. 2014
201442066	20.12(b)	Dec. 2014
201443021	20.12(a)	Jan. 2015
201444043	24.9(c)	Jan. 2015
201445015	32.3	Jan. 2015
201446025	28.1(b)	Jan. 2015
201446026	32.3	Jan. 2015
201446028	4.11(b)	Jan. 2015
201448026	4.5(a), 12.4(a)	Feb. 2015
201449002	23.5(b)	Feb. 2015
201450023	15.1(b)	Apr. 2015
201451030	15.1(b)	Mar. 2015
201452017	4.11, 20.12	Mar. 2015
201452018	20.12	Mar. 2015
201503016	4.11	Mar. 2015
201503018	30.2, 30.7	Mar. 2015
201503019	21.10	Mar. 2015
201505040	4.11(b), 6.3(a), 7.12, 8.1	Apr. 2015
201505041	20	Apr. 2015
201507023	4.3(a), 4.4(b), 20	Apr. 2015
201507026	4.11, 20.12	Apr. 2015
201508011	16.2	Apr. 2015
201509001	19.22(b)	May 2015
201509039	4.11, 6.3(a)	May 2015
201512006	18.3, 25.3	June 2015
201514011	20	June 2015
201515035	15.1, 20.11	June 2015
201515036	18.3	June 2015
201518018	13.2(b)	July 2015
201519023	26.1(a)(iii)	July 2015
201519027	19.22(c)	July 2015
201521017	28.1(b)	July 2015
201523021	23.2	Aug. 2015

Private Determination	Book Sections	Newsletter Issue
201523022	20.5(h)	Aug. 2015
201524026	4.5, 20, 23	Aug. 2015
201525007	14.1	Aug. 2015
201525011	4.11	Aug. 2015
201525012	4.3(b), 4.11	Sep. 2015
201525014	4.3(b), 6.3(a), 26.1(a)(i)	Sep. 2015
201526020	4.11, 20	Oct. 2015
201527043	6.3(a)	Oct. 2015
201528010	19.22(b)	Oct. 2015
201528038	18.3	Oct. 2015
201529010	14.2(a), 14.2(c)	Oct. 2015
201531022	=7.7	Oct. 2015
201533014	4.11, 6.3(a), 81	Oct. 2015
201534016	27.3	Oct. 2015
201534020	6.3(a), 7.4	Nov. 2015
201535019	4.11, 20.4(c), 24.2€	Nov. 2015
201537019	19.22(b)	Nov. 2015
201537025	10.4	Nov. 2015
201538027	7.6(f)	Jan. 2016
201539032	28.19(a)	Jan. 2016
201540016	4.11	Dec. 2015
201540017	14.2(c)	Jan. 2016
201540019	32.10(b)	Dec. 2015
201541013	20	Dec. 2015
201543019	20.12, 27.3	Jan. 2016
201544025	24.5(i)(i)	Jan. 2016
201544028	4.5(a), 20.5(h)	Jan. 2016
201545026	18.3	Mar. 2016
201545029	4.11, 20.12(a)	Jan. 2016
201548021	4.11(d), 20.1	Feb. 2016
201548025	4.11(d)	Jan. 2016
201550043	4.3(a), 8.1, 20.12(a)	Feb. 2016

Private Determination	Book Sections	Newsletter Issue
201551010	20.8	Mar. 2016
201552033	19.2(a)	Mar. 2016
201603032	12.4(c)	Mar. 2016
201604018	4.3(a), 4.5(a), 20.12	May 2016
201605019	19.6	Apr. 2016
201605020	14.2(a), 14.2(c)	Apr. 2016
201605021	15.1	Apr. 2016
201609006	4.11(a), 10.3, 20, 27.3	May 2016
201609008	19.9	May 2016
201612014	15.1(b), 15.2	May 2016
201613014	24.2(b)	May 2016
201613015	24.2(b)	May 2016
201613016	19.9	May 2016
201614038	20.12(a)	June 2016
201615014	4.5(c)	June 2016
201615016	20	June 2016
201615017	27.6(b)	June 2016, Sep. 2016
201615018	6.3(i), 20.12(a)	June 2016
201615021	15.3	June 2016
201615022	7.6(m), 7.7	June 2016
201617010	4.11, 14.2(c), 20.2(a)	July 2016
201617012	4.11, 20.12(a)	July 2016
201619010	4.3(a), 11.2, 20.12(a)	July 2016
201620011	7.16(d), 20	July 2016
201620014	19.5(b)	Aug. 2016
201620015	6.3(i)	Aug. 2016
201621017	14.2(a)	Aug. 2016
201622033	14.2(a)	Aug. 2016
201623013	13.2(b), 20.8	Aug. 2016
201624023	7.4, 20.12(a)	Aug. 2016
201626004	25.1(a)	Sep. 2016
201626025	20.12(a)	Sep. 2016
201627002	20, 21.4(c)	Sep. 2016
201629009	27.6(b)	Sep. 2016
201630016	13.3	Oct. 2016
201632020	20.12(a)	Oct. 2016
201632021	4.11(a)	Oct. 2016
201632022	7.14(a), (b)	Oct. 2016

201633032	24.4(a), (b)	Oct. 2016
201633035	4.11(a), 20.12(a), 14.2(c)	Oct. 2016
201633037	14.2(a), (c)	Oct. 2016
201634012	19.22(b)	Oct. 2016
201634029	20.12(d)	Oct. 2016
201635004	19.22(b)	Nov. 2016
201635006	20.12(a), 28.20	Nov. 2016
201636042	24.2(b)	Nov. 2016
201636043	24.2(b)	Nov. 2016
201637017	6.3(a)	Nov. 2016
201638028	15.1(b)	Nov. 2016
201639016	14.2(b), 14.2(c)	Nov. 2016
201640019	6.3(a)	Dec. 2016
201640022	20.5(e)	Dec. 2016
201641021	7.15	Dec. 2016
201641023	20, 27.3	Dec. 2016
201641026	20.12	Dec. 2016
201641027	4.11, 20	Dec. 2016
201642001	12.4(a)	Dec. 2016
201642036	15.1(b)	Dec. 2016
201643025	21.16	Jan. 2017
201643026	20.5(i)	Jan. 2017
201644019	30.2, 30.5, 30.7	Jan. 2017
201644021	15.1(b)	Jan. 2017
201645011	12.3(c), 12.4(c)	Jan. 2017
201645017	4.11(d)	Jan. 2017
201645019	19.9	Jan. 2017
201646007	7.7, 13, 16, 27.3	Jan. 2017
201647008	5.7(c), 20.1	Feb. 2017
201648019	6.3(a)	Feb. 2017
201648020	20.5(d), 20.5(i)	Feb. 2017
201649015	————	Feb. 2017
201649017	14.2(a), 14.2(c)(i), (ii)	Feb. 2017

Index

INDEX